YOU <u>CAN</u> COPE WITH SUCCESS,
ONE PARADOX AT A TIME.

Throughout women's lives, they receive many confusing, contradictory, and absurd messages telling them how "society" thinks they should act. Be smart, but not too smart. Be good, but not too good. Be like men (sometimes), but always be a woman (whatever that means today).

It all boils down to success with guilt.

But Celia Halas and Roberta Matteson have changed everything. No longer does a woman's life have to boil down to guilt—they have broken it down into thirteen clearly definable, and *conquerable*, paradoxes. The proof of their success is in the women's lives they have changed. No woman needs to be alone in her struggle to be herself and to be a success. This book is filled with women ready to help you by the examples of their own lives.

And no woman needs to wait for success any longer. Paradox by paradox, you can free your life from guilt and anxiety and replace them with happiness and fulfillment. Soon, you will be able to do <u>so</u> well *and* feel <u>so</u> good!

I've Done So Well—Why Do I Feel So Bad?

CELIA HALAS, PH.D. &
ROBERTA MATTESON, PH.D.

BALLANTINE BOOKS • NEW YORK

In memory of our mothers:
MARY FABRITZ SCHAUB,
who by her courage, fortitude, and hope provided a
model to follow,
and
HILDA MITCHELL HOEY,
whose quiet strength represented love and safety
and served as an example for encountering life.

Library of Congress Catalog Card Number: 78-3403

ISBN 0-345-28553-0

This edition published by arrangement with Macmillan Publish-
ing Co., Inc.

Printed in Canada

First Ballantine Books Edition: January 1980
Second Printing: October 1982

Contents

RESOLUTION OF PARADOXES

Preface

This book is an expression of the love and respect we have for women, especially those we have known as friends, clients, and seekers of personal growth and awareness. In thanks for all the trust they have invested in us, and the joy and satisfaction we have received from being associated with them, we offer to them these pages which reflect the understandings and concepts they have helped us to acquire.

As we worked with women who were struggling for increased self-worth, autonomy, and effectiveness, we saw the same double-binds occurring in their lives over and over again. In looking at these common experiences as paradoxical conflicts, we formulated a framework within which to examine and understand women's distress.

We found ourselves talking more and more about how paradoxes shape women's lives and found our friends and clients saying, "That describes me perfectly." As the paradoxes became clearer to us, we realized that they exist not only in the lives of our clients, but are familiar to all women, for paradoxical conflicts are central to the experience of being a woman.

Just as we have been concerned by the distresses and dilemmas of women, we have also been concerned about the misunderstandings between women and men. We have received strong support from the men with whom we have shared the material in this book. They sometimes saw themselves reflected in the paradoxes, too, and welcomed our concepts as a guide to help them understand themselves and to empathize with the women they love. We hope that other men will feel the same way.

We think fellow professionals who work with women will find helpful information in these pages, too. The opportunity to contribute to our colleagues in this way increases our pleasure.

We want to give special thanks to two women, Dee Gunn and Bea Trudelle, who worked enthusiastically and dilligently in the preparation of the manuscript. Our husbands, Mike and Archie, have cheerfully endured our months of preoccupation; we are grateful for their patience and pleased with their pride in our accomplishment. And to Therese Halas and Johnnie Matteson, warm hugs for the unqualified encouragement, delight, and admiration they have showered upon our efforts.

C. H. and R. M.

Phoenix, Arizona
February 1978

CHAPTER I

Paradoxes: Key to Women's Distress

At a brainstorming meeting ideas were being tossed about in a search for ways that psychologists could be most helpful to women. It became apparent that women do not have a framework for self-understanding and for the resolution of their distresses when the puzzle pieces of their lives do not fit. The stimulus for this book came from that meeting.

In the following chapters two themes are developed. One is the destructiveness of certain paradoxes in the female experience; the second is the report of our experiences as psychotherapists in helping women to develop self-mastery by recognizing paradoxes in their lives and resolving them with strength and autonomy.

The models of traditional psychology have included concepts such as the nature of man, personality characteristics, and theories of personality. The focus of psychology has been on fitting people into categories and stereotypes that have been based on research with male subjects. When measured by such standards, women have been seen as different, and *different* has been judged *deficient*. As a result, women's ledger sheets show many debits and few credits. Women, too, have inadvertently colluded with the rest of society in selling out their own authenticity, whatever the consequences.

In using paradoxes as a framework for a new model, we focus on how women behave, how they see themselves, and how they see the world around them. This model is based on components that can be examined in therapy—the self-contradictions, the false messages, the absurdities, and the double-binds that make up the fabric of a woman's life.

It is difficult to talk about women without comparing them with men. It is important not to do that. Nevertheless, when we talk about socialization, we must talk about how roles have been developed in a society in which men have dominated, have made the rules, and have been the decision-makers. It is true that we live in a male-dominated culture. By describing this reality, we are not assigning blame or saying that men have caused terrible things to happen and women have allowed terrible things to happen. We are saying that this is reality and we must start from there if women are to renovate the structure of their lives.

Although the socialization process has created paradoxes for both women and men, a greater burden has been placed on women as a result of paradoxical injunctions. Since over 90 percent of all women in the United States marry, it is not surprising that many of the paradoxes of the female experience involve male-female alliances. It follows that many of the issues in this book focus on relationship conflicts. Women have been overloaded with conflicts spawned by the allure of the easy magic of love. Once women understand these paradoxical issues, they will be able to invest their energies and abilities in many areas of productivity rather than focusing single-mindedly on relationships.

To be born female and live in this culture is to receive certain messages throughout life. Some of those messages are paradoxes that confuse, disarm, bind, push, or contort women into becoming caricatures of what they could be. The paradoxes in women's lives are of two kinds: self-contradictory, absurd, or inconsistent messsages that are nevertheless true; or contradictory messages that seem true but are, in fact, false.

Each of the next thirteen chapters examines one paradox. Some of them are double messages with which, in various ways, women have been fettered since they looked through the bars of their cribs. Others are interpretations that women have made to explain conflicting messages to themselves. They have all become internalized by women, integrated in such a

2

way that women are no longer aware of the relentless coercion that dictates much of their conduct.

These are the paradoxes:

EQUALITY: *"How can I be both equal and inferior?"*

Women are defined as inferior solely because they are born female. They are seen as subordinate to men. As is the case of all inferiors in a dominant-subordinate relationship, they have been delegated the roles and behaviors that the dominants do not want. The paradox is that even though women are told they are equal to men, they are treated as if they are not. They are expected to facilitate men's lives by doing all the things men cannot do or do not want to do. Ironically, as subordinates, they have been charged with responsibility for the qualities most important in the enhancement of human life: love, children, and interpersonal relationships.

SELF-ESTEEM: *"I've done so well—why do I feel so bad?"*

Self-esteem is acquired through achievements and feedback from others. Women have successfully and enthusiastically adopted the roles and behaviors society has dictated for them. They have nurtured children, cherished relationships, been helpmates, and have not asked for too much. Shouldn't they feel good? The paradox is that no matter how hard women try, how well they do, or how much they achieve, they still feel bad. The roles and behaviors assigned to women have not been highly valued. Women do not get the positive messages needed for a sense of high self-esteem.

AFFILIATION: *"Without you I'm nothing; with you I lose my sense of identity."*

A primary relationship is seen by a woman as the center of her world; so much so that her efforts may be directed almost exclusively to enhancing and facilitating that relationship. The paradox is that without an-

3

other person in whom to invest herself, a woman may feel empty and useless, yet in investing herself completely in another person, she becomes an extension of that person and loses her own identity. Women have confused the *capacity* for affiliation with the *need* for affiliation. It is true that women have a great capacity for intimacy and sharing with others. They are enhanced by, and do enhance, those to whom they are connected. Nonetheless, affiliation is not a need, nor is it a firm foundation on which to build one's identity.

DEPENDENCY: *"I have to destroy myself in order to survive."*

Having a man on whom she can depend has been the central element of security to a woman. Dependency has been seen as appropriately feminine and has reinforced men's patterns of superiority. When women become financially and emotionally dependent upon someone else, they give up the power to be in charge of themselves and to direct their own lives. The paradox is that what starts out to seem good fosters resentment in both the giver and the receiver. The giver feels taken advantage of and the receiver loses her sense of self.

EMOTIONALITY: *"I can be emotional, but I mustn't upset anyone."*

Women are defined as emotional; they are rewarded at times for feeling free to express themselves. However, only positive feelings are allowed; negative feelings are discouraged. The paradox is that although women are told they are emotional and cannot help being that way, they have been charged with responsibility for how others react when they express their feelings. They feel guilty if they express emotions to which others react with discomfort. The fact is that this discomfort reflects the inability of others to handle their own feelings and is not the responsibility of the woman who is expressing herself.

4

PERCEPTION: "I don't see it the way you do, so I must be wrong."

Men have described how the world is. Because they are subordinate to men, women are supposed to agree with them. But women's perceptions tell them that things are different; their reality is not as it is defined by men. Women are comfortable and confident in how they perceive things until they are challenged. When that happens they tend to back off and assume they are wrong. The paradox for women has been that when they cannot trust their own perceptions, they do not know how to act. The challenge, "How dare you see it the way I don't?" is enough to immobilize most women.

CONFLICT: "I have to resolve differences without facing the issues."

It is not an accident that women are called peace-makers. They have been charged with creating harmony, making everyone happy, and preserving tranquility. They are told to be feminine, yet never to act with anger or directness, as men might do. The paradox is that women are charged with doing the impossible; conflict cannot be resolved without addressing the issues, and women are not psychologically prepared for conflict. They have learned and have been encouraged to use indirect ways to handle things, thereby perpetuating the paradox.

GUILT: "I'm responsible for everything and powerless to effect change."

Women are able to control very few of the things for which they feel responsible. Important decisions are made by others without consultation with them. Yet they feel guilty about other people's failures, other people's feelings, other people's choices, and about circumstances and situations not of their own making. The paradox lies in the notion that responsibility and power can exist independently of each other. They can-

5

not. Yet, in our culture, when things don't work out and someone is sought to take the blame, women accept that responsibility.

MYTHS: "I lose, especially when I win."

Unrealistic hope has set the stage for women's disillusionment. Because they have believed many romantic notions about fairy-tale futures, women have given up aspirations and achievement goals that could provide real success. They have designed their lives to fit a mythical model in which Prince Charming and Cinderella live happily ever after. The paradox is that they lose even when they win; there is no way that achieving a goal based on fantasy and myth can result in a satisfying reality.

MODELS: "My models are not to follow."

Modeling is a most influential source of a child's learning. Children learn to be like the significant adults whose behavior has impressed them. Lucky is the woman who has had positive models whom she admired in her early life and whom she wants to be like. The paradox is that many women grow up knowing that they do not want to be like the adults who were available as their models, yet they have no one else to emulate. As adults, women are burdened with the task of erasing their dysfunctional ways of behaving and developing positive patterns that will make life more rewarding.

SEXUALITY: "That is the way men like women, but I don't dare be that way."

Women see men reacting positively to sexy, alluring, glamorous, and seductive women. This model of sexuality is held out as an ideal for which women should strive. The same men, however, give the message that they expect their women to be modest, demure, and virtuous. The paradox is the double message: A woman should be both a whore and a madonna. This

6

expectation has caused women to feel distressed and confused about their own sexuality.

PSYCHOSOMATICS: *"Getting sick isn't so bad; there's a lot of strength in being weak."*

For one who has no other way to exercise power, sickness can be a useful tool. The paradox for many women is that when they are sick they receive the love, attention, and cooperation that they do not get at any other time. Sometimes sickness results in gaining a control over others that is unattainable when one is well. Although this paradox is rarely verbalized, it has been experienced widely, often without one's realizing it.

FEAR: *"I want to want to, and I won't."*

Women have not been encouraged to see themselves as courageous, nor to take risks in order to grow. They have been expected to suffer in silence when life is unpleasant. Their fears increase, and they become immobilized. They may develop a pattern of expressing desires upon which they never act. The paradox is that women tell themselves they are undecided when, in fact, their fear guarantees that they will not do anything. Such women exemplify the adage, "Not to choose is to choose not to."

The messages of socialization are among the first and strongest in a woman's life. A little girl learns very early whether she should play with the tea set or the Tonka toys. Girls do seem to accept their sex roles with less enthusiasm than boys, and this divergence increases with age. Those who question this fact might try this experiment. Ask a little girl to pretend she is a boy. Then ask her what she would like to be when she grows up. She will probably say that she would like to be an astronaut, a doctor, a cowboy, or some current television hero. Ask a little boy to pretend he is a girl and then ask what he would like to be when he grows up. Chances are he will say, "I wouldn't *want* to be a girl."

7

The devastating thing about socialization is that it indoctrinates one to choose and to like the characteristics and roles that society says one should have. For women, this means that they accept the contradictory message of the first paradox, which says they are equal to men, whereas they are treated as if they are not. Women translate this message to mean that they are innately inferior to men and that it is appropriate that their aspirations, goals, and choices reflect that inferiority.

The second paradox follows inexorably. If women are inferior, then what women are and what women do are not highly valued. Then, of course, the messages they get from others are likely to be less than positive. Since these messages form the basis of one's self-concept, we can expect women in general to have lower self-esteem than most men. No matter how hard women try, they do not feel good about themselves because the roles they fill are not highly valued. Because they feel this way, the third paradox becomes a logical next step.

Women's need for social approval has been generally accepted and identified as a need for affiliation. They say to themselves, "If I don't feel good about myself, perhaps I can become connected to someone who will give my life more meaning." Women tend to center their lives around relationships and identify themselves in terms of those to whom they are connected. In doing so they lose their own identity and are placed in double jeopardy. The threat of total loss if the relationship should end results in behavior in which they push aside their needs, aspirations, and goals in order to preserve the relationship. Thus, they are set up for the fourth paradox, dependency.

If a woman has confused a capacity for affiliative relationships with the need to be affiliated, dependency is an easy step away. To cling to someone for emotional and material support seems to offer security, but to experience the feeling that one cannot exist without some other person is a devastating experience. This leads to pain and to giving over one's power and strength to someone else in order to survive. A feeling

8

of powerlessness promotes more dependency and helplessness. Women are then set up to be judged and to judge themselves negatively in terms of the fifth paradox, emotionality.

Not feeling good about oneself and feeling unwilling to risk terminating "life-sustaining" relationships can cause one to be cautious about expressing the full range of one's emotions. Women begin to be very selective about those they do express—that is, only positive ones. This is especially confusing since women are also told that they are expected to be emotional, that emotionality is part of the "female nature." This confusion creates self-doubt and leads into the sixth paradox, perception.

Although their perceptions tell them many times that things are different from the way someone else describes them, women tend not to trust their own perceptions. If women are inferior to men, do not feel good about themselves, need relationships to feel whole, must depend upon someone else to survive, and cannot accept the full range of their emotions, why should they trust their perceptions when they differ from someone's else's? If women do not know where they stand because they cannot trust their view of things it is understandable then that women would not be prepared for the seventh paradox, conflict.

The resolution of conflict is the starting point of growth. If one is to arrive at that position, one must courageously face the issues involved. When women do not trust their own perceptions, they hesitate to take a confident stand. Their diffidence comes from feeling responsible for creating harmony and keeping everyone happy. Women resort to indirect ways of handling things, trying to meet the need to act while ignoring the necessity to face the issues. The results are unsatisfactory and the resultant feeling of powerlessness leads to the eighth paradox, guilt.

Women recognize that they are caught in this paradox when they see that they feel guilty for things for which they are not responsible and over which they have no control. It is not easy to clarify the nurturant role into which society has cast women. To do so in-

9

volves allowing others to make their own mistakes, to hurt at times, and to struggle with problems. In short, it means allowing others to take responsibility for their own lives while women confine their concerns to areas in which they have both responsibility and power, areas in which they can, therefore, properly be held accountable. The distress that comes from the paradox of guilt sets up women for the ninth paradox, myths.

Women's experience with parents, educators, peers, and society at large all emphasize a mythical reality. There is little in women's early training to prepare them for the realities of life. Most women in our culture are urged directly and indirectly to marry. Their early training emphasizes that once a woman marries she will live happily ever after. Marriage can be and is a rewarding experience for women who are prepared for its realities. For most, however, unrealistic hopes set the stage for disillusionment. It takes hard work to recognize a fantasy and to put it aside in order to work out a satisfactory reality. Having experienced the conflicts of the tenth paradox, models, makes the task doubly difficult.

If a woman has good models to follow, she has inspiration, guidelines, and confidence in her choices of what to be and how to behave. She has touchstones along the way; she can expect to become like those people she admires as she follows their manner of doing things. Some fortunate women have had positive models and have not experienced a modeling paradox. For others, however, the scenes of childhood are bad memories. They lack the habits, personal characteristics, and skills to be the kinds of adults who relate well to others and are happy in their own achievements. It is difficult to erase dysfunctional ways of behaving, to replace them with positive behavior patterns that will facilitate growth. One of the biggest voids in modeling seems to be in an area of essential importance, sexuality. Because of this void, women experience the confusion of the eleventh paradox, sexuality.

Because every cell in a woman is female she should feel good about her sexuality. Unfortunately, the totality of a woman's sexuality has received shabby treatment.

10

Issues of sexual development, care and understanding of one's body, reproduction, and hormone influences are seriously neglected. The emphasis of society has been on women's sexual performance. Women have been further confused by the double message that they are to be both seductress and virgin. There is both power and powerlessness in the way women handle this challenge. The confusion and frustration women feel as a result of trying to deal with this and other paradoxes can lead to the twelfth paradox, psychosomatics.

It sometimes comes as a surprise to women who feel helpless, powerlesss, alone, and unloved that when they get sick, lots of good things happen to them. Love, attention, and cooperation, which were granted only grudgingly while they were healthy, are now showered upon them. These rewards make it difficult not to use illness, either consciously or unconsciously, to resolve paradoxical conflicts in which thev feel ineffective and powerless in their alliances with others. This fragile means of resolving conflicts generates fear.

The thirteenth paradox, fear, is a link connecting all of the paradoxes in women's lives. Unresolved conflicts generate more self-doubt and feelings of powerlessness. As a woman's fears increase she is unable to think, to make decisions, or to act. The fear itself then becomes another paradox as she attempts to handle her distress by not handling it. Immobility is the final indignity.

Many variables contribute to the dysfunction that women exhibit. Moreover, these variables are comnlex, subtle, and greatly misunderstood. In traditional therapy, based largely on concepts developed by Sigmund Freud, it is assumed that the distress people experience is generated internally through some personality deficiency. In this approach, in which women are seen as inferior to men, therapy consists largely of teaching women how to adjust to subordinate roles and to accept second-place status in a male-dominated society. In reaction to this position, some therapists in recent years have focused on the external, or situational, causes of women's distress. They have explained all of women's problems in terms of social and political vari-

11

ables. In our view, both approaches are simplistic and limited. The distresses of women are the result of both internal and external factors. These diverse agents work hand in hand, the demolition accomplished by one adding to the destruction wreaked by the other.

For women who are in psychotherapy with us, the experience is a three-faceted process. First, we help our clients see that they came to their distress through no fault of their own, but by way of the process of socialization. They learn not to blame themselves for society's sleight of hand.

Second, we help them to examine the coping styles they have developed in order to survive, to jettison old dysfunctional habits, to preserve those that serve them well, and enhance their skills and talents. Third, we provide emotional support for clients as they take charge of themselves in a process that involves making choices, taking risks, and gaining confidence through action.

We have identified five stages of growth during psychotherapy. The first stage may be either anxiety or depression. Women who are shaking and frightened are experiencing anxiety. Their symptoms signal that there is turbulence on a deeper level, although it may not be clear what is wrong. Depression may be an attempt by women to move away from grief or anger by turning those feelings in on themselves. Depression can also be generated by feeling hopelessly entrenched in paralyzing situations over which one has no control and is powerless to change.

Identifying the sources of distress allows a client to move to the second stage, dealing with her anger. Many emotions with which women deal at this stage of therapy are disguised as anger. These include rage, blame, grief, disillusionment, and feelings of powerlessness.

After anger comes confusion, a stage of uncertainty. This involves vacillation between choosing the relative comfort of being rooted in the unacceptable familiar and striving for the vaguely envisioned substance of what might be. During this stage women clarify their thinking, search for direction, examine alternatives, and weigh the consequences of their choices.

After doubt and confusion are reduced, the next stage is risk-taking. During this time women test out new behaviors. They implement new skills generated from rusty or revitalized talents. They add up the pluses and minuses of the risks they have taken, evaluating the success of their changes.

As the process continues, women move into the fifth stage, competence. This stage is marked by trusting their perceptions and feeling confident that the plans they have made and are acting on are cut to their measure. At this point the goals of therapy have been achieved.

Central to our approach to the psychology of women is the conviction that every woman knows herself better than anyone else does. The answers to her questions are within herself; as therapists we provide opportunities for our clients to explore their uncertainties and arrive at their own answers.

Not that we believe every woman needs therapy. Some women have been fortunate enough to have had experiences that enhanced their self-esteem and sense of competence. They have felt successful and happy with their lives. They, too, have experienced conflicts, but have been able to handle those conflicts in such a way that destructive problems have not been the result. Other women who have chafed under the constriction of paradoxes have found diverse ways to work themselves free. It is our hope that this book will be for all women a source of support and will provide for some women sufficient insight to help them break out of the pressure of paradoxes and move into the freedom of self-direction.

THE PARADOXES

CHAPTER II

Equality

"How can I be both equal and inferior?"

Women are defined as inferior solely because they are born female. They are seen as subordinate to men. As is the case of all inferiors in a dominant-subordinate relationship, they have been delegated the roles and behaviors that the dominants do not want. The paradox is that even though women are told they are equal to men, they are treated as if they are not. They are expected to facilitate men's lives by doing all the things men cannot do or do not want to do. Ironically, as subordinates, they have been charged with responsibility for the qualities most important in the enhancement of human life: love, children, and interpersonal relationships.

Read the following unfinished story involving a difficult decision and decide how you think it should end. In a few sentences write your own conclusion to it. The way you finish the story says something about how the paradox of equality has affected you. The significance of your ending is explained at the end of this chapter.

Joan and Robert are married and have two children. Robert works hard to support the family and there is little money available for recreation. Joan keeps house and is going to college. They are both looking forward to her working after she graduates.

It is Sunday afternoon. Robert has been given free passes for the zoo and wants to take the family for an outing. Joan has a big exam tomorrow and had planned to spend the afternoon studying.

The socialization process underlies all the paradoxes examined in this book. It is the real villain in the paradox of equality. It creeps up on women with subtle imperatives that account for women's acceptance of second-class citizenship. The basic message of socialization that becomes the paradox of equality is that women are innately inferior to men, and men and women's lives and relationships should reflect this. The social, cultural, and hereditary influences of a woman's parents are joined by those of the rest of society to teach her what she should and should not, can and cannot do. Human potential combined with social experiences account for what an infant grows up to be.

We can look at socialization in terms of its definition and in terms of its effects. By definition, socialization refers to the habits, customs, beliefs, and practices that influence an individual as she or he grows up and takes her or his place as women or men in society. If we examine this definition, we can predict the effect. The process of socialization causes one to want to be and to accept the way that one has been reinforced to be by subtle influences originating outside of oneself. In the case of women, this means they have been influenced to accept themselves as inferior to men.

A small girl learns, by the time she is two or three, that she is a girl. Her books tell her with big pictures and little words what girls are like and what course she is bound to follow. Girls can become mommies, nurses, or teachers. The books do not show sisters leading brothers. They do not show girls making discoveries, creating inventions, making important decisions; boys do these things! Girls learn early that what boys do is better.

Children get spoken and unspoken messages from

16

their parents that communicate the relative value of blue and pink. Parents have very different ideas about what is appropriate behavior for girls and boys. Their expectations influence how they treat their children and have a snowball effect on the small differences between children when they are born.

Proud fathers teach sons to chin themselves on the shower rod before they can walk, whereas girls are handled with a hesitancy more suitable to the care of a fragile flower. As early as nursery school, little boys and little girls know their places. Boys go directly to the corner where the skill-building and action games are. Girls content themselves with make-believe objects: toy irons that do not get hot, play stoves that do not cook, and dolls that serve as imaginary children. Often, while little boys play, little girls watch. While boys are learning independence, mastering skills, and gaining confidence in their abilities (in short, acquiring the "masculine" traits), little girls are learning to stay safe in loving relationships. Such little-girl behavior is translated as *feminine*.

After nursery school, girls and boys are educated equally for a while. Girls sit in the same classes and learn the same subjects at the same time from the same teacher. They often make better grades than boys and respond as enthusiastically to a teacher's challenge. At the age of ten a girl may still outswim or outrun a boy. She may even dream of adventurous or challenging careers, but not for long.

Subtle changes have been taking place. By ninth grade, many more boys than girls are thinking of careers in math and science. By high school a girl knows that being smart guarantees her place among the wallflowers. Attracting boys is what counts now! She puts aside other goals and concentrates on this exciting pursuit.

"I'm not so equal after all."

During the metamorphosis from baby doll to social butterfly, a girl experiences poignantly what it means to be equal in the paradox of equality. She gets the message in her home, in school, and from her peers

17

that boys are valued more highly than girls. Research studies have shown that even in the first year of a child's life, parents show bias in favor of boys, although few parents realize that they are doing so. Little boys are allowed to cross streets and play farther away from home at a younger age than little girls are, even though boys tend to be more impulsive and less careful than girls. Boys generally can stay out later at an earlier age than girls. They are allowed to use the family car more often and to keep it out later. If there is only enough college money for one child, in most families it is used for a boy's education. In spite of the fact that female infants are generally sturdier than male infants, it is widely believed by parents that girls are more fragile than boys and must be protected.

For anyone who questions that there is parental bias in favor of males, it is easy to do some informal research. Ask a group of parents whether they wanted a girl or a boy when they were expecting their first child. About seven out of ten will say they wanted a boy.

The notion of female inferiority is as old as Adam and Eve. Somebody must have noticed after they left the Garden of Eden that Eve was not as strong physically as Adam. Actually, some women are larger and stronger than some men, and females do have greater endurance, longer life expectancy, and less susceptibility to life-endangering diseases than males do.

Differences between the sexes in size and musculature are generally found in all animal species, but it is only in humans that these differences have been seen as evidence of female inferiority and male superiority. The basis for this generalization cannot stand up under scrutiny. Larger muscles do not destine men for financial, vocational, social, political, intellectual, and emotional superiority. In the day of the caveman, brute strength was very important; today there are few areas where muscles are an important factor in a man's performance. Men have to jog or go to gyms to tend all those muscles, which they find largely superfluous in their daily living.

What are the pervasive messages in women's lives

that prepare them for lower rank and keep them there? Added to those they experience as children are those they find in the working world. There is a message of inferiority in the fact that there is no expectation that a woman will earn as much as a man does. A trained nurse earns less money than a bus driver; women who do exactly the same jobs as men are not paid as much. Nor do token titles compensate for inequities in paychecks. When salaries are discussed, we often hear the remark, "That's a good salary for a woman." We personally have never heard the parallel, "That's a good salary for a man."

There is a message of inferiority when women are talked down to. One of us remembers the remark of a workman with whom she was negotiating for a house-painting job. He looked directly at her and said, "I am a bonded painter. You probably would not understand what that means, lady, but I know your husband would." There is a message of inferiority when businesses, banks, mortgage companies, and insurance companies are reluctant to deal with women. They insist upon having "the man of the house" present when financial considerations affecting the family are discussed. There is a message of inferiority when a single woman has difficulty opening charge accounts in her name or getting a mortgage on a house. Although legislation has been passed to change such inequities, reality has not yet caught up with the law.

"I'm supposed to do what no one else wants to do."

It is not because women are inferior that they have been assigned submissive, low-status, and unwanted roles; it is because these roles involve doing things that men do not want to do or cannot do. How many men would compete with a hotel chambermaid for the job of cleaning up other people's dirt; a nurse's aid for the chance to empty bedpans; a secretary for the tasks of typing, filing, and "pleasing" the boss; or a housewife for the drudgery of her daily routine?

Men have assumed the power to do the assigning; women have acquiesced. Since women have been taught to be other-oriented, they have accepted the appropriateness of doing whatever is asked of them. Their compliance has freed men to use their resources and to expect support in being self-oriented. Women have made it easy for men to put themselves first.

Women have been told that they are responsible for the emotional climate of the family, while men are responsible for the family's financial upkeep. Society has tremendous respect for the male task of meeting the monetary needs of the family. There is very little appreciation for the significant contribution of nonemployed homemakers to the economic well-being of their families.

There is also little recognition of the fact that over 40 percent of all married women are employed and contribute significantly to the family income. Such women have two full-time jobs, one at home and the other at work. Nevertheless, they are often accused of neglecting their families and working only for self-fulfillment, or in order to get out of the house. Family members may support the myth that a wife's earnings are insignificant, in spite of the fact that this income may provide for family clothing, vacations, furniture, or a new car that could not otherwise be afforded. The problem is that women's financial contributions are made light of or taken for granted because they are usually smaller than men's earnings. And society puts a greater value on men's higher earning power than it does women's traditional tasks.

In the world of work, secretaries enjoy neither the salary nor the status of their bosses, yet it is often the secretary's complex and essential skills that are responsible for harmony, efficiency, and productivity in the business world. We could add examples of nurses and doctors, teachers and administrators, clerks and managers, in which women's contributions are no less significant than those of men, yet status and reward differentials prove the existence of the paradox of equality.

Power, advancement opportunities, and high-salaried positions are more open to men than to women. This is compounded by the fact that women are not inclined to call attention to their achievements and to request advancement. Women often remain at low-level, assistant jobs because they have internalized the notion that they are needed there. At a recent workshop on employment, we asked how many men and women would stay on a job once they had mastered it. All the men said that of course they would strive to move on. They were astonished at the response of most of the women that they would hesitate to move up if they were needed where they were. It was a perfect example of the paradox of equality in action.

"I'm the heart of the family."

Having credited men with the economic support of the family, women have inherited by default the complementary role of being responsible for the emotional climate in the home. With the suavity of the confidence man, the aphorism, "The man is the head of the family and the woman is the heart," disarms women.

The socialization process begins very early in a girl's life to prepare her for this role. Girls tend to be more obedient than boys, partly because being good has been so strongly reinforced. Girls enjoy being the kind of model that people like, being helpful at home, cooperative at school, and nice to the teacher. Mothers say, "My daughter has never given me a minute's trouble." This is often one of the highest praises bestowed on a daughter. Mothers praise boys for their accomplishments, for having ambitions, for being good in athletics, for doing things that people admire. When mothers give little girls messages that they are not giving their parents any trouble, what they are really saying is, "I love you when you are compliant."

Men are taught in many ways to gain skills, to earn a living, and to fill the position of the head of the family. When a man is seen as the *paterfamilias,* his role is to make decisions and to give permission. A subservient wife follows his rules. This puts wives always in the "Yes, sir" stance. Their focus is on finding ways to please their husbands and to make their lives easier.

21

Women are described as being "by nature" sensitive, nurturing, loving, soft, submissive, gentle, compliant, and emotional. They are seen as extensions of men and are expected to be fulfilled by taking their place as man's complementary-but-equal helpmate in a dominant-submissive relationship. Men are the thinkers and doers, women are the helpers and givers. Telling women they are complementary keeps them doubletiming to stay in place.

When women are assigned subservient roles, the necessity of tailoring themselves to fit those roles creates feelings of inferiority. They fear punishment, disapproval, and sanctions if they fail to please. Because they feel less-than, they become dependent upon other people's approval to flesh out their sense of self-esteem. Because others do not value their efforts and they get few positive messages, they see themselves as inferior. They believe that subservient roles are the only ones they *can* fill. The circular process of devaluation is complete.

What is it like to be the heart of the family in our culture? Women have to depend upon the modeling of previous generations to learn how to be the family heart. They do not have a clear recipe to follow, but they realize that the ingredients include being supportive, understanding, and loving in exactly the right proportions.

For Faye, being the heart of the family meant devoting herself to the physical and emotional needs of three children and her husband Roger, who was away from home fifteen hours a day "in order to get ahead." In addition to kissing hurt fingers and bandaging cuts and bruises, it meant making trips to emergency rooms, budgeting the household finances, being there when the children came home from school, and listening to the confidential complaints of a growing family. It also meant cooking a second dinner when her husband came home late and changing her plans on a moment's notice for business-related social functions.

Faye made an art of taking these adjustments in stride, and she enjoyed most of the things that filled her days. What did trouble her was that she could not explain to her children the emotional void they felt because of their father's continual absence. She thought she had to defend Roger's actions; he was working so hard for his family. She had stifled her own feelings of disappointment, but it was harder to live with her children's unhappiness.

Faye conveniently avoided acknowledging that her husband probably would have behaved the same way if he had not had a family. He was deeply gratified by his success and much preferred to spend his time at work, where the praise, adulation, and deference that he received reassured him of his value, than at home. If Faye suggested, "But the children need you, too," he replied, "I work hard to provide the money. It's your job to take care of the rest of the family's needs. Buy whatever you want."

Roger became more and more a distant figure. The children felt alienated from him; they knew they could not look to him for either companionship or direction. Faye could not turn to Roger in her frustration. Both he and society expected that she dredge up from within herself the resources to single-handedly resolve the complexities that exist in any growing family. Faye had always expected that theirs would be a marriage of mutuality, a joint venture, but it did not work that way. As Roger became more occupied away from home and as the children's needs lessened, Faye found herself pulling in single harness.

When Faye came to therapy, it was because, as she expressed it, the "bottom of my world has dropped out." Quite by accident she had discovered that Roger had a mistress. Confronted with her discovery, he admitted it. The reason he gave for his wandering was that he found Faye dull, and he felt he deserved some spice in life. Unless their marriage could be revitalized, Faye feared that she had thirty-five years yet to live with nothing to look forward to. The paradox of equality had surrounded her. Being the heart of the family lasted only as long as Faye was subservient, cooperated with everyone else's plans, and was still seen as desirable by her husband.

23

Just as men have delegated to women functions they do not want or value for themselves, they have ascribed to women the emotions they do not want or value for themselves. Such characteristics as sensitivity, passivity, submissiveness, fearfulness, weakness, and timidity have been reserved for women, along with the positive characteristics of being nurturant, loving, warm, friendly, and supportive. Many of the qualities used to describe women are seen, at best, as less than ideal, whereas male qualities, such as dominance, competitiveness, and aggressiveness, are seen as healthy and desirable. If the emotional qualities ascribed to men are indeed superior to those of women, then it would be appropriate for men to be in charge of society's emotional health. Since women have been assigned this awesome task, we can only conclude that this is further evidence that women have been charged with doing what men are unable or unwilling to do.

Many women are beginning to recognize that the emotional relationships for which they are held responsible are much more difficult to develop, more tenuous to hold, and harder to turn loose at declaration-of-independence time than are the relationships that men develop in the course of providing for the economic needs of their families. The rules, criteria, and guidelines are fairly well defined in economic relationships. A man knows when he has adequately filled his role; a woman is not so sure.

A woman client put it this way:

I was always told that child-bearing is a woman's most important accomplishment. We are expected to develop loving, supportive, cheerful relationships with our children so that they can look to us for the right kind of parental guidance. We are to help them to grow and develop beautifully and never go astray. Our children are supposed to be our primary concern; next to our husband, the most important involvement in our life. Yet, ironically, we are not to invest too much of ourselves in them, because when they grow up we are to turn them loose emotionally.

24

No one has much sympathy for the conflict that this produces in women.

The fact that women bear children has been used as the starting point to say that they should also be better equipped than men to nurture them. This is a handy argument for men, who generally do not want to be involved in the day-to-day care of children. Responsibilities that both parents should share are often delegated to mothers. The parenting task is often seen by men as less important than others they choose for themselves, and they put other responsibilities ahead of their children.

To further the injustice, child-rearing occupies only about the middle third of a woman's life. When her children are raised, her husband is usually involved in the most demanding years of his career and has little time for stoking the home fires. If a woman's sense of self-esteem has come largely from the fact that she is a wife and mother, she is likely to come to the bitter realization that her role was not sufficient to last an entire lifetime. The capriciousness of the paradox of equality has left her empty.

Up until the twentieth century, few women lived past the age of forty-five. Although large families were the rule, many children died young. A woman felt her life was complete if she was fortunate enough to live until her surviving children were adults. The situation is changed now, and that is the source of the pain many women experience in their middle years. Their role is gone; their capacity to fill it remains. Full of their emptiness, they ask themselves, "How am I going to fill the rest of my life now that the children are grown?"

"I do what he lets me do."

The paradox of equality is self-serving for men. They have conditioned women to be subordinate in areas where men want to be dominant and maintain control, yet to be adult and capable on signal. Business and industry are controlled by men because they want it that way and they have the power to make it happen.

25

In these fields women hold positions characterized by lower pay and little opportunity for decision-making. Politics is also still a man's world. The prestige offices go to males, many of whom are elected largely due to women's dutiful activity on their behalf. Even in education, where the majority of employees are women, women are most frequently represented in the least prestigious, lowest-paid jobs. School principals, college executives, and other decision-makers are usually men.

In marriage, where it is claimed that women make as many decisions as men do, the virulence of male domination is barely beneath the surface. Investigation shows that more husbands than wives control the money. Many men decide upon the large purchases without discussing them with their wives, and most husbands claim the right to put their foot down and have the last word about family decisions.

Paradoxically, although a woman's value is affirmed by her subservience in most situations, a woman is supposed to be adult and capable in areas where men are well-served by her competence. This is most clearly seen in the home, where men often choose not to participate in the nitty-gritty routine. Although housewives are rarely credited with having executive skills, the challenges involved in running a happy home efficiently certainly require high-level executive abilities.

In order to be an effective homemaker, women are challenged with financial decisions; they often must struggle heroically to balance the budget. They need to be time-stretchers, jockeying into their days the variety of needs of all the family members. They must be specialists in interpersonal relationships, calming tempers, negotiating arguments, settling disputes, and maintaining harmony with family, in-laws, and friends. In their spare time, they write the letters, handle the social calendar, wait for the repairmen, and see that birthdays and holidays are rewarding times.

Our clients demonstrate the many ways that a woman's strength serves her husband well. When a child is sick, it is the mother who takes over the chores that the father largely avoids. Mary was expected to have whatever physical and emotional stamina was needed to add nursing care to her schedule. She sat up night after night with her sick son. This was a task no one shared with her, no matter how heavy the burden was.

If a woman is sick herself, it is a special problem. Most women do as Norene did: she handled her own illness while staying on her feet. After a serious operation and only a few days of recuperation, she got back in harness, snatching a little rest between meals, laundry, and car pools. No one in the family urged her to take longer to recuperate.

When Connie's husband's business folded, she was his main emotional support. Her love for him motivated her to listen while he lightened his load of failure by sharing his disappointment with her. Connie found, however, that he could not be supportive of her when her feelings about their loss spilled out. He became visibly upset and explained that he did not want to be reminded that he had failed her. Her role was to be strong when he needed her.

In another instance, Alicia's husband regularly gave her messages that he made the decisions because he was the capable one. Whenever they took trips, he did all the driving while she attended to the children's needs. When his job required that the family move across the country, he moved first. Alicia was expected to drive alone with the three children to the new city. Her capabilities were not questioned when he needed her to take over.

Women are more flexible than the paradox of equality would suggest. Problems arise when conflicts are resolved by identifying the subordinate role as the model for women's behavior. Wives do enjoy filling executive roles in a family. They also accept subordinate roles; at times they may even choose them. Combining some executive and some subordinate functions suggests that there is a healthy interdependence in a relationship that defies the paradox.

"He's going to be the breadwinner."

The paradox of equality has forced women into positions of ambivalence. From their earliest years,

27

many women see the model of self-sacrifice as being appropriate for them. Achievement goals are directed away from fulfillment except in traditional female roles. This in itself produces discomfort in women as they grow up.

Women cannot say, "I want to be married and I am going to marry this particular man." Traditionally, women are picked by men. One of our clients was in love with a man and was certain she wanted to marry him. She told him so. He responded with, "*I'd* like to do the asking." This chilling message had a double edge: it cooled her ardor while it put her back in her place. She felt that he was justified in chastising her for being forward.

In thinking about what she wants for herself, a young woman realizes that she must maintain a position of flexibility. This means that she must keep herself available and sufficiently attractive to a variety of men so that one will eventually pick her as his bride. A woman also has to recognize that maybe she never will get married, and she needs then to plan a self-supporting future for herself. The paradox of equality has thus set up seldom-acknowledged dissonance for women that is not experienced by men. A man thinks that he probably will get married some day, that in the normal course of events he will acquire a wife and children. For women it is not that simple. Women expect to get married, but on the off chance that they do not, they must be prepared to support themselves.

The ambivalence continues into marriage. A wife must stay flexible because her marriage may not turn out as she expected. If a wife dreams of staying home and raising a family, she may find that there is not enough money. She may have to find a slot in the job marketplace, or her husband may become ill, or die prematurely. There is a good chance that the marriage will end in divorce. Each of these contingencies becomes a reality for some women, and the chance that one might is enough to produce anxiety in every woman. At the very least, women can expect that they might outlive their husbands by several years. It is folly for women to close their eyes to that frightening fact.

Ambivalence in a young woman extends to believing that if she marries a man who has a promising career the actualization of her own career goals is no longer necessary. A large percentage of the women we see in therapy are those who have swung from a career course to the relationship route. Many have put their husbands through school by working at jobs far below the achievement level they once expected for themselves.

Abby had intended to work for a degree in business and was enrolled in a university program; instead she quit college and became a secretary to support her husband while he went to school. Mandy was preparing to become an interior decorator, but put it aside and took a job as a salesclerk when she married; she saw her own vocation as no longer a valid goal. Abby and Mandy are typical of many young women we see in therapy. Self-sacrifice seems totally in order for them; they hope to achieve their goals through marriage.

"I'm just not happy like I thought I'd be."

Many women who have awakened to the paradox of equality come for therapy. They are in a transitional stage. They are in the process of examining their development and meaningful participation in life. We often find among these clients women who have fulfilled traditional roles and, some years later, have identified a stirring in themselves, an awareness that in choosing the traditional role they passed over their potential for achievement in other areas. They are feeling that reentry time has come.

Among these are young women who, having been married several years, feel guilty because they are uncomfortable with the wear and tear of matrimony. They come to us saying, "I don't know what's the matter with me. I have a husband and three lovely children, and I'm not happy." Those who once had high achievement needs share certain similarities. They have been able to satisfy some of these needs in their own homes. They are known among their friends as having the best-decorated houses. They are good cooks and give large, successful dinner parties. Their children are bright, well-liked, and well-mannered. Their husbands are usually occupied with successful careers. When these women were growing up, they were encouraged to see themselves as achievers and were given every indication that whatever they did would be satisfying. It was after they were married that they discovered that marriage did not tap many areas of their potential and that they felt vaguely restless and unfulfilled.

Nora was thirty years old when she came to therapy, disappointed and feeling guilty that she was so unhappy. She described her marriage as finished. She felt sexually turned off by her husband, hated the house she had once been so proud of, and found herself very short-tempered with her three children. She no longer enjoyed socializing with her neighbors, who seemed to Nora to be happily involved with homes and children.

Nora was very bright. As a child she had been encouraged to develop her considerable musical abilities and had dreamed of a career as a concert pianist. When Nora met Rick, however, she realized that she had other dreams, too—dreams of a home and family, which suddenly seemed more desirable than a music career. Limiting herself to a choice of either/or, she picked marriage.

Although marriage had been rewarding, there came a point in Nora's life when her earlier aspirations began to surface and she felt that she had been cheated. She saw that her role as wife and mother did not earn the status or rewards that men enjoyed, nor was it as rewarding as the role to which she had once looked forward for herself. Although she could not identify it, Nora's conflict was with the paradox of equality: She did not feel equal.

Nora learned in therapy that women can plan complex lives for themselves. They can combine traditional values with contemporary aspirations and enjoy the rewards of both. Husbands, who at first may feel threatened, soften when they see the positive results of their wives' achievements. Children admire and respect mothers whom they see as happily occupied.

Nora will never become a famous pianist. She examined this goal in therapy and explored other options. She realized that she was as interested in composing music as she had once been in performing, and she decided to pursue that goal. In doing so, she combined her commitments to her family and to herself, issues of equal importance to her.

For older women who put aside achievement goals in favor of traditional roles in their early years, the pain of the paradox of equality is extreme. We frequently see women in therapy who have sacrificed themselves for other people all their lives. This is a grievously heavy investment. All of their socialization messages told them that self-sacrifice was appropriate behavior for them and that it would bring great rewards. These women are bewildered and shocked to find in their later years that their efforts are discounted. Instead of being appreciated, they feel rejected by those from whom they expected the greatest rewards. They react with indignant resistance when they learn from their therapists that they have been filling a martyr's role. They are offended at the suggestion that every martyr expects a payoff. Historically, Christian martyrs sought salvation. In a modern family, the martyr usually wants appreciation, affection, and recognition that her sacrifices are valued.

There is no way that a woman of sixty can relive her life and choose not to invest so heavily in serving others. Having put aside her achievement goals in her youth, an older woman may feel remorseful when she confronts the fact that her opportunities are lost forever. This realization is complicated by her conviction that since she did so much for the members of her family they should now be grateful. It is difficult for women to comprehend that their children, believing that sacrifices were freely made, see no reason to reciprocate. The recognition that no one has a right to put a mortgage on the future of those she has served is a bitter pill to swallow.

"This is the way women are, and don't forget it."

Stereotypes that box women and men into precast

roles support the paradox of equality. The rewards and pressures of our experiences encourage us to internalize stereotypic qualities. Women are supposed to be nurturing, loving, gentle, patient, tender, and caring; that is the female stereotype. Yet the truth is that all these qualities are present and desirable in both males and females. Some males are more nurturing than some women. They also may be more gentle, loving, patient, tender, and caring. Other stereotyped qualities that are used to describe women are plainly negative, qualities like passivity, dependency, submissiveness, and indecisiveness. These are seen as weak and unattractive. They, too, apply to both sexes.

Men also are stereotyped with certain qualities: bravery, strength, intelligence, resourcefulness, energy, and competence. Although considered masculine, these are characteristics that are essential to the effectiveness of women as well as men.

It is important that all women be seen as people with qualities that everyone values, not as stereotypes. Women must enhance the positive attitudes they have and reject the negative stereotypes applied to them. If they believe that negative descriptions accurately fit them, they will continue to feel inferior and caught up in the paradox of equality.

There is another difficulty in the assignment of stereotypical characteristics based on sex. Women have felt that they must deny in themselves the positive qualities that are ascribed to men, lest they appear masculine and seem to be challenging men for their dominant position. By accepting the less ideal "female" characteristics, women collude with men in defining themselves as inferior and perpetuate their submissiveness. What women need if they are to communicate and become comfortable with men is a central issue in this paradox; relationships do not have to be based on a dominant/submissive model. Moving to peer relationships with men is a way to break out of the mold. Cooperation, not competition, is the mark of equality.

The main message of socialization for females is that they should grow up to be happy wives and mothers.

But even women who want to fill this role to perfection have little preparation for the realities of marriage. The most specific modeling they have is from their mothers, and few women want to live as their mothers did. Even with the best of examples, one generation cannot anticipate all of the realities of the next generation.

As children, young girls identify with the fairy tales they read. Cinderella, Snow White, Rapunzel, and the Ugly Duckling are the stuff of most girls' dreams. Although these characters have humble beginnings, they are rescued, through no efforts of their own, and led to a happy life. These fairy tales are further embroidered by little girls' imaginations, which overload their ability to sift out truth from fancy. Marriage is seen as a magnificent event, the final goal. It is not seen as a continuation of the growth process.

For many women, the fairy tale stops with marriage. When we see these women as clients, it is usually some years later. We see them as victims of sex-role socialization. These women feel bewildered, bitter, confused, disappointed, and guilt ridden. If often comes as a surprise to them that what they thought was going to be a beautiful reality was only a fantasy.

We have seen in our practice that when women marry very young they cannot predict what they will want for themselves when they are older. Lack of knowledge and experience precludes their even knowing what the opportunites for growth and development are. They report that they expected to get complete fulfillment from family life. Many women do experience years of satisfaction and happiness in raising families, but for other women the reality differs from the dream. They had not thought about the stacks of laundry they would wash, the piles of dirty dishes standing on the sink, the number of diapers they would change and wash, the toilet bowls they would scrub, the hundreds of hours of interrupted sleep, the years of weekdays filled with children's chatter and unrelieved by adult conversation.

When these women come to therapy they feel overwhelmed with guilt; they are unhappy, and they think they should not be. They believe that if changes are to occur in their lives, they must bring them about. Burdened with low self-esteem, they cannot see any viable way of improving their lives. They also feel guilty about experiencing anger and reproachfulness, feelings they have been taught are unfeminine. Sometimes it is hard for them to recognize that sex-role socialization is the thief that has robbed them, that this is at the root of their problems. When they do see this, they taste bitterness. For the therapist, it is one of the times when she must point out the real injustices in women's lives. Socialization has led women to believe a lot of lies.

"I should . . ."

The paradox of equality requires that a woman examine many issues. Does she accept that women are by nature inferior and that men are somehow more important than women? Does she aim as high in her occupational goals as she would have if she were a man? Does she break an engagement with a woman for a date with a man? Is she willing to work at the same job with a man but for less pay than he gets? Does she like most men better than she likes most women?

For a married woman, additional questions surface. Does she believe that complementary male and female roles are equal? If she has accepted this notion, has she allowed her partner to do what he found most important in life while she filled in the holes and made his way easier? Has he gained recognition and status in the community while her value resides in being his wife? Are his opinions sought out and listened to whereas hers are seen as unimportant? If he decides to leave her for a younger woman, how will their life-style differ? Will he continue to enjoy the status and prestige that he has earned with her support? In the case of a divorce, at what level of status and salary will she enter the job market?

The purpose of the story you were asked to complete at the beginning of this chapter is to demonstrate the extent to which typical socialization messages can influence the way people react when role conflicts arise.

34

Readers unconsciously identify with people in a story like this, and women, even though they are unmarried, tend to identify with Joan. For most women, the socialization pressures toward marriage have been so strong that the feelings they have about a woman's role in marriage are reflected in their opinions about how other women should fill this role.

The issue involved in the story is acceptance or rejection of a subordinate role in a conflict situation. If there is a conflict, subordinate women tend to put themselves last and to meet their needs only after the needs of others are met. Even the slightest pressure encourages them to resolve conflicts in another person's favor. In cases where they make a conscious decision to take care of their own needs first, they tend to feel guilty and lose much of the pleasure that could accompany their choices.

The story could have been completed by resolving Joan's dilemma in either a submissive or a nonsubmissive way. Which you chose will tell you something about yourself. A submissive solution would be that Joan puts aside her personal plans and goes to the zoo with the family. This means that at some level you feel it is appropriate for a woman to fill a subordinate role. The choice of such an ending reveals that you believe that a woman's plans are not as important as those of other members of the family. If you elaborated on this by having Joan pack a picnic lunch or stay up half the night to study, it suggests that you believe that a woman should please her family first, and then meet her own needs by extraordinary efforts.

A nonsubmissive solution would have Joan look objectively at her own needs, recognize her and Robert's goals, and decide to stay home and study while Robert took the children to the zoo. If your story also includes Robert cooperating with Joan's effort, you reveal appreciation of true equality and not the paradox that, although Joan's rights are said to be equal to Robert's, she should give in when there is conflict.

If your story did not resolve the dilemma, then it is important to consider whether in your life you back

35

away from situations in which your rights conflict with the wishes of other people.

The paradox of equality will not be totally resolved for women until their socialization experiences change. But it is time for women to challenge the contradictions of this paradox. If women are equal to men, they should receive equal treatment. If they are inferior, then not so much should be expected of them in tremendously important areas.

Women are not inferior to men. They should not be treated that way. Complementary does not mean equal. Women and men can appreciate each other's differences, see each other as equals, and enjoy respectful relationships. Unfortunately, at the present time, women's experiences with the paradox of equality are likely to be exacerbated by the next paradox, which is concerned with the issue of self-esteem.

CHAPTER III

Self-Esteem

> *"I've done so well—why do I feel so bad?"*

Self-esteem is acquired through achievements and feedback from others. Women have successfully and enthusiastically adopted the roles and behaviors society has dictated for them. They have nurtured children, cherished relationships, been helpmates, and have not asked for too much. Shouldn't they feel good? The paradox is that no matter how hard women try, how well they do, or how much they achieve, they still feel bad. The roles and behaviors assigned to women have not been highly valued. Women do not get the positive messages needed for a sense of high self-esteem.

If you feel good about yourself, you have high self-esteem. If you feel bad about yourself, you have low self-esteem. The difference between high and low self-esteem is as simple as that.

Self-esteem can be defined as a positive or negative attitude toward oneself. This self-evaluation is learned in two ways: through one's achievements and in one's interactions with the significant people in one's life. As individuals do things and experience success or failure, and as family members, teachers, friends, and peers give them positive and negative messages concerning how they are seen, individuals make decisions about whether they consider themselves good or bad.

Even under the best of circumstances, acquiring positive self-esteem is difficult for women. Growing up in a male-dominated society, without being consciously aware of it, women come to regard themselves as innately inferior to men. Women reveal their self-abnegation not only in important matters, but in countless little ways as well. For instance, without even thinking they stop talking when a man interrupts. They do not seem to respect women's opinions, but listen attentively when men say the very same thing. Or they turn to men for advice, "just to be sure," when they have already decided what they want to do. Each little incident that confirms a woman's subservience is not traumatic in itself; it is the accumulation of years of little put-downs, negative messages, and being regarded as subordinate that eats away at a woman's sense of self-worth until she ends up feeling bad.

Because women are seen by others as inferior, they come to see themselves that way. They are assigned to and fit themselves into subservient, childlike roles, primarily those of helper and giver. Unfortunately, helping is seen as not doing anything important. A woman may refer to herself as being just a housewife, just a secretary, or just a teacher, even though whatever she just is can become her reason for being. Her *justs* go unchallenged; her second-rate standing is silently affirmed.

Once installed in their discounted callings, women are expected to demonstrate characteristics, such as passivity and dependence, that confirm their lowly status. Their functions are not highly valued by other persons, and their achievements in carrying out their duties frequently are taken for granted or go unnoticed. Nevertheless, they are to accept their "proper" places and, having done so, they are supposed to feel good about themselves, even if their roles are not especially rewarding.

It does not work. Inferiority is a flimsy foundation upon which to construct positive self-esteem. Women's achievements do not serve as a source of pride and self-respect. Instead, they become a graveyard for unrealized potential, deferred hopes, and forfeited identities. Searching for an alternative base upon which to build a belief in themselves, women turn to affiliations with other people. They make heavy emotional investments, hoping their unselfish commitments will pay generous dividends in the form of love and appreciation, which will in turn boost their sense of self-worth.

All too often, their relationships go bankrupt. After a while a woman says to herself, "I've done everything that was expected of me. I've raised the children, been a loving wife and a helpmate, and I haven't asked for much in return. How come I feel so bad?" Thus do countless women express their experience with the paradox of self-esteem.

Riddled with self-doubts and constricted by narrowed images of themselves, women struggle within self-imposed and other-prescribed limitations to maintain a sense of dignity and worth. Th rocky ground of low self-esteem has not been fertile soil for women's growth. For some women, maintaining their faith in themselves has required that they wage long battles involving extraordinary maneuvers that have ultimately failed to provide them with inner strength and positive self-regard. Being dependent, not trusting themselves or anyone else, blaming and rejecting others, and becoming helpless are tactics that provide only the thinnest veneer of protection. The paradox of self-esteem continues to eat away below the surface.

"No one will ever love me."

Happy, healthy children are vivid examples of individuals with high self-esteem. Their shrieks of laughter, shy giggles, mischievous pranks, tender affections, quick tears, and joyful sprints, leaps, and somersaults all shout the unmistakable glad tidings that they feel good about themselves.

How did they acquire their sparkling eyes, curious minds, and spontaneous emotionality? As they grow up, children develop self-worth in part by integrating content and process messages from others. A content message is what is said and a process message is how it is said. Children evaluate themselves and then act in response to how they see others viewing them. For example, if a teacher tells a student that she is artistic, the student is likely to test out her teacher's perception and may come to think of herself as artistic, too. She will probably feel encouraged to draw and paint, and may develop creative skills that are praised by others. The student's self-esteem is enhanced in two very important ways: first, through her successful accomplishments, and second, because of the positive communication she receives.

Incongruencies in the messages people send create confusion and self-doubt. When a little girl hears, "I love you," said with a frown, she is likely to ignore the positive words and wonder what the frown means. She does not have to wonder what is meant by, "I love you," when it is said with a smile and a hug.

Parents are the most influential storehouse from which children draw supplies for building self-esteem. When the material is spoiled with negative messages, children evaluate themselves harshly unless they have many rewarding achievements to fall back on. When parental messages are positive, high self-esteem is stockpiled even when successful achievements are absent, although strong reliance on close interpersonal relationships may also develop. When *both* positive feedback and enriching achievements are lacking, children generally feel unloved and rejected, and suffer from low self-esteem.

Jan is an example of the paradox of self-esteem. She grew up in a home where esteem enhancement was absent. Jan's parents never intended to give her the message that they did not value and appreciate her, for they loved their daughter very much. Unfortunately, their own upbringing taught them that to spare the rod was to spoil the child, that loving parents guided and controlled their children and kept them safe from harm and disappointment, then passed them into their respective roles: work for the boys, marriage for the girls. They were reserved, unemotional, and stingy with praise. Worse yet, perhaps, they seemed to be saying that any man Jan could attract would probably be inadequate, so she should develop secretarial skills in case she needed to take care of herself. Jan interpreted all of these messages as rejection.

Jan had determination and perseverance despite almost overwhelming feelings of low self-esteem. A spark of self-actualization burned in her, and she refused to accept what she believed to be her parents' notion of her self-worth. In high school she worked hard to maintain her grades so she could get into college, even though she thought of herself as a mediocre student. Not long before graduation, she was astonished to learn that she was second highest in her class. No one had told her before how well she was doing compared with the other students. She had thought her classmates were much more intelligent than she was and were surely doing better work. This boost to her confidence did not last long.

College was an ordeal for Jan. She worked full-time at evening and weekend jobs to support herself. Her greatest difficulties, however, centered around her fear of other people. Anxiety became a deep freeze that kept her locked up inside herself. Her opinion of herself was so low that she interpreted most questions or comments from her professors as subtle messages that she would never measure up to their expectations. This created a new obstacle: As Jan's fragile confidence in her academic abilities plummeted, her test-anxiety soared. Her grades reflected her distress, for her anxiety made it impossible for her to concentrate on her studies.

Jan experienced college as an ongoing nightmare in which she blindly scurried from one test performance to another. The single redeeming event was meeting Cliff, a fellow student, in her junior year. He had suffered much the same childhood as Jan had. Each found safety and solace in the other—at long last someone from whom each of them could receive comfort and praise.

When Jan graduated from college, jobs in her field were hard to find. She saw her failure to get a job as the final confirmation of her fundamental lack of worth. She slid quietly into the consolation of marriage. A few months later she learned, with much relief, that she was pregnant; this justified her continuing to find refuge in her homemaker niche.

During her second pregnancy, Jan came to therapy feeling vulnerable to any real or imagined slight. She knew she felt worthless, but that was only the tip of the iceberg. Low self-esteem provided a frigid platform beneath which lay the heavy load of emotional pain accumulated over many years of silence. In therapy this hurt and disappointment poured out.

As long as Jan felt incapable of doing whatever was necessary to update her skills, homemaking was her only option. She felt trapped; her refuge turned into a prison and she became resentful and angry. Her guilt and her belief that she was a horrible person, unworthy of her family's love and affection, added the ball and chain to her confinement.

Therapy ended for Jan when she rearranged her perceptions of herself and her life so she could enjoy both a career and a family. This thawed out long frozen, benevolent parts of herself and freed her energies so that she could let go of past hurts, focus on the present, and plan for the future. Jan's resolution of the self-esteem paradox provides an example other women can examine as they wrestle with the contractions and expansions of their own images and select self-enhancing routes to change.

"If I feel bad, I will prove that I am bad."

Problems revolving around self-esteem are presented by almost every client who comes to therapy. When

41

women express feelings of defenselessness, passivity, hostility, dependence, lack of identity, anxiety, manipulation, control, and projection, the underlying issue involves lack of a sense of positive self-worth.

For a few women, the paradox of self-esteem takes a curious twist. Instead of trying hard and feeling bad, they feel bad and try hard to prove just how bad they are. They do things to confirm that their evaluation of themselves as no good is true. They behave in ways that force others to respond with negative messages; such messages confirm their fears that the black demons, which they suspect live barely restrained within themselves, do indeed exist.

Penny was such a woman. She came from a family in which boys were encouraged and girls were only tolerated. Women were expected to provide support services, whereas men were expected to achieve whatever goals they might establish for themselves. When Penny was eight years old, her only brother was killed. She felt burdened with guilt; in her little-girl wisdom, she felt somehow to blame. She knew, too, that the ambitions her parents had hoped to fulfill through their son could never be realized by a daughter.

Feeling bad about herself, Penny set about proving the truth of what she thought. She became disobedient and disrespectful of her parents, proving that she was a bad daughter. She stopped studying and got bad grades, proving that she was a poor student. In her teens, she had sex with several boys, proving that she was dirty. Having accomplished all of this, she withdrew socially, proving that nobody liked her.

In her young adulthood, Penny covered up her badness long enough to attract a husband, a man who was dominant, wealthy, and powerful. She became compliant, subservient, and nonassertive, confirming that she deserved to be mistreated. She became bitter and hostile, confirming that she was a bad wife. She thought of running away and committing suicide almost daily. Her abject misery drove her to seek therapy.

Once she began therapy, Penny discovered that her self-defeating behavior was her way of punishing herself because she felt completely worthless and blamed herself for her brother's death and her parents' grief. It was a tortuous uphill climb for her to change her self-punishing and demeaning patterns, a painful process of destroying the negative images she had projected so convincingly. She had to acquire a brand new self formed from positive values and rewards that would nurture her self-esteem.

Penny's therapist knew that the long struggle for self-forgiveness was over when she received a drawing Penny had done. In it she had sketched herself as a woman giving her eight-year-old self a warm and loving hug.

"I thought being with you would make me feel good."

Women have been told that they will be fulfilled once they have a man to love and be loved by, that a girl becomes a woman when she is chosen as someone's sexual partner. For countless women, the most believable and satisfying confirmation of their self-worth comes from a man's approval. Their successes as well as their emotional supports center around their close relationships. The other achievements they attain usually do not mean much to them if they do not have at least one other person with whom they are affiliated. Their sense of self-worth, their identity as adult women comes from belonging to someone else.

Women who lack a healthy, separate identity are afraid of rejection; if they lose the people who love them, they lose the reservoir of positive messages from which they draw their belief in themselves. The affirmations of others are essential to confirm their worth; negative messages can undermine their confidence and trigger fears of repudiation and abandonment. For women who have accepted the notion that they will be real people, that they will be fulfilled and certified as okay when they are loved by men, it is exceedingly hard to accept the possibility that they may never find someone to love them and take care of them. When this dilemma is heaped on top of low self-esteem, this contingency is so frightening that they may refuse to examine the issue at all.

Maxine's life provides a vivid example of the paradox of trying hard and feeling bad with which women must struggle in their efforts to develop positive self-esteem. She was the oldest daughter in a family of eight. Her job from early childhood was to take care of the other children; girls were good for that sort of chore, and for cooking and cleaning. Her family scoffed when she said she wanted to go to college, and insisted that Maxine pay her own way because college was wasted on females. Being a wife and mother, the only job for which women were suited, did not require educated brains.

Maxine used grit and ingenuity to get her degree and establish herself in her career. At the same time, she felt internally generated commands to establish an intimate relationship. Her low regard for herself dictated failure. Afraid no man could ever genuinely love her, she settled for a series of casual sexual encounters. Maxine believed that only by offering sex could she keep a man. She was plagued with loneliness because the intimacy and love she longed for were missing.

As Maxine rapidly climbed the career ladder to become the director of a community agency, her feelings of failure supported her belief that she had to choose between her job and marriage. Men seemed unresponsive to her workaday competence, and disrespectful of her afterhours playfulness. It seemed to her that love and a career were mutually exclusive, that the more she succeeded in her work, the less likely were her chances of finding a loving relationship.

When Maxine began therapy, she was confused about why she searched so desperately for intimacy, since all the love affairs she had known had ended in heartbreak. She gradually came to the realization that the debilitation of the paradox of doing good and feeling bad determined these outcomes.

In all of her relationships Maxine became dependent, hoping in this way to elicit a commitment from her partners. Probably because initially they were drawn to her by her independence, they reacted with anger and withdrawal when she took the one-down position. This reinforced her estimation of herself as

44

being unworthy of love. Feeling rejected, she attempted to hang on by becoming pleasing, possessive, and placating. They withdrew even further; her anxiety increased, but she tried to act less demanding. Then they began to take her for granted. Maxine's self-esteem hit bedrock each time she tried to please a man, since the more she tried the more she felt rejected.

Maxine summed it up in her women's therapy group: "When I'm dependent upon men, I feel anxious and possessive and angry because they are not what I demand they must be. Then they get angry and go away, and I feel helpless and worthless. I say to myself, 'Obviously I'm no good, because no one loves me.'"

Ben, the last man with whom she did this careful balancing act before she came to therapy, often dropped in without calling, expecting that she would "cook a nice little meal" and then "jump into bed." The final eye-opener came one Sunday afternoon when Ben dropped off his two small children for Maxine to babysit while he went to a party at a friend's apartment.

In therapy, Maxine focused on the low-down side of herself and her kick-me behavior with men. She learned to value herself and in turn to value other women. Establishing friendships with women meant that she was freed from depending exclusively upon men for positive messages. She started seeing her career achievement as a powerful affirmation of her self-worth. To her delight, her inner-based, self-generated appreciation of herself acted as a magnet for other people. Again, Maxine summed it up: "I used to long for someone to be with and despaired of ever finding a man of my own. Now I could choose from among three or four men if I wanted to have a permanent arrangement, and I have so many friends that my problem is finding time for myself."

Doing good and feeling happy replaced doing good and feeling like a failure.

"Anyone is better than no one."

When we ask our clients to list their positive characteristics, they often laugh nervously. They cannot think of anything good to say, or even as they are thinking about it, they cancel out each positive attribute with a negative one. For instance, Jackie said, "Well, I'm good at my job, but it's so easy any fool could do it." Carolyn described herself as a friendly person, then added, "I'm afraid not to be because I can't stand to be by myself." Lettie decided she was pretty, then took back the statement by saying, "But you should see me in the morning without my makeup."

Although they may disqualify themselves, many of the roles women fill are a source of self-enhancing messages. As therapists, we know that there are many rewards in the helping professions. Our clients give us positive messages and society values our achievements. Teachers feel excited and reinforced when students' eyes light up at the pleasure of learning something new. Nurses are happy when their patients get well.

For some women, being wives and mothers is the primary confirmation of their self-worth. One of our clients always felt loved and needed when she held a new baby in her arms. "Maybe," she laughed ruefully in recognition of the truth of what she was saying, "I had all seven of my kids because having a baby made me feel important. It was my one great achievement. Besides, they all loved me, especially when they were little."

Having no other source from which to gain the longed-for superlatives of their self-worth, many women expect to be rewarded for filling their homemaker roles. Their other-generated sense of themselves is dependent upon the successes and failures of their husbands and children. When children grow up and leave home, they feel an immediate, bewildering sense of role loss; the underpinnings of their self-esteem are gone, replaced with depression, anger, and emptiness. On the other hand. women who have developed positive identities look forward to the years when their children have moved into adulthood as a time to fulfill previously unused potential. Resources of time, energy, talent, and money that were invested in others are now available for consignment to new, self-oriented endeavors.

Tragically, some women crippled with the pain of low self-esteem are so uncertain about their value that they are easily influenced by what others think. They accept someone else's judgment of them as gospel. They are unable to see that problems often have more to do with another person than with themselves.

This was Joan's dilemma. Twenty-two years old and married for three years, Joan reported in therapy that her husband Bert had never settled into his wedlocked state. He spent several nights a week out with the boys or other women. When he did come home, he treated Joan as if she were a trash can for dumping all of his hostilities. Joan recalled what she described as "an incident that will give you a sample of my life with Bert."

A few weeks ago I waited three hours in a broiling sun for Bert to pick me up after a doctor's appointment. I was afraid to wait inside the office where it was cool, because if he came and I failed to jump into the car as he slammed on the brakes he was likely to gun the engine and speed off without me. When Bert did come for me, he said with mock apology, "Sorry I'm late. The engine was a little rough, so I had it tuned up." When I said that I wished he'd come for me first, he said, "You women like to keep men waiting. Now you'll know how it feels if you're ever tempted to do it to me."

Unlike many women, Joan was not financially dependent upon Bert. She worked as a reservations agent for an airline and earned a good salary. This achievement, however, meant nothing to her. She was convinced that there must be something wrong with her or Bert would not be treating her so badly. Trying hard and failing big with Bert was a daily occurrence.

Joan's feelings of low self-esteem were deeply

ingrained from years of childhood abuse by a cruel father. As an adult, she felt as weak and helpless as the kittens she had once been forced to watch her father drown, one by one, in a bucket of water. Joan reacted to her husband as if he were her father, the person who had horrified her days and inhabited her nightmares.

The paradoxical glue that kept Joan attached to Bert was that any little elevation in her self-esteem originated in his infrequent endearments or offhand kindnesses. Her hope that she was lovable rose and fell like a barometer in response to his moods. Feeling full of emotional hunger, she looked to Bert for positive messages that would affirm her value. Despite the fact that she tried hard to please him, for the most part Joan failed to get even crumbs of the kindness she needed to nourish her self-esteem. Feeling as if her worthlessness would overtake her diminished identity completely if she let go of Bert, Joan failed to resolve the paradox of self-esteem.

Children of cruel or rejecting parents like Joan's are characterized by feeling bad about themselves. They experience bottomless pits of yearning for the love and sense of belonging they have never known. Some grasp at common, everyday courtesies as if they were promises of lifelong devotion. Others armor themselves with frozen masks and impenetrable defenses. Many come to see themselves as unworthy of being loved, for it is unthinkable to see their parents as unloving persons. To do so would open the floodgates of overwhelming fears of abandonment and helplessness at a time when a child does not have the intellectual capacity to understand or the emotional stamina to prevent drowning in sorrow.

Only twenty-two when she began therapy, Cindy looked old beyond her years. Her clothes were nondescript, her hair dull and limp, her skin pale and lifeless, and her movements were curiously slow yet uncertain.

For Cindy, her feelings of grief and not belonging anywhere were similar to those that originate in parental rejection, although the cause was different. She described her distress to her therapist in a low, tired voice.

I don't know what's wrong with me. Maybe I'm a terrible person. I feel bad and I don't know why. I've tried to ignore my uncomfortable, miserable feelings, thinking they would go away. When they didn't, I decided to come for therapy. As a child I was always having to say good-bye to people and places that I loved. My father was so important to me, but he died when I was only eight years old. I still think about him and miss him very much. After he died, my family moved from town to town. It seemed I would finally feel comfortable at home, and the next thing I knew I was leaving friends and familiar surroundings behind again. My older brother and sisters grew up and left home, too. Then when I was eighteen, my mother remarried and I thought I should strike out on my own. But I've been feeling bad ever since.

Cindy's feelings were the result of choked-back grief. She had suffered so many losses that she had accumulated a reservoir of dammed up tears. Because she felt bad, she interpreted her emotional state as proof that she was bad, and she suffered from low self-esteem as a result.

"I can't trust anyone."

For some women, low self-esteem leads to lack of trust in others and consequent avoidance of intimacy. They feel threatened and anxious whenever they associate with people, fearing that they will not be liked. Their mask of indifference hides an inner uncertainty, for the relationship between self-esteem and interaction with other people is a circular process. Low self-esteem not only results from, but it also increases interpersonal tension and anxiety. Staying away from closeness with others breaks the circle of self-doubt. By avoiding commitments, one can elude any barbs that might come

49

one's way, lest such remarks confirm a poor self-image and increase disappointments in oneself. To salvage some vestige, no matter how dim, of her own identity, a woman may explain this behavior by saying, "Well, I'm just different."

When women ache with the encumberance of low self-esteem, they translate feeling *different* as *being bad*. They shrink back from others so no one will catch sight of the voided condition of their inner selves. It is then an easy, logical step for some women to project negative feelings onto other people without checking to see if that is where they belong. They end up disliking other people as well as themselves.

Francene was such a woman. Her parents were European immigrants who had settled timidly in a large city. They sacrificed their own comfort to live in a middle-class neighborhood so that their four children could have advantages they, the parents, had never known. Francene's father worked at two jobs to pay the bills. Her mother spent her days cleaning up relentlessly after everyone. She urged the children to visit "nice" friends, go to "good" movies and "big" dances, and to stay late for "important" after-school activities, all in the interest of making friends whose connections would serve them well as adults.

Francene did not share her parents' view of the good life. She suspected that their hard work and sacrifices for their children were handy rationalizations, for they seemed afraid to do for themselves the social climbing they urged their youngsters to do. They clung to home-country clothing and customs and rarely ventured far from the uneasy safety of their neighborhood. Without realizing it, they transmitted their fears of everything new to Francene. She grew up feeling timid and different and ashamed of her family's ways.

Francene's low self-esteem was well established by the time she began college. She did little to improve it and much to keep it down. She shunned close relationships with college men because, she said, they had none of the qualities she valued in a man. No one ever asked her what those qualities were, unfortunately; had she discovered she could not list them, she might have realized what she was doing to herself. She felt uneasy and competitive with women, describing them as critical, bitchy, and trivial. She felt jealous when another woman seemed prettier, more confident, or more intelligent than she was. Francene failed to recognize that these feelings reflected a lack of trust and caring for herself.

The approach to intellectual enhancement Francene took was as tentative as her attitude about relationships was hostile. She remained convinced that she could not possibly be intelligent or successful, and did her best to sabotage her college career. Nevertheless, she outwitted herself by graduating near the top of her class. Although she won a scholarship to graduate school, she firmly believed that it was an accident, that she had not earned it even though she had been urged by the graduate school to apply.

Having reluctantly accepted the scholarship, Francene worked hard but was seldom satisfied with her efforts. She refused to turn in less than perfect work, and so began to fall behind in her studies. At last her self-doubts were confirmed. Threatened with failure, she dropped out of school. The prophecy which her low self-esteem had dictated had been fulfilled.

Both of the avenues to enhancing her devalued image were closed to Francene. She discouraged affirmative affiliations with her haughty mask of scornful indifference and dictated academic failure with her disguise of perfectionism and procrastination.

"Don't blame me!"

Low self-esteem is fertile soil for seeds of querulous discontent and defensiveness. Quite often people who have poor opinions of themselves pick partners who feel bad about themselves, too; they hope that someone who feels as they do will understand how wretchedly forlorn they feel and that together they can experience the splendid magic of feeling good together.

Sharon was a handsome, trim woman of forty-two who took a no-nonsense approach to life. Looking at Sharon on the surface, one would describe her as confident, aggressive, and outgoing. Her friendliness was a ruse, however, for she maintained a stubborn stance of defensiveness that made sharing and self-exploration difficult. She felt self-righteous and abused because of an unhappy marriage. Sharon's complaint when she came to therapy was that her husband Dan was treating her badly and she would like him to change from an ill-tempered miser to a benevolent lover. She did not want to leave the marriage, even though she felt contemptuous of her husband and blamed him bitterly.

In a moment of unaccustomed candor in her therapy, Sharon listed the low-esteem symptoms of her troubled spirit. "I feel so bad about myself that I blame everyone else, especially Dan, for how I feel; I interpret whatever he says about me negatively. I even resent people who feel good about themselves. I'm so sensitive that I know I need to change."

Sharon was surprised when her therapist identified feelings of low self-esteem as underlying the dysfunctionality between her husband and herself. As a matter of fact, neither Sharon nor Dan felt good about themselves when they had married. Both had looked upon marriage as the natural course of events that would provide an easy escape from the unpleasantness of their parental homes. Being together would automatically provide an out-of-the-pits boost into a full-grown expansiveness of positive feelings about themselves and each other. This was to ensure self-contentment and everlasting happiness.

Neither Sharon nor Dan felt she or he had a right or even knew how to express directly these strong but vague hopes. As bitter disappointment replaced optimistic hopes, a mutual pattern of manipulation and punishment became firmly entrenched. Rather than tell Dan beforehand what she expected, Sharon waited until after the damage was done and then berated him for his shortcomings. Instead of speaking up, Dan sought the imaginary protection of avoided conflict by coming home as little as possible.

By the time Sharon started therapy, Dan had made a 100-percent emotional investment in his business and she felt their marriage was bankrupt. Wanting revenge, Sharon found it difficult to evaluate herself and her behavior. She would have preferred to spend her time in therapy blaming Dan for their unhappiness.

Defensive clients are shielding themselves from the vulnerability of low self-esteem, and they deserve empathy, understanding, and time to work through their problems. They do not need criticism for the distresses they are feeling. When you have a broken leg or an appendectomy, others can accept your infirmity. Women suffering from the psychological distress of low self-esteem deserve the same kind of consideration.

In her therapist Sharon found someone who was willing to listen and would give her time to work through the dark storm of her rage and confusion. She began to understand that the sex-role socialization she had been exposed to had created her foundation of low self-esteem. She had been tricked into thinking that she did not have to take an active part in providing for her own happiness; Dan's expressions of love were to have established her value. Once her worth was established, happiness was to have followed automatically. Sharon had deposited all of her hopes and dreams in Dan, expecting to earn high self-esteem in return. When he failed to live up to her expectations, the paradox of self-esteem provided the rationale for insisting that everything was Dan's fault.

Sharon came to understand that Dan was not a well of positive self-regard from which she could replenish herself. She had many untapped potentials of her own from which she could draw, and she had to begin nurturing her own resources. At forty-five this seemed like a difficult but not impossible challenge. By focusing on her own positive qualities and capabilities, Sharon gradually generated an image of her own design that did not depend upon Dan for fulfillment.

"I'll have to make someone else do it."

When a woman has low self-esteem, dealing directly with anyone creates a hornet's nest of what-if catastrophes that defeats her long before she steps forward.

She retreats into dependence upon other people to provide what she wants without her having to ask. Since no one can do a good job of reading her mind, disappointment in her reward. At this point, she may respond in various ways. She may become angry and overtly punishing; she may withdraw and feel self-righteously bitter and distrustful of everyone; she may use the powerful lever of guilt-induction to force things her way; or she may become resentful and behave in indirect ways to try to force her family and friends to be responsive to her and responsible for her. Other people understandably react by sidestepping these tactics as nimbly as possible.

Rose was a beautiful young woman. Unaware that she was making such a decision, she responded to the wretchedness of low self-esteem with helplessness, unexpressed anger, and indirect messages. She did not even come for therapy on her own, but was delivered at the appointed time by her brother, a fatherly, gruff man who sensed that something was very wrong. Rose burst into tears at the slightest provocation; she constantly complained of feeling sick and had fainted several times at work; she was worried that she would not be able to hold her job because she was making so many mistakes. In every square foot of the constricted space of her life Rose was rapidly regressing to helplessness.

Rose had been living with Jim for six years. She yearned for marriage and children, while Jim seemed comfortable with the status quo. The thought of telling him that she was unhappy was unthinkably difficult and anxiety-provoking. Her behavior was an attempt to make Jim give her the positive messages she knew intuitively that she desperately needed.

Most of her life Rose had reacted to others with hostile passivity and dependence. She had manipulated them into making the decisions and setting the emotional tone of their relationships. Jim had his own self-esteem problems, carbon copies of hers. Neither felt comfortable with direct conflict or anger, so Jim became peevishly silent while Rose constantly cried.

Rose had decided that she would have to find a replacement for Jim, a man with whom she could share her home-building dreams. Being without a man was unthinkable in her helpless state. Only through someone else could her rescue from worthlessness be achieved.

Rose resisted tenaciously, with the please-mother-me tyranny of the weak, her therapist's gentle and firm insistence that she confront her low self-esteem and interact directly with her world. Rose spent several therapy sessions practicing how to say what she wanted to say to Jim as well as others. At first, she burst into tears at the thought of verbalizing her feelings. When she understood that her tears encouraged Jim's silence, she began to accept responsibility for the way her behavior damaged their relationship.

After arduous practice, Rose gave voice to her newly acquired self-confidence and told Jim what she was feeling and what she expected from him. He responded predictably at first, with sullen anger, and listed all the things she had done that he did not like. He said that she was irresponsible and did not love him. Rose agreed that she had been irresponsible in not asserting herself. She was delighted with her courage, and he was shocked out of his blaming when Rose said that their relationship would have to either improve or end. For the first time since they had known each other, they sat down and discussed many of the things that had troubled both of them.

Rose continued with therapy in order to develop her capacities and effectiveness as an adult woman. She learned to express her thoughts and feelings assertively instead of with passive-aggressiveness and manipulation. As her anxieties lost their urgency, her energies were diverted from self-preservation to becoming more efficient at everything she did so she had free time for herself as well as for Jim. As she became less sensitive and concerned about what other people said or did, she was more pleasant to work with and coworkers began reacting warmly to her. Rose actively assumed responsibility for resolving the paradox of self-esteem. Her helpless pleas for deliverance gave way in the face of belief in herself. Rose's work, home, financial security, and a relationship with Jim based on honesty and affection were enduring strengths upon which to establish positive self-regard.

The key to the resolution of the paradox of self-esteem is that a woman must learn to feel good about herself. Given increased self-esteem, she is able to see herself in realistic terms, to verbalize expectations she has for herself and others and to identify her rights and act on them. Feeling better about herself gives her the capacity to effect changes in situations where once she felt powerless. The sense of being in charge of herself in this way in turn increases her self-esteem in a benevolent, slowly widening, circular process.

"I'm feeling better about myself all the time."

Many women who have low self-esteem are unable to break out of their timidity and change their lives because rejection threatens. They seldom think about having any rights so they have no experience in acting on them. They are reactors, not actors on behalf of themselves. In therapy, they focus on the messages that rob them of self-confidence and result in a vicious, downward spiral that bottoms out in their inability to act.

All women can initiate change by interrupting the spiral at any point; they can do it by behaving differently, thinking differently, or feeling differently. When women behave in new ways, they find that their attitudes and feelings change, too. Or they can consciously make a decision to approach a problem, themselves, or their lives with a different attitude, to find that their feelings and behavior are altered also.

The women described thus far in this chapter changed their behavior and their attitudes as a result of developing feelings of positive self-esteem. Others have chosen to behave differently, and have found that their feelings about themselves improved as a result. For instance, Chris was a young career woman who wanted to enliven her social life. She changed her I'm-a-loser opinion of herself when she changed her actions. She began smiling and speaking to her coworkers and people she chanced to meet; she took pains with her appearance and began an exercise program, even though she felt depressed. Her attitude toward herself and toward friends and acquaintances changed, and others began acting differently toward her. Once she felt better about herself, she was less offended by negative messages sent her way. She no longer stored up hurt and resentment, and her relationships became spontaneous and present-time oriented. She had energy available for living because she had interrupted and reversed the direction of the self-depleting, downward spiral of her life.

Shelley is an example of a woman who recognized that her low-esteem spiral could be diverted upward when she consciously decided to replace her old attitude of distrust with a new one of trust. Shelley announced as she sat down for her first therapy session, "I picked your name out of the phone book because I liked the sound of it. I know that if I am going to solve my problems here, I have to trust you. I just made up my mind that I would, even though it is something I have never dreamed of doing before. I'm usually extremely cautious about letting people get to know me, but I've decided to tell you everything about myself so we can do whatever has to be done to help me."

Shelley recognized that she could establish an environment in which she could grow, and that is exactly what she did. In her newfound resolve, she seemed like a beautiful, strong, and healthy sunflower; she used all the skills and resources she could command from herself and others around her to ensure rapid and positive exploration of her complete self. Her emotional, intellectual, and physical components became integrated and available to promote her own well-being and to provide warmth and nourishment for others.

It is important for women to build their self-esteem on solid foundations: education, achievements, and roles and relationships that are positive and self-enhancing. They can have complex, busy lives in which they can fill many functions while still maintaining their own identity. They can be deeply committed to and gratified by the traditional roles for which women have been socialized. They can be flexible and comfortable in both traditional and contemporary roles, and pioneers in those based on female equality and leadership. Women who have resolved the paradox of self-esteem are not likely to become victims of the next paradox, affiliation.

CHAPTER IV

Affiliation

> *"Without you I'm nothing; with you I lose my sense of identity."*

A primary relationship is seen by a woman as the center of her world; so much so that her efforts may be directed almost exclusively to enhancing and facilitating that relationship. The paradox is that without another person in whom to invest herself, a woman may feel empty and useless, yet in investing herself completely in another person, she becomes an extension of that person and loses her own identity. Women have confused the capacity for affiliation with the need for affiliation. It is true that women have a great capacity for intimacy and sharing with others. They are enhanced by, and do enhance, those to whom they are connected. Nonetheless, affiliation is not a need, nor is it a firm foundation on which to build one's identity.

All human beings have a capacity for affiliation, the formation of rewarding alliances and the commitments to significant persons in one's life. It is the friendly bonding with someone else's openness to intimacy, love, respect, companionship, caring, intellectual exchange, and sharing. It is the connection with someone else's power that relieves our sense of disconnectedness. It becomes a paradox for women, however, when, drawing from the strength of others, they bask in that second-hand light and their own glow is extinguished.

Affiliation is an essential capacity in fully functioning people; humans are social beings not intended to live in isolation. An examination of how affiliative conflict follows on the heels of the paradox of self-esteem makes it plain that having a poor opinion of oneself can lead to affiliative problems. If a woman does not feel good about herself, it makes sense to hitch her wagon to someone who does, hoping that the union will give her life value and meaning. Thus, the first half of the affiliative paradox: "I am nothing unless I am connected to, valued by, and approved of by a significant other person." By attaching herself to a person more secure than she is, a woman tailors her life according to that person; the second half of the paradox, "With you, I lose my sense of identity," becomes a reality.

Since a primary relationship is seen by most women as central to their existence, they look to attachments to forestall emotional impoverishment. They focus most of their attention and energy on enhancing and facilitating their interpersonal bonds. Without sharing with at least one other person on an intimate level, women feel empty and useless. The absurdity of this paradox is that since this is so, they tend to trade off their opportunities for self-enhancement through their own achievements and accept instead identities as extensions of the people they love. The price they pay is the forfeiture of their own self-actualization.

The focus of this chapter is on the ways that women commonly lose their identities through affiliation with others. It is essential that we first clarify a confusion between the supposed *need* for affiliation and the *capacity* for it. To see affiliation as a need freezes women into a helpless position with great yawning needs no one can be expected to meet, with sieve-bottomed buckets that can never be filled. To see it as a capacity is to recognize it as a positive quality, enhancing to both women and the people they love.

In striving for affiliation, women confuse a desire for connectedness with other rewarding achievements.

59

Even when they do well, their motivation is often to please others rather than to master some task or skill. The efforts that men put into a career are matched by the efforts women put into nurturing and loving. In our country, men have aspired to be vocationally successful, whereas women's highest aspiration has been to marry such men. While boys and young men are stretching to develop vocational capacities, girls and young women are discouraged from learning skills that would enable them to be independent. When women do have personal goals, they are not expected to aim very high. They are rewarded, however, for being pleasant and cooperative, qualities that will endear them to everyone. The message is clear: "Women's joys and rewards are to come largely from affiliative relationships."

"Girls are made of sugar and spice."

Our second chapter asserts that the paradox of equality, generated by socialization factors in our culture, underlies the stresses of each of the other paradoxes in this book. The ways in which boys are raised differently from girls explains why women are more concerned about affiliative "needs" than men are. When a baby boy is born his parents think in terms of teaching him how to catch a ball, helping him to ride his first two-wheeler, teaching him to defend himself and to work for what he wants. In short, a baby boy is thought of as a little man from the beginning. Goals for him are related to competencies, achievements, physical prowess, and success. In most families in this country, however, the emphasis for a baby girl is upon dressing her up, teaching her manners, encouraging her to please others, and reinforcing her for being mother's little helper. She is often thought of as a little doll. Generally, she is carefully protected, taught to be loving and to enjoy being loved. Goals for her are related to becoming cooperative and nurturant. The hope is that someday she will have a happy marriage, be a loving wife, and be blessed with children. We say this in spite of current efforts to change the narrow socialization of women. It will be many years before the effects of sex-role socialization, which have encouraged women to go in traditional directions, will disappear from young women's lives.

As children grow, a girl's desire for affiliation increases while a boy's decreases. Boys' rewards come more and more from the games and the tasks they master; boys receive clear messages that they are achieving and competent because they are mobilizing their own efforts and proceeding in a clearly defined direction. If a boy builds something with an erector set, he can see what he has done and is proud of his achievement. He is well on his way to developing a sense of self-worth that is minimally dependent upon other people's approval. He is developing achievement capacities that will, throughout his life, move him toward specific and chosen goals.

On the other hand, a little girl who plays with her doll all day does not know anything more about herself at the end of the day than she did at the beginning unless someone tells her that she has been a good mommy. She is well on her way to learning the importance of other people's approval as her route to happiness. She is developing affiliative *needs*. This lesson involves the first half of the paradox, "Without you I am nothing." The second half follows easily as she sacrifices occupational skills, autonomy, and education in favor of the comfortable feeling of being connected to somebody. For the rest of her life, she may get her primary satisfaction and feelings of fulfillment from pleasing others who are important to her.

The development of affiliation is important to a girl's evolution as she grows up. In a home where there is a good feeling between family members, affiliation is experienced and enjoyed as a natural part of the growth process. At first, the roots provided by affiliation with parents are all-important to a child, and rightly so. As a child grows, though, she needs encouragement to develop wings and to fly. She then enjoys relationships with a wider group of friends while still feeling accepted at home. Thus, when the time comes to stand alone, she feels safe to take chances and to make commitments to others with courage and confidence.

Most young women bow to strong societal pressures to marry. A girl who has had a good affiliative relationship with her parents is likely to have a good one with her husband. Benevolent experiences at home have prepared her to move on and invest emotionally in others. Along the way, her relationships outside the family have been varied and rewarding. She does not need to cling to one person in a primary commitment and looks instead to many people for different pleasures.

A woman who has developed in this way may be fortunate enough to avoid the conflicts connected with the paradox of affiliation. She has known and enjoyed affiliative experiences, and has not let them dominate her life. Since she has never experienced the feelings reflected in "Without you I'm nothing," she has not needed to look to others for an identity. Thus, the second half of the paradox, "with you I lose my sense of identity," does not describe her either. Although this model of development is the ideal, it is not what happens for most women.

"I'm still their little girl."

Some parents tie the knot so tightly that a woman finds it hard to break loose, even as an adult. Needing constant reassurance of her value from her parents, she tiptoes through life in fear of displeasing them. We saw this in one of our clients, Shannon.

Shannon was an attractive professional woman who had never broken out of the affiliative pattern developed with her parents. She recalled the pleasant days when she had been a favorite child and felt greatly loved by a mother and father who were delighted by their firstborn daughter. Her family life had been happy and loving. Both she and her sister were close to their parents. The strictness in their home seemed normal to her since she knew no other way to live, and Shannon grew up accepting her parents' rigid standards concerning right and wrong. Sex was never discussed except to reinforce the taboo against premar-

62

ital alliances. As a sure-fire precaution, Shannon was generally discouraged from being friendly with any young men.

When she went to college and later joined the working world, Shannon found that her values differed uncomfortably from those of her friends. She was now associated with people whose life-styles were much freer than the one she had learned at home. She was caught midway between two sets of values. To the extent that she accepted and clung to those of her parents, she felt different from her friends; to the extent that she joined her peers and moved away from her parents' values, she felt guilty. Her need for parental approval finally won out. She backed away from her own generation and made an uneasy truce with obedience. Not confident that adult relationships could replace the affiliative rewards she bought from her parents at the price of freedom, Shannon became emotionally immobilized. She dated men only briefly, quickly finding a reason to break up with them. She was critical of most people; it was easier to criticize others than to examine her affiliative patterns.

When Shannon came to therapy she was forty years old, still tied to her parents and rationalizing her need for them by explaining that she could not build a life independent of them because *they* needed her!

"My parents never did love me."

Other women report that they did not feel valued in their homes when they were young. They felt the need to find someone with whom they could feel important, to whom they could be connected, and with whom they could experience the rapture of feeling special. Because they did not experience affiliative rewards with their parents, something that is important in everyone's life, they experienced their deprivation as an unmet need.

As an adult, Shannon continued to expect her parents to fill her affiliative needs; she could not break away from the feeling that her parents should be all-important in her life. In contrast to her, we see many young women who, at a very early age, have moved away from home emotionally, looking for satisfaction from anyone but their parents. These women felt minimally connected to their parents as they grew up. Often they became involved early in sexual relationships, hoping that this would help them to feel related to someone. They explain their behavior by saying that in cooperating sexually they felt cared for and loved. They seldom say that their motive was sexual gratification; they tell us that they had sex simply because "he wanted it" and they were afraid they would lose him if they did not cooperate. Their actions say, "Without him I am nothing."

Susan is an example. She was truly devoted to Tom, the first boy who showed a romantic interest in her. Her home life had been bleak. She was the third of six children, a quiet withdrawn child who was no match for her outgoing and demanding brothers and sister. At her earliest opportunity, she moved out of her parents' home, got a job and an apartment, and spent as much time as she possibly could with Tom. She cleaned his apartment, turned down other dates, and sat waiting when he did not call. Although he openly dated others, she consoled herself with the dream that they would get married someday. Her identity as Tom's girl filled her need to be loved and to be somebody. When it became apparent that Tom was bailing out emotionally, Susan felt devastated and clung desperately to the remnants of their relationship. He took her for granted and responded to her jealous outbursts by threatening to break away completely. He had become so important to her that she believed her life would have no meaning without him.

For Babs, the paradox of affiliation was no less painful. She was a mature woman when she came to therapy, divorced after twelve years of marriage. Babs had never thought that her parents cared for her. She was like a ragdoll, a pathetic little girl. She made no close friends until she was in college; then she met Glenn and fell deliciously in love. They shared with each other their feelings of having been unloved in their own homes and swore undying devotion to each other. Their relationship was built upon an affiliative

64

need that Babs felt strongly and upon her belief that Glenn had the same need.

Unfortunately, Glenn's affiliative bond with Babs was not strong. He found someone else before long, leaving Babs feeling unloved and desolate as she had had never felt before. It seemed to her that without him she was nothing. She had told herself that with him she was somebody, although the truth of the matter was that, paradoxically, she had lost her own identity by being a somebody with him. She promised herself in her anguish that she would never care so much about anyone again, that way she would avoid being so badly hurt.

Babs did eventually meet and marry someone. After living with him for twelve years, however, she realized that she had consigned herself to limbo when she had determined to protect herself from pain. She was angry at herself because she had not let herself love freely; this had kept her from putting into her marriage the involvement that might have made it work.

What had happened to Babs was that early in life she had identified as a need her capacity to be affiliated. When she was hurt, she tried to tell herself that affiliation was not important; henceforth she would avoid it. She realized belatedly that she had been cheated out of closeness and love, that she had locked the door and left herself outside.

"I have a capacity that I thought was a need."

The affiliative paradox generates conflicts for women when they place so much emphasis on relationships that they become confused about their capacity to relate meaningfully to another person. They see their capacity as a need to have someone relate to them, and they feel incomplete if that need is not met. This transforms a strength into a weakness and leaves one feeling dependent for her well-being on the responsiveness of someone else. Clients who feel this way seem to look at the world and everyone in it through the eyes of other people who are important to them.

One client noted that thirteen times in one hour she

had asked herself what her father would think about something. Another client said, in response to a comment about herself, "but my husband wouldn't like that." Saddest of all was a widow of many years who said, "Charles and I *do* it this way."

One of the women we know told a sad story of a visit to a family friend in a nursing home. She went in and said to her friend, "Hello, Katie." She was taken aback when her friend burst into tears. She understood, however, when Katie explained, "No one has called me by my name for so long. When you said, 'Katie,' I realized that it seems as if I'm not even me anymore. I'm Mrs. Young or Granny or Mother. It's been so long since I've been Katie to anyone." In her relationships with others, Katie had lost her self.

This feeling that women are nothing if they are not affiliated with somebody, that their identity comes from being connected to someone, explains why our clients frequently describe their most intense pain as a feeling of emptiness, a yawning hole in themselves that they want someone else to fill. These women exemplify the paradox of affiliation. Only when they have resolved this paradox by finding resources of strength and power within themselves will they feel whole. In order to do this, it is important not to confuse a capacity for affiliation with a need.

Rosella, an idealistic and enthusiastic young woman, had made this confusion. The course of love was not running smoothly for her. She described herself and her problem in this way: "Sharing deeply with the person I love is very important to me. I can't live without the nourishment that a close intimate union gives me. I'd as soon starve physically as die of emotional thirst in an arid relationship. But my husband looks at me in disbelief, groans, and goes back to reading the paper when I bring up issues that seem terribly important to me. I *need* to share with him, but he doesn't seem to need to share with me." Rosella felt her "need" so strongly and was so helpless to plumb her husband's depths that she had begun to see herself as lacking. She felt frustrated; in her urgency to relate in what she described as a meaningful way she had used every approach she could think of to elicit a response to her "need." She was now searching for the fault in herself.

In therapy we asked Rosella to alter her statement slightly and to say, "I have a capacity to share with him. He lacks the capacity to share with me." We used this analogy: A capacity to share in an affiliative relationship is like the ability to play the piano. If your audience does not want to listen to music, you may choose another audience. Your skills are well developed; the lack of responsiveness of others does not diminish your ability and you can use it elsewhere.

Two people in an intimate relationship often have different capacities for affiliation. This does not mean that the relationship is hopeless. The reality is that affiliative relationships are usually more important to women than they are to men because men have not been urged as women have to see relationships as all-important. It helps women to be comfortable in male-female alliances when they understand this. Many women can make a ninety-degree turn and resolve their feelings of being unloved when they accept that different does not mean lacking.

After being severely offended because her mostly silent husband rarely expressed affection verbally (as she did and as she wanted him to do), Mary Ann came to realize that he was indeed a nonverbal person. Sweet talk would never roll easily off his tongue. His ways were different from hers. She saw, though, that he did for her the things that he considered expressions of love. By standing in his shoes, she could appreciate his intentions and be happy with his efforts even if he did not do things the way she would have done. She understood that what she had resented as his limitation was really a difference between them for which he should not be blamed.

For women, affiliative relationships are so important that they tend to center their lives around them. They see affiliations as tender flowers to be cherished, tended, and nurtured to full bloom. These delicate flowers are a source of much pleasure, and women rarely resent the care required for their upkeep. In contrast, men see relationships as more like sturdy bushes that may need a bit of care when they are first planted, and perhaps a shot of fertilizer once in awhile. By and large, however, they can be expected to grow on their own and stay healthy with minimal attention. For a man affiliative relationships are sturdy things and can be depended upon always to be there.

"If I'm good, I'll be liked."

A woman learns early in life that the best way to feel rewarded in a relationship is by behaving in pleasing ways. Janet was a good example. She sought therapy after years of an emotionally frazzling marriage; her vitality had been drained as she tried to march in step with the rules she had grown up with. She was depressed and bewildered, not yet aware that she was living out the self-destructive paradox of "With you I lose my identity."

Janet had learned early in life that she was loved because she was good, not just because she was a person. As the youngest child in a large family, she had many people to please, and she lived in fear that her older and bigger siblings would punish her if she was so incautious as to resist their demands. She was so careful in her behavior that she became a model child and never counted the cost of making others happy. Her good-girl behavior was reinforced and everyone loved her. It seemed that a child who was such a comfort could always look forward to being cherished.

It was no accident that Janet married a man who was attracted by her compliance. He enthroned her in his world as an extension of himself. She felt comfortable being connected to him and enjoyed the status she gained from being his wife. Of course, he was not perfect, but it was not safe for Janet, the good little girl wife, to see him realistically. Like many other women, she filled her wifely role of devotion by attributing to her husband sterling qualities he did not have. In her mind she replaced his clay feet and testy disposition with a manliness cut from pure imagination.

Because she needed to see him as successful, when he failed in business she explained away his financial incompetence as bad luck. Because she needed to see him as loving, she excused his bad temper as being caused by business pressures. Because she needed to see him as strong, she did not notice his dependence upon her. He was jealous and insisted that she stay home in case he came for lunch. She denied being disappointed when her plans were constantly frustrated, choosing instead to blame herself for inadequacies. Suffering from feelings of low self-esteem, she believed that there was something fundamentally wrong with her when the truth of his inadequacies tugged uneasily at her.

Janet's story involves a critical issue with which many women deal in therapy. Since relationships are often seen as tenuous and experience shows that even a lifetime certificate of commitment provides no absolute assurance that they will last, women do not risk testing relationships by making demands. Demands might push loved ones to reject them. Better to close one's eyes to reality than to take the chance of having no one to turn to in order to feel whole. Since Janet could not hazard displeasing her partner, she found herself always capitulating to his wishes and anticipating his demands. Such one-sided yielding creates anger; it did so in Janet. Although she was unaware of it, she felt resentment toward her husband. Unable to recognize her anger for what it was, she had turned its energy in on herself and experienced it as depression. It was this condition that brought her to therapy.

In therapy Janet gained an understanding of her nice-girl patterns and learned to see her husband as he was in fact, an oppressive tyrant. She learned that she did not have to put up with his criticism of her cooking, his badgering of the children, his suspiciousness about her activities, and his sexual punishment. She became courageous enough and had the necessary support to confront and challenge him when her rights were abused.

She learned that he would not abandon her when she used her affiliative capacity in constructive ways without allowing her identity to be wiped out. Today, with a year of therapy and two years of school behind her, Janet has a job with a future and she has many friends. She is still married, having found that her husband's patterns changed when her weakness and fear no longer reinforced them.

"I have to have a man."

It is in adolescence that women usually make their first conscious choices to be affiliated with a mate. Until that time, most girls enjoy other girls and are not concerned with marriage, although they are subtly and not so subtly influenced in that direction by daily experiences related to the paradox of equality. During their teenage years, girls are transported giddily into the world of social imperatives. Having dates, or the lack of them, becomes a criterion by which girls value themselves. Popular young women date, have fun, and their jubilance gives the impression to less fortunate friends that the attention of men makes the difference between happiness and gloom. From then on the path is clear. In young women's eyes achievement in other than traditional roles usually takes second place to successful relationships with men. Educational plans are put aside or modified. Even women who go to college have traditionally joked about going there to get a Mrs. degree.

Time and affiliation march on. During their formative years, when young men are primarily concerned with preparation for occupational goals, young women are increasingly subject to societal pressures that encourage them to look to men to fill their lives. The messages of television and other media overwhelmingly stress acquiring and holding fast to a man. School functions facilitate dating. Even parents encourage and enjoy their daughters' social conquests; they see popularity as insurance for success. Inherent in all the messages is the suggestion that marriage will provide the affiliation that makes women whole. No wonder so many women we see are distressed.

Single women who describe their problems as a desperate search for their identity do not, indeed, know who they are in terms of the affiliative paradox: They are nothing without somebody, since they do not have anybody. The pain of the conflict for them is intense; convinced as they are that they need a man, they feel bitterly left out without one. Often they are not able to find suitable partners. More and more young men choose to marry late or not to marry at all. For these men, a relationship is nice, but their affiliative needs are not as strong as those of women, and this produces the conflict.

Some young women come to therapy because they feel intensely unhappy without a commitment to a man. They believe there is something wrong with them because they are unattached. In therapy they come to see that they are also angry. They have been raised to believe that all women can look forward to receiving their greatest joys in alliances with men. They feel that they have been cheated; it does not seem fair that there are not enough good men to go around.

Mary told her group how unhappy she was in spite of a life that sounded enviable. She was an attorney moving up in her field; she had rewards from her work that many young professionals would have considered first rate. But deep down she felt empty and lonely because she was not married. It was embarrassing for her to go to company functions where everyone else was half of a couple. She found herself avoiding weddings because of the questions of well-meaning relatives: "When will we be invited to your wedding?" or, "Are you going to be the next one?" People seemed to be giving her the message that she was somehow to be pitied because, to them, success in her career was no substitute for what they saw as essential to a woman's happiness.

Sherry, at twenty-two, was still a student, yet she could not devote herself wholeheartedly to academics. She had seen school as a good place to spend time until she got married. She was preparing for a career, but did not take her work seriously because she did not look upon it as a lifetime commitment. It was something she was going to do only until the right man came along. She had grown up shy, introverted, and not too happy at home, although her ties to her parents

71

were strong. She continued to look to them for guidance and direction far beyond the age when most young women have left home to wrestle with life on their own.

What Sherry was doing was biding time until she could transfer the dependence she had upon her parents to a husband. Not having had a healthy affiliative relationship with her parents had deprived her of the kind of stretching-out experiences she needed to develop the peer relationships that serve as a transition between home and marriage. She began to feel anxious in social situations, afraid to risk and to give cues to other people that she was ready to be their friend. She did little to inspire people—especially the young men she wanted to attract—to see her as a promising friend. Until she could do that, she could not expect to move on to love and marriage.

Toni was another young woman for whom the right man had not yet come along. The paradox of affiliation took her by surprise and she found herself facing unexpected challenges.

All her life Toni had been delightful, friendly, and loving. She was also entertaining and amusing, an asset to any party. Her friends made sure she was included in everything because she could be counted upon to add fun to any occasion. Rewarded by such social support, she had not felt a need to study much, to achieve in school, or to look to a future that might require more than winning ways to succeed.

By the time she got to college, Toni discovered that her poor study habits, which had been just passable in high school, were a serious handicap. At the same time, not having found a husband, she was beginning to think of a career, and achievement needs surfaced in her. In graduate school Toni began a hard struggle to make up her deficiencies, and often felt discouraged that other students seemed to know how to get the top grades that eluded her. She felt frustrated because at twenty-three she was trying to learn study skills that she could have learned at an earlier age had she turned her attention to them. Everyone had expected her to marry young, and she had never considered that she might need to support herself someday; her efforts had not been directed toward such mundane pursuits. Rather, she had enjoyed the affiliative rewards that had been reinforcing to her since she was a little child. It was a disappointing revelation to her than an overemphasis on those rewards had put her in such a position that she had to work very hard as an adult to discipline herself to work effectively. Ironically, what had seemed so good in her childhood had shortchanged her as an adult. Many paradoxes do.

Some young women who come to us in therapy are in relationships to which they are committed but their partner is not. Like Barbara. She had gone with a man for four years. She wanted to marry; he did not. The conflict for her was one of affiliation. She could not stand breaking off with him, yet she saw her life slipping away as she clung to his slender support. She knew that if she spent the next few years with him, she would reduce the likelihood of finding someone else who would want to marry her. She explained it well when, after some time in therapy, she was able to say, "I know that the issue for me and many other women is to look to the day when we do not see men's approval as our most important source of self-esteem, social status, and financial security. We need to get to a point where we can save some of the energy we have so frantically invested in trying to develop lasting commitments with reluctant men and to direct this energy and our talents toward our own growth. If we develop our own tools, we will find within ourselves the resources to fill our emptiness."

It had seemed to Donnette that she was one of the lucky ones; at age twenty-one she was engaged. She was sure that she would marry and live happily ever after. Tragically, her fiancé was killed in an accident. Heartbroken, she found sanctuary with a sympathetic man who responded to her loneliness and convinced her that she could be a whole person—she could care for him and have the children she had dreamed of.

Eager to trade her sadness for a chance at happiness, Donnette did not think about any other criteria for a happy marriage. She married on the rebound and

73

regretted almost immediately her hasty decision. Once married, it was plain that there was little love between them. Their temperaments were incompatible, their goals were different. His sympathy wore thin when she expressed her disappointment in him, but neither could say, "This is a mistake." The panic of separation, of not belonging to anyone, had to be avoided at all costs. In order to survive, Donnette learned not to feel, to become numb rather than take the chance of having negative feelings that would threaten the delicate balance of her marriage. Their life together became unrewarding and stagnant. They communicated on only the most superficial level.

The saddest part of Donnette's story is that it took her thirty-three years in a sorry marriage to understand that she had lived out a paradox. During all those years she had merely existed with her husband. Although affiliated, which she saw as essential, they found little satisfaction in their association. By existing with him in order not to be alone, she had quieted any stirrings of autonomy in herself that might have given her life broader dimensions. In focusing upon belonging to someone, she had lost her identity.

"Three is a crowd."

The fear of losing her man to another woman is related to many of the feelings of inadequacy we see in women clients. Women have had the firm conviction since childhood that their success depends upon being happily married. If they are not successful in their marriages, they look to themselves to find the source of the blame.

Kathy had been a trusting bride who believed that her marriage would be considerably different from what it turned out to be. She expected her husband to be staunchly loyal, forever devoted, and to have eyes only for her. It was a shock when she found that she had a rival for his affections. She felt betrayed and helpless; it seemed that her whole life was shattered. As do many women in a similar situation, after experiencing grief she felt an overwhelming distrust. She be-

74

lieved that she would never be able to trust her husband again. The rejection, humiliation, and emptiness she felt were barely tolerable. Even worse, she felt hopeless and worthless. She searched within herself for the villain responsible for the break in this important affiliative bond. She told herself, "If I were not lacking in some way, he wouldn't have strayed." "Without him, I am nothing" rang bitterly in her ears.

Women's fury when they find that their partners have been unfaithful may be as overwhelming as their grief. Men's infidelity seems doubly painful since women do not have the mobility and opportunity to attract other partners as readily as men do. Women may be pregnant and tied down with small children, or they may be older and less attractive than their younger rivals. But that is only part of the problem.

As a man gets older he has a wider choice of feminine companions. In our society, a man of fifty-five feels free to select a mate from an age span of twenty to sixty. On the other hand, a woman fifty-five would be hard pressed to find a mate even a few years younger than herself. Society frowns on and the average woman is reluctant to have an intimate relationship with a man even a few years her junior. The result is that, as women and men get older, men's sources of potential mates increase greatly while women's are much diminished. No wonder the spurned women clients we see are so often filled with rage. Part of their anger stems from their feelings of betrayal, not only by the men they trusted, but by members of their own sex as well. This seems to be the ultimate indignity.

On the other side of the affiliative coin are the women who come for therapy because they are the "other woman." They have a different story to tell. Many of them have been so convinced that their happiness lies in liaisons with men that they have closed their eyes to the potential hurt their actions may inflict on other women. Some women would never intentionally become involved with a married man; they have done so believing that he is unattached. Others have bought the oft-told tale of woe: A cold, rejecting wife has driven away a good husband. Some women seem to have rejected identification with other women to the extent that they knowingly enter relationships with married men without regard to the complications and consequences of such behavior.

One of the values of a woman's therapy group is that women learn that a betrayed wife is not the only victim; the "other woman" is a victim too. Therapeutic groups provide women opportunities to see the commonality of the female experience. In sharing, women overcome their distrust of other members of their own sex and learn to cooperate to work out problems, rather than to compete with each other. In time, they can resolve the paradox of affiliation by coming to see themselves, not as extensions of men, but as persons with identities of their own.

As women share their experiences of joy and anguish they cut through the superficialities that have been the basis of their dislike of each other. Best of all, they develop affiliative relationships with other women, affiliations based upon a capacity to share and enjoy, rather than on a need to survive.

"My children are my life."

In addition to forming strong affiliations with men, women invest heavily in other people, children in particular. Because having a child does increase a woman's sense of self-worth, it is understandable that mothers develop strong bonds with the children who depend upon them. This can be warmly rewarding for both mother and child. When mothers draw their sense of identity from their children, however, the paradox of affiliation can cause trouble.

Kitty, an unmarried mother, came to therapy because she was lonely. Throughout her life she had never felt she belonged to anyone. Although her therapist saw her as a warm, likable, and affectionate person, she had a miserably poor opinion of herself and thought she was unlovable.

Having decided several years before that she was too unattractive to expect to marry, she told herself that if she had a baby she would never be lonely again. Kitty intentionally became pregnant, expecting that having a child to love and being loved in return would make her happy. Unfortunately, Kitty discovered that an infant, for all the joy she or he brings, cannot alone meet an adult's needs for a full life.

Some mothers experience the pain of the paradox of affiliation when they put aside their own rights in order to provide lavishly for their children. Georgia did that. She was so pleased with her adopted daughter that nothing was good enough for her child. Although the family was not well-to-do, little Janey lacked for nothing that children from wealthier homes enjoyed. Georgia cheerfully wore shabby clothes and deprived herself of things she could have afforded had she not been trying to give the child all the "advantages."

As Janey grew up she came to take for granted things her mother had so generously sacrificed to provide. Since Georgia had enjoyed playing the martyr role, it was hard for her to stop giving things at that point.

Georgia demonstrated another problem that can develop when mothers affiliate too closely with their children. She expected her child to accomplish the goals and dreams that had eluded her in her own childhood. Janey, however, did not want to be a dancer or an actress, two of her mother's girlhood ambitions. Conflict flared between mother and child as Janey became resistant to Georgia's pressures and firmly refused to cooperate in ways that bewildered her mother. Georgia could not understand why her daughter had rejected the many advantages Georgia had provided. What she did not see was that she was placing unrealistic expectations on the child. She saw in Janey abilities that her daughter did not see herself as having.

It was Janey who came to us for therapy when she was a young woman. She explained, "I feel confused and anxious because I don't know who I am. My mother has always told me that I am very talented, yet when I compare myself with my competition, I can see that I don't have as much talent as they have. I remember my mother always telling me that I am a leader and should act like one. I never felt like a leader, and still don't. Yet I feel guilty when I don't want to step out in front. I really feel more comfortable as a follower."

Other affiliative problems between mothers and children come into sharp focus when there is not an appropriate transition from affiliative childhood experiences to a capacity for adult affiliation. In Marian's case, this produced multiple problems. Although she did not feel sweet and happy, she was told by her parents that she was and she felt obligated to behave as if she were. The conflict between what she felt and what she thought she should be produced qualms of self-doubt. She wondered what her parents really thought of her because she did not believe that they liked her as much as her siblings. She saw herself as stupid in school, and she believed that since she did not get good grades she probably could not excel in anything. She would have to be the way her parents believed her to be if she were to have any worthwhile identity.

When Marian came to therapy as an adult, she had not grown beyond feeling that she had to please everybody. She was still questioning her every motive, struggling mightily to make decisions, and feeling at everyone's mercy. She saw herself as an inadequate mother, daughter, and friend. She was burning up all of her energies trying to meet affiliative needs. This left her with no vitality to formulate goals that would fit her potential rather than her parents' prescription.

Sometimes mothers of grown children are apprehensive when their children defy their maternal expectations and resist growing the way the twig was bent. In addition to the issues of guilt and responsibility that mothers must resolve, there is an affiliative issue involved. These mothers have permitted their children to become so important that they see them as extensions of their own selves. It is agonizingly painful for these mothers to accept their children's differentness. Different, to them, means deficient.

Gretchen had this problem. She and her daughter, Terry, had diametrically divergent values. Gretchen

78

was conservative, hardworking, frugal, and methodical. Terry was lighthearted, easygoing, and was, in fact, irresponsible for a woman of twenty-three. Describing her vagabound life-style, she said, "I like it. I travel around a lot and don't worry about security in a job. I seem to get along. There is always someone to bail me out when I run into difficulties. Things would be much better between my mother and me if she would just stay out of my business. She is too worried about my life." On the other hand, Gretchen, frightened by some of Terry's escapades, fretted daily, convinced that a good mother should be able to influence her daughter toward more conservative ways.

Among the important realizations that everyone must come to is that there is a difference between generations, that times do change. Clinging too tightly to a previous generation's values prevents personal growth. Many of the youthful decisions made by women who are now mothers and grandmothers seemed shocking to their parents. It once was considered risqué to to wear bobbed hair, to dance the Charleston, to frequent a speakeasy. Today's daughters face similar value choices. But it is important for parents and children to realize that many things represented as having moral overtones are, in fact, cultural norms imposed by people who are fearful of change.

Although Terry felt comfortable with values that differed from those of her parents, it is surprising how many adult women never achieve that ease. Fearful of parental objections, they are secretive about their lives. As adults, they do not move beyond the childhood level of affiliative ties; they fail to make the transition to peer status with their parents. They continue to see their parents, particularly their mothers, as unreasonably threatened by their choice of values different from those of their parents.

We often see women who cannot separate themselves from what is happening in their grown children's lives. They consult us because of their children's problems—they are anxious because they would like to help and cannot do so. What these women do not realize is that the problem they are experiencing is their own.

Their task is to accept that their grown children have unique identities and can be trusted to work out their own lives. In doing so they may see things differently than their parents do. For a woman who has been influenced to believe that her children are her life, it is exceedingly difficult to sit back while her children may be suffering. She must learn to trust that the investments she has made in her children have prepared them to meet life's challenges.

"I am expendable for the man I love."

Women's talents and capabilities are frequently seen as readily expendable in the face of men's ambitions. Nowhere are these renunciations so apparent as in the area of affiliation, where women sell their talents short in an effort to gain the satisfaction of belonging to someone. It is not uncommon for a woman to claim that her sacrifice is "no sacrifice at all, just a natural impulse to cooperate with the man I love." The trouble is that by sitting on her own potential while boosting her man to the pinnacle of his, a woman's abilities stagnate. Her unjelled plans are put aside in favor of her man's goals, with the explanation that he needs to get skills and an education to reach his vocational potential, which will, in turn, benefit both of them. Long-range objectives are made for him; short-range jobs to help him are found for her. The fallacy of this arrangement can be disguised for years.

Aline dropped out of college in her first year to marry Matt, an economics student whose energy and ambitiousness seemed to guarantee reward enough for both of them. Their dream was that he would become a professor of economics; their plan was that she would help him do so. She held a variety of office jobs, fitting in three pregnancies with hardly a pause. Creative and imaginative, she opened a secretarial service, which she operated from their home. This enabled her to sandwich in the children's needs and to give them time and emotional support. Aline disregarded opportunities to expand her business since the full-time involvement required would detract from her role as helpmate. Her focus was still on achieving their dream for Matt.

The tragedy for Aline was that when Matt reached the pinnacle of professional success for which she, too, had struggled and hoped, he announced, with easy disdain, that he had grown and she had not, and that they no longer had anything in common. After thirty years of marriage, Aline found herself cut off from the security of the agreement by which she had lived and he had profited.

Aline recalled in therapy her many years of struggle, doing things that were difficult and unpleasant while Matt involved himself with work he thoroughly enjoyed. She felt that somewhere along the way her halo had slipped over her eyes and obscured her vision. To go on without Matt seemed overwhelming, although it was obvious that she was a highly capable person. She had received so little positive reinforcement during her marriage that she did not believe she could function adequately, except as an adjunct to him. She was uneducated, tired, and completely lacking self-confidence. Bitter at being rejected, she said, "I am the one who should have had the doctor's degree; I'm the one who worked hardest for it."

Aline is representative of countless women in our society who realize belatedly that they are victims of the paradox of affiliation. They are vulnerable to premature endings of the relationships from which their identity comes. Years of being other-oriented and putting their needs last has done little to develop their potential as interesting, challenging people to grow old with. Their status-seeking or achievement-oriented husbands frequently prefer younger and "more stimulating" women with whom to enjoy their success.

Women abandoned at this point in life feel bewildered and grief-stricken; they have been cast aside after having unstintingly devoted their lives to the role society says is women's highest achievement. Women who have focused primarily on being loving and supportive mothers and wives feel deeply wounded and misunderstood when their husbands and children ignore them. No one ever told them that, if their value

81

came from an association with someone, then they would be valueless when that someone no longer needed them.

"Any old port in a storm will do."

Belonging to someone can be so important to a woman that she is willing to settle for a relationship that has no future. Roxy, an intelligent young woman in her twenties, hooked into a clandestine alliance with a married man and said good-bye to a good job and a wide circle of friends to follow her lover when he moved up in his career. She relocated to a large city and settled down in a new job and a love-nest apartment. Although theirs was primarily a sexual relationship, Roxy was not his mistress in the usual sense, for she provided all of her own financial support.

When she was asked in therapy what she was getting out of life, Roxy became anxious and depressed. It was humiliatingly clear that her heavy investment in their love affair was not matched by any pledges on his part, but it was safer not to see the painful facts since it was so important to her to feel cherished by someone. Intellectually, Roxy knew that she was only peripherally important to him, that he would never leave his wife and children for her, and that she was reading promises into his vague and meaningless remarks. Nonetheless, hope dies hard and Roxy continued to trust that someday, somehow, she would be rewarded for her patience. While Roxy hoped for a future commitment, her lover behaved as many men do. He believed and acted upon his conviction that it was possible to maintain his marriage while having an affair. The affair lasted five years.

Although there are exceptions, the experiences of the women we have known show over and over again that a man seldom divorces his wife for a woman with whom he is having an affair. Her hopes that he will are based on wish-fulfillment, not on the reality of the situation. She rationalizes her hope by saying, "It will be different for us."

A woman can also get hooked into a job and gain a sense of identity from that connection. For a woman with no other source of self-esteem, this is another way of living out the "Without you I am nothing" paradox.

We saw this in Celine, a woman who had worked twenty-nine years for a service organization. Her reinforcement had come from the recognition that she was doing a good job; she could not have been more devoted to the company if she had owned it. Her customers appreciated her friendly manner and cooperation, preferring her meticulous attention to that of newer and less dedicated employees; her employers made it plain that they had never had anyone who was more effective in her job. While less capable people sought and received promotions and new people came in to fill higher positions, Celine never requested advancement. She had the feeling that if she changed jobs, she would be letting down her customers.

After twenty-nine years, there was a change of administration. The new director wanted to bring in his own team of younger people. To her complete bewilderment, Celine was replaced. Without retirement benefits and unable to compete with younger people in the job market, she did not know where to turn. She was cut off from the only identity she valued. Having lulled herself with the false security that her job would not leave her, she had not left it. In this way she had passed up opportunities to develop skills and gain experience that would have enabled her to compete for management level jobs. But at her age many of those doors once open were permanently closed.

In making her self-defeating liaison, Celine also accepted the myth of female inferiority. She had seen a low aspiration level as appropriate and had been willing to fill a helping rather than a leadership role. She had been satisfied to know that she was effective in her job, and the affiliative rewards that she received gave her a sense of importance. A man in her position would have expected to move forward after mastering his job. Celine and her soul sisters are the indispensable administrative assistants, the loyal secretaries, and hard-working bookkeepers whose talents and dedication often exceed those of the people around them who are promoted.

Among our clients we have seen how affiliative conflicts reinforce low aspirations in women who are afraid that they would endanger close relationships if they were to focus on their own goals. Capable, intelligent women often let their talents lie fallow while they live with the frustration that comes with trying to bolster a less talented partner. As therapists, it is our pleasure to see women grow to expect more of themselves and their own resources and to depend less upon the benevolence of affiliative bonding to add to their stature and satisfaction.

Believing that affiliation is a need creates in women a compulsion to connect that diverts their energy away from other goals and rewards. This produces conflicting feelings and destructive alliances that, if left unresolved, can lead to emotional problems. Helping women to resolve the paradox of affiliation begins by helping them to see that affiliation is a capacity, not a need. As a capacity, properly developed, it enables women to enjoy trusting, loving relationships.

In therapy women learn that enjoyment of their affiliative capacities need not preclude the development of other capacities. Women who are vocationally skilled, educationally confident, and socially active do not have to depend on affiliative bonds to define themselves as people of worth. They can let go of relationships that limit their self-development, they can take risks to improve their relationships, and they can enjoy to the fullest the rewards of social interaction. They need not experience the conflicts that come with the next paradox, dependency.

CHAPTER V

Dependency

"I have to destroy myself in order to survive."

Having a man on whom she can depend has been the central element of security to a woman. Dependency has been seen as appropriately feminine and has reinforced men's patterns of superiority. When women become financially and emotionally dependent upon someone else, they give up the power to be in charge of themselves and to direct their own lives. The paradox is that what starts out to seem good fosters resentment in both the giver and the receiver. The giver feels taken advantage of and the receiver loses her sense of self.

There are two kinds of dependency, only one of which produces paradoxical conflicts. *Evolving dependency*, in which needed help is provided at appropriate times, is functional and rewarding. It leads ultimately to autonomous, effective behavior. In evolving dependency children rely upon their parents, as is appropriate. The parents' task is to encourage their children to move from needing to lean upon someone to a position where they can be effectively in charge of their own lives. Other times when evolving dependency is appropriate include times of crisis, when various types of support enable one to meet current hardships without emotional crippling. A helping hand to a person who is sick, financial support at critical times, comfort when there is grief all provide help while encouraging the receiver to move on to self-determination and effectiveness at the earliest possible moment.

There are even certain times in psychotherapy when

it is appropriate for a client to be dependent upon a therapist; times of anxiety, depression, and confusion in the early stages of therapy are examples. The therapist's task is to help a client evolve and gain the skills she needs to take charge of her own life so she no longer needs someone else to help her find alternatives and support in decision-making.

Wilma was a client who needed support. She started out in therapy being typically dependent. She was a frail woman of thirty who had come for help after her second divorce. Confused and shaken, her thin body and timid manner revealed the strain she had been under. One divorce had been bad enough for her; the second had driven her self-esteem to the depths. She did not know where to turn. She described herself as feeling totally dead. She knew she needed to get a job, find an apartment, and start to make new friends, but it seemed her mind had stopped, like a run-down clock. She sat abjectly, waiting to be started up. She told her therapist, "I feel like a lost child. I hope you can convince me that there is some reason to live, because I can't see any. I also need you to help me see what I have been doing wrong all my life so I will never make the same mistakes again."

Wilma went on to describe haltingly her feelings about her second husband, Ralph.

He almost destroyed me. If I had lost any more weight I would have been blown away. And my nerves are shot. Before we were married he acted like it would be all peaches and cream; he told me how wonderful I was for him and promised me the sky. But as soon as I was dependent upon him, he picked and picked at everything I said or did or wore. He wanted to control me completely. I couldn't stand up to him because he was like a Mack truck, always bearing down on me. My only defense was to shut down and to stop feeling in order to preserve myself. Eventually I had to get away from him to survive. I need help now because I don't feel I have any resources left.

In the course of therapy Wilma could draw support from her therapist when she needed it, encouragement when she took risks, and validation as she put together some plans for her future. All the while her therapist's objective was to move her toward eventual self-support. It was a happy day when Wilma said in a session, "This is my last session. Now I can call you by your first name. I felt I had to call you Doctor at first, but now I know I don't need you anymore and I can think of you as a friend." She was no longer dependent. She had found her own power.

At various times, certain dependent roles fit well for partners in a marital relationship. If the roles are freely chosen and both partners are comfortable, there is no problem. In that case, the union is built on interdependence. Interdependence involves a mutuality; each person gives to, and gets from, the other. Interdependence is a mark of a healthy relationship. In such an alliance, each shares, supplements, and supports the other. By mutual consent, a division of responsibility is based upon likes, abilities, and other carefully considered factors. Each is able to lean on the other *at times*. There is, however, independent activity in which each spouse is effectively involved without the other. From the independent activities comes a sense of autonomy, freedom, and effectiveness, while the interdependence affirms their commitment to, and cooperation with, each other.

One of our clients has worked out an interdependent relationship in her marriage: she works at her profession, does the cooking, laundry, shopping, and some housework and gardening, while her husband also has a job, does the dishes, yardwork, cares for the cars and lawn, and shares in the housework and gardening. Each day has scheduled time they share, and weekends are reserved for special times together. Other couples may need a very different plan to please them.

The paradox of dependency in women's lives results from being in a state of *static dependency*. Such a state is destructive because it locks women into childlike roles that undermine their growth as adults. They feel

87

powerless because their ability to act is controlled by someone else. In this helpless state they do not dare to take risks lest they lose their security. Passiveness replaces spontaneity and a zest for life. Anxiety replaces trust. At times dependence is reinforced by alluring trade-offs; others gain by our needing them. A woman who describes herself as dependent feels helpless, powerless, childlike, inadequate, ineffective, trapped, and uncertain; she can see no way to get out of her misery. A static, dependent relationship becomes a life sentence to which a woman submits when it seems that she has no other alternatives; she must stay in it to survive. The paradox for women is that in doing so they destroy their best qualities and, ultimately, themselves.

"I'm helpless."

When a woman is in a dependent relationship, she exchanges the power to be in charge of herself and to direct her own life for the comforting sanctuary provided by someone else who will take care of her. This reliance upon others has been encouraged in women because it has been seen as appropriate feminine behavior. Women have been encouraged to see such a retreat as positive because it promises them security and freedom from responsibility. The helplessness it generates is not anticipated.

Theresa was a forty-two-year-old woman who was referred for psychotherapy after she swallowed a bottle of sleeping pills, then panicked and called an ambulance to take her to the hospital. Everything about her behavior was typical of the helplessness that accompanies dependence. She came to us in tears; indeed, she spent most of her early sessions crying. Theresa was word-poor as she tried pathetically to express her feelings about her husband of nineteen years who had deserted her. It was hard for her to talk at all because each thought brought wracking sobs. She sat in her chair, wringing her hands, repeating, "I just don't know what I am going to do. I can't understand how he could do this to me. I just can't understand."

Theresa truly believed that she could not survive

alone. Desperate in her loneliness, she saw suicide as the best way out. Like other dependent people, she was filled with suppressed rage. She had turned this rage, which she was unable to express, in on herself. The depression that resulted triggered her attempt to escape a life that seemed worse than death.

It was obvious that it would be some time before Theresa would be able to make serious decisions about her future, or even to get her present life into comfortable balance. She presented a helpless picture, which suggested that she wanted her therapist to tell her what to do. It was as if she hoped to transfer her dependence from her husband, on whom she could no longer lean, to anyone else who would take responsibility for her. She simply had forgotten how to make plans and decisions during the many years she had lived with this autocratic man who traded material comforts for her dutiful compliance with his wishes.

Theresa's feelings of helplessness were not exaggerated. For many years she had lived a life of middle-class comfort; a large home, cars, friends, swimming pools, and trips were an accepted part of her life. Now she did not know what to look forward to, but conceded that it would be harder to live on a poverty level after having had so much luxury. For her the bubble of security had burst. It would be fair to say that dependency had destroyed her spirit, her hope, and her future.

Theresa needed supportive therapy until she got over some of her grief and worked out some realistic plans for the years ahead. These plans took time since she had no marketable skills. Before her marriage she had been a waitress. Now varicose veins made that job impossible. Getting a job at forty-two was difficult, at best. The property settlement she was to receive would be minimal, and Theresa knew she could expect to have to work for the next twenty to twenty-five years.

Other helpless women whose dependency has destroyed a part of them are the women who have "temporarily" put aside careers only to find that their skills have rusted with disuse and are finally too out of date to be marketable; wives who have cut off their own family relationships because their spouses wanted their undivided attention; mothers who have looked to their children as the source of their self-esteem rather than engaging in ego-involving activities that would be there even after their children had grown up and gone; and daughters who have remained at home with aging parents, doing nothing to develop peer relationships that will survive after their parents are gone. All such women can expect the day to dawn when they will be without the supports they have leaned on so heavily. Unfortunately, they can expect that their resources will have been destroyed by the paradox of dependency, the subtle villain that masks long-range destruction by flaunting short-term rewards.

Being dependent is not new to most women. They have had lifetimes of reliance, moving from being dependent upon their fathers into marriages where they assumed the same position with their husbands. For them dysfunctional dependency is the logical outgrowth of affiliative bonds. Since they must be connected to someone in order to feel of value, it is logical that they attach themselves to someone bigger and stronger than they are, to someone who seems to have qualities that they lack, in the hope of gaining a sense of security from such a fortuitous association.

When a woman moves from dependence upon her father into a similar position with her husband, she is rarely aware that this is happening. Not until she feels surrounded and restricted does she realize what has happened. Such women are unaware that childhood dependence can evolve into adult ineffectiveness; that a woman's relationship with her husband should be one of equality, rather than of submission and dominance.

"I need you for love and security."

The paradox of dependency is manifested in many forms and can involve either psychological or financial reliance, or both. In this chapter we focus on both psychological and economic dependency since both are reinforced from a woman's earliest years. Even a young girl learns that the smile of pleasure on her father's face as he grants her simple requests has something to do with his liking to be needed. She learns early to depend upon him and thereby to cement their relationship.

One reason it is psychologically destructive for a woman to depend upon another person to give her a sense of value is that she feels abandoned when confirmation from that other person does not come. Furthermore, if the person she is dependent upon leaves her life, her sense of self-worth exits with him or her.

Vivian, a young married woman, depended psychologically on her husband Bill, although she did not need him financially. She had a prestigious job and earned as much money as he did. But when she came to therapy after Bill had asked her for a divorce, she was sure she could not survive without him.

It had not always been that way. When Vivian and Bill met she had seven years seniority in the department store where she was a buyer. She had a home, a daughter, and many friends. Until Bill swept into her life and swept her off her feet she considered herself stable and secure. She was not prepared to resist the enchantment that life with him promised. She put her child, her job, her friends, and her own security out of her mind as she threw herself enthusiastically into Bill's plans for the two of them. After they were married and Vivian was deeply committed to him, it became clear that Bill would not be friendly to the child. Loving her daughter dearly and not willing to see her suffer, Vivian reluctantly gave custody to her ex-husband. This was her hardest choice and moved her closer to the dependency paradox.

In the few years that they were married Vivian quit her job and went with him to a strange city, leaving all her friends behind. Gradually she lost touch with them. She also broke completely with the rest of her own family, whom Bill did not like. She eagerly invested all of her energy in developing closeness with him; loving him took the place of all the emotional supports she had before she knew him.

As whirlwind romances often do, the love affair soured. For three years Vivian clung to the shreds of it,

91

knowing that she had closed all other doors when she married Bill. When Bill left, it seemed that Vivian's will to live went with him. Psychological dependency had destroyed it.

To the Vivians that we work with in therapy, we point out the debilitating web of paradoxes that have trapped them. Because affiliation with Bill was so important to her, Vivian threw away her own identity, certain that once she was connected to him she would need none of her previous resources. She had even given up her daughter. Doing so made her more dependent upon Bill and vulnerable to loss of him.

Vivian need not have invested so lavishly in Bill. She could have loved him and still held on to her child, her job, and her friends, the emotional supports she had developed over the years. Her love for Bill could have built upon what she had, all valuable resources that could have helped her to avoid the paradox of dependency.

Nancy differed from Vivian in that she was both psychologically and financially dependent on her husband Sam. They had been married eighteen years when Sam died suddenly and left virtually no estate. Nancy panicked about the future. She did not see how she could support herself since she had never worked outside their home and could not imagine what kind of employment she might get.

Nancy was one of those trusting but misguided women who had thought she was totally secure because she was happily married and her husband's job provided a good living, a comfortable home, and college educations for their children. As a wife, Nancy never worried about the future. Sam took care of the money and assured her he would always provide for her. This seemed reasonable since he was a good worker and generous with money. Sam did not share the details of their finances with Nancy. She never knew that they spent every penny he earned and that they had very little property and no insurance. Having been dependent upon Sam while he lived left Nancy helpless at the very time she needed resources to draw upon.

Many of our younger women clients who are married and have small children are also both psychologically and materially dependent upon their husbands. They tend to be more realistic than Nancy. They know they are dependent and have fears about the future; they would be hard pressed if they had to support their children, who are dependent upon them to meet evolving needs. These uneasy feelings gradually erode a woman's sense of security, rendering her anxious and destroying the base from which she can develop skills and reach out and enjoy other people. Feeling powerless, dependent women recognize that they need to please in order to feel safe financially and emotionally; they become extremely timid about expressing themselves or taking any risks that may threaten their already shaky security.

Static dependency also engenders hostility and resentment on the part of both the giver and the receiver in a relationship. It is not unusual to resent someone on whom we must depend. That person has too much control over our lives. It is also likely that persons depended upon feel hostile or resentful if they see themselves always giving and getting little in return. It becomes burdensome to carry someone else's weight all the time.

Rita resented her wealthy husband Samuel. He used money to control everyone and everything, including Rita. Perhaps she would not have resented him so much if she had not been dependent upon him. With three small children she had no choice but to go along. Samuel made it plain that if she "asked nicely" she would be more likely to get what she requested. Rita told her therapist she felt that she was prostituting herself to ask for things that should be rightly hers since she was his wife. She believed it was her role to care for their home and the children, and that she should have some freedom of choice in how she did it. She did not think it unreasonable to buy clothing and pay for necessary household repairs without "asking nicely" for the money to do so. Just as he was paid for his labor, she believed that, by carrying the role they had mutually agreed upon for her, she earned the right to the use of the money he brought home. She knew that his income was impressively large, and she would have liked to plan together how they would use at least a part of it.

Because she felt so controlled in the area of money, where she had no power, Rita began resisting in areas where she could avoid confrontations with Samuel. She found more things to do away from home without him. This further angered him; like other people who buy loyalty by being available to be depended upon, Samuel felt taken advantage of. He saw himself as being used because he was generous.

When Samuel told his side of the story it was plain that money provided him the only power he saw himself as having in their marriage and he used it to maintain control. He thought it only proper that a man be the dominant one in the family, and he felt Rita's resistance. He did not see that by carrying out her agreed-upon role she earned any automatic right to money he worked for.

Money was only the first battleground in Rita and Samuel's power struggle. The war eventually extended to Rita's freedom, which infuriated Samuel. He saw himself as bound by an inflexibly demanding business at which he worked hard all day. He envied the flexibility she had in her life, her freedom to fit into her days a variety of things she enjoyed. Their marriage was faltering because Rita had sensed the destructiveness of her dependence and was trying to resolve the paradox. Eventually they divorced, since Samuel would not budge from his position and Rita refused to be controlled, which to her was tantamount to being destroyed.

"Is somebody gaining by my weakness?"

We tell our clients that static dependency in adult relationships puts a burden on the other person, which no functional person enjoys. Anyone who is in a dependent relationship needs to examine whether something psychologically dysfunctional lies beneath the facade of harmony and cooperation. Is someone benefitting in an unhealthy way by having another person rely upon him or her?

Often women come to us with other concerns, unaware that this is happening to them. Some of them have viewed dependency as a plus in their lives. They have delighted in having a marvelous benefactor to do everything for them. For them it is hard to face that no matter how attractive it looks, dependency is destructive when someone else benefits inappropriately from being needed.

Lanny had not seen that this was happening to her. She was an attractive woman who had been married for fourteen years to Norm, an advertising executive. She would have told anyone that she did not know how she could get along without him. She was used to the affluent life marriage to Norm provided. Although he had a bad temper and could be unpleasant to be around, he made it plain that he did not mean the things he said when he was angry. He lavished her with gifts and money. At the same time, he kept her on a jealously short leash in every other way. He was suspicious and possessive of her time and attention, and Lanny felt obligated to humor him.

Trained as a nurse, Lanny had not had a paying job since she married. She knew that her profession had changed so much that, if she ever chose to go back, her skills would be outdated. An outside job was not important to her anyway. She was kept busy entertaining Norm's business contacts and friends, and being an all-around social asset to him.

Norm often told Lanny he was proud of her, and he reveled in the knowledge that other men envied him his stunning wife. She knew it was important to live up to the image and dedicated herself to doing so. What Norm was getting from Lanny's dependence was a boost for his ego. At her expense. He had a free hand to indulge his possessiveness and enjoy the reflected glory of Lanny's beauty. Not feeling good about himself, he used her to make up for his inadequacies. A question she asked herself in therapy was, "Can I depend on Norm when I can no longer depend on my good looks?"

Mary, another client, also depended upon her husband Joe, unaware that he was using her. She saw him as a cooperative, thoughtful spouse. He cheerfully balanced the checkbook, paid the bills, looked after her car as well as his, negotiated with all the repairmen, and protected her from the intrusion of any unpleasantness. Joe loved having Mary turn to him whenever she needed him.

Before they met, Mary had seen herself as capable; she lived alone and took care of her life. When she met Joe he impressed her with his helpfulness. Learning to lean on him was mutually rewarding; he delighted in anticipating her wishes. Dependency became a comfortable way of life for her, and Mary leaned more and more. It was easy to go along with Joe's cues that she needed him to do things for her. What Mary did not realize was how much Joe was getting out of her helplessness. He had grown up not feeling sure of himself. When Mary accepted his attentions, he felt good. By seeing Mary as less adequate than himself he could do things for her that reassured him of his value.

Both Norm and Joe gave strong cues to their wives to stay dependent. Accepting these cues and adopting dependency was causing both women's confidence to rust out from disuse. It was likely that they would drift deeper into passivity unless some unexpected event disrupted their lives and forced them to reclaim their own strengths.

It is only when women recognize the dynamics that are taking place in their dependent relationships that they can begin to stop destroying themselves in order to survive. Once they see dependency as their problem, they are halfway to having licked the paradox. When they harness their own strengths and power they find many ways to take steps toward greater autonomy. As one of our clients aptly put it, "Awareness may not resolve all of life's problems, but without it there is no hope at all!"

"I don't want to grow up."

Some dependent women stay children forever,

destroying their potential for adulthood. Being a child is fine at the appropriate age. A child can be irresponsible, not having to weigh the consequences of her behavior or tangle with difficult realities as adults do. Growing girls should, however, be taking steps toward maturity by assuming increased responsibility with each year. A grown-up child-woman cannot know the joys that come with adult accomplishments and self-actualization.

Liz was such a woman. Although she had been married four years when she came for therapy, she had not outgrown the ways of a child and she used them even in therapy. She spoke in a tiny, questioning voice and tilted her head coyly as she talked.

Liz's parents had encouraged her to remain girlish and emotionally immature. As a child she had only to be pleasant, entertaining, and good in order to be liked. She was encouraged also to be cooperative, attractive, complimentary, and to delight other people rather than to seek achievements for herself.

It was no surprise that Liz married Tom, who liked the way she played up to him. He invited her coy behavior; it made him feel important. He was charmed by the way she danced around joyously when she was pleased, spoke to him in a little-girl voice, teasing and cajoling him into cooperation and out of bad moods. He was amused by her pouting lower lip when she did not get her own way. What neither of them saw was that in behaving like a child, Liz was steadily eliminating any likelihood that she would become a mature woman who would one day behave responsibly. By depending upon Tom to get by, and not developing her adult capacities, she was destroying her potential to grow.

Some men marry a child-woman for the reasons that Tom did and later become frustrated and discouraged when they see that the realities of marriage are too much for her. This is what happened to Tom. The very qualities that were once alluring lost their charm when Liz's irresponsibility about money caused problems, when housework and children seemed overwhelming to her, and when she seemed disinclined to play and carry out any goals for the family. They came for therapy after a big blow-up that left Liz in tears and Tom locked outside the house. Both of them knew they could not go on that way.

In therapy we asked both Liz and Tom to examine what they were doing to keep Liz in the role of a child. What was she doing to perpetuate her immature behavior and to keep him acting as her daddy? What was he doing to maintain a parent role and reinforce her childish ways? Recognizing these behaviors and attitudes in themselves showed them what they needed to change.

In therapy, Tom became aware of how he had enjoyed making the decisions for both of them, giving permission to Liz, and being indulgent when she elicited favors. He liked handling the money and making the plans. If he never saw Liz as an adult, he would never need to treat her as a peer and share these powers with her. Liz realized that by using little-girl ways, she was asking for a daddy to indulge her. She would thus not need to accept responsibility for her actions and accept the consequences of her behavior as an adult would.

All women need to see that childlike dependency reinforces bad habits in the people they rely upon. As in Liz's case, each time Tom got rewarded through being her "parent," there was less likelihood that he would ever change. And each time she exercised her "child" ways, she dug herself deeper into the destructiveness of the paradox of dependency.

"What happened to my ambition and good nature?"

To have self-rewarding ambitions and to achieve the goals connected with them puts women beyond needing to look to others for emotional and material support. Since girls and boys study the same subjects in their early years in school and some girls recognize that they are more capable students than most boys, it is not surprising that these young women expect *not* to take a backseat to men when they grow up. They want to achieve in ways that will maximize their abilities. Long before their ambitions are tested, however, girls hear clearly the message that happiness for women comes most surely when they put aside their ambitions and find someone else to depend upon.

There has been much talk in recent years of women's fear of success; it has been shown that women tend to avoid achievement lest their accomplishments cost them their popularity. Social acceptance becomes the most important criterion of success in a young and adolescent woman's life. What follows is a crazy message that says that, although women must prepare for careers, they must not take the task too seriously. To do so would suggest that they are not seriously interested in affiliation. To invest heavily in a career would jeopardize their chances for future relationships and would reduce their marriageability. Yet achievements, more than anything else, can help women find their way out of the paradox that says women must destroy themselves in order to survive. A capable, achieving woman does not have to depend upon anyone.

Having made the decision to seek their happiness in affiliations, most women in our culture marry and move into dependence upon their husbands. It is not unusual for women who have been dependent in marriage to discover after a few years that they have somehow been cheated. They never worked in the careers they prepared for, and marriage has not proved to be as delightful as they expected. When this happens, the disappointment, disillusionment, frustration, and guilt they feel takes its toll. They act in ways they do not like. They may even become the kinds of people they once avoided. The first quality to go is their pleasant disposition.

That is what happened to Noreen, who came for therapy remembering wistfully the dreams she had once had. She and Peter had gone together since she was in ninth grade, and they decided to marry as soon as she graduated from high school. Noreen never even considered preparing for a career other than marriage; class work and study took second place to the fun they had together. They were young and idealistic when they married. They hoped to have a large family because both of them loved children. Although Peter's job as a bus driver would limit them financially, they were not deterred. They discussed their future and agreed that they were not afraid of poverty. They were sure that theirs would be a marriage where love would conquer all.

When the reality of babies, diapers, hard times, and fatigue hit, Noreen's patience wore thin and her positive qualities waned under pressure. She yelled at the children, felt hostile toward her husband, and complained about the things they could not afford. Worst of all, she disliked herself. It was because she saw that she was so unpleasant to be around that she came for therapy. She felt trapped in a morass of never-ending demands with no way to work herself out. Anyone asking Noreen what was happening to her would have gotten the answer, "I am being destroyed."

A functional person does not enjoy being around someone like Noreen who no longer shows many positive qualities. If a man marries a woman because of her dependence, he can expect to feel burdened when he tires of carrying her weight as well as his. That is, unless he is gaining something from her weakness. If, as sometimes happens, a man marries a woman because he is attracted to her independence and then forces her into dependence, he will find he no longer likes her because she has changed. The very qualities for which he married her are gone; an important part of her is destroyed.

"Maybe it will go away if I don't look."

Dependent women often find it virtually impossible to face realities for which they are not prepared. They have been shielded from encountering the unpleasant and the difficult by those whom they trusted. Theresa, whom we discussed earlier in this chapter, was still telling herself that she would be reconciled with her husband long after he had made the decision to divorce her. He had refused to explain his reasons for wanting a divorce, but she knew that he did want one. She was still asking herself why he had moved out in the middle of the night without a word, although he had told her plainly that he did not want to hurt her more by talking about his decision.

While they were married, Theresa's husband had discouraged any efforts she made to find a job outside their home or to involve herself in activities that would have developed competencies she might cash in on now. Her husband enjoyed having her at home. He wanted her free to travel with him, something a job would have prevented. In addition, she functioned beautifully as a showpiece and social secretary. She eventually had come to believe she had no other skills. She had slipped steadily into passivity.

Because of the helplessness she felt, Theresa did not see how she could live without her husband or build a life on her own resources. It felt better to deny her need to do so. Even though she admitted he had not been a great prize, life with him looked far better than life without him and she still hoped he would change his mind. She was like a person adrift in a raging river, going over a waterfall clinging to a piece of wood; her hope was totally without foundation.

In her dependent state the reality of a divorce and life alone seemed too difficult to face. Like the proverbial ostrich, she stuck her head into the sand; she tried not to notice that the weeks were passing and the time drawing nearer when she would have to move from her home and do something about getting a job. She resisted making any plans that did not include her husband. Although she was faced with a real financial crisis, she acted as if it would go away if it were not acknowledged. She would delay taking a hard look at reality until it crept up on her. The paradox of dependency had left her both passive and helpless, waiting for the future to strike.

Passivity such as Theresa experienced has been seen as a normal personality characteristic for women. It fits the stereotype of what is feminine; it is part of the triad: passive, dependent, and submissive. As therapists, we see passivity in most of the dependency-related problems of our women clients. What it does, in fact, is inhibit women's motivation toward action, causing them to back off into inactivity, which seems safe. But once it becomes a habit, as it did for Theresa, it buries a woman in the paradox of dependency without any tools with which to dig her way out.

Passive women find ways to comfort themselves in their inactive roles. They sit silently in the midst of problems that need to be solved and say to themselves, "I won't have to do anything. Someone else will surely take care of it." In the face of abuse they tell themselves, "I don't have to get angry; let others make waves." If there is a chance to be taken, they let someone else do it, assuring themselves, "I don't want to risk making a mistake." And they sit placidly through controversies that rage around them, saying, "I won't have to take a stand." Passivity, which is a coping technique, destroys the capacity to flourish and sentences women to the periphery of other people's lives.

The paradox of dependency builds on the paradox of affiliation and operates in many women's lives to lull them into false security in dependent marital relationships. All women need to know that wives can expect to outlive their husbands by several years, and they should be prepared for this eventuality. Looking to their husbands to give their lives meaning is folly; women must not ignore their own individual development or close their eyes to the vagaries of the future. For those who do and are faced with widowhood for which they are unprepared, the sadness they feel at the loss of their spouses is compounded by the exacting challenges they face in the strange, real world.

The authors have known many older women who, at their husband's deaths, had no understanding of their family's financial situation, had incomplete knowledge about family possessions and obligations, had no plan for survival without a husband, and lacked the necessary skills to provide for their years alone. They are the widows of prominent men, once photographed at their husbands' sides and now no longer recognized; and of brilliant men who did not want women to trouble their little heads with business details; and of chauvinistic men who did not want to share their powers. These women are legion. Some are eking out an existence on social security, others have been bilked of their resources by fortune hunters, while many of them live sad lives lightened only by memories. Dependency, which kept them from looking at reality, has destroyed the so-called golden years of their lives.

"It's more comfortable not to risk."

Another way dependent women destroy themselves in order to survive is by not rocking the boat, by remaining compliant and never offending; this relieves the anxiety that comes with taking risks. After all, a risk might bring feedback that would suggest a need to take action. Backing off and moving away from getting reactions from others may feel safe, but it is impossible to grow in a static situation. Women who do this become so used to being dependent that they pass up opportunities to be independent and thereby destroy their chances to enjoy new growth experiences.

Roseanne did this. Dependency did not seem bad to her at first; she came for therapy after the destructiveness of the paradox had caused a serious rift between herself and her husband. In the early years of her marriage, when she had three small children at home, she enjoyed her dependent role as a wife in the suburbs, where it seemed that the good life flourished. She felt secure financially and knew she could count upon her husband Charles for emotional support. There was heartwarming satisfaction in their usual give and take. She pleased him, and he rewarded her efforts with a grateful response. When decisions were difficult for her to make, she had only to turn the problem over to Charles; she admired the dispatch with which he smoothed feathers and negotiated differences. As each year passed, the contrast between her role as follower and his position as leader became more apparent; he made the decisions, she expected him to make them.

When Roseanne was forty-three she inherited a large sum of money and the big question arose, "What will we do with it?" The children were grown and

Roseanne now had time and money to do some of the things she previously could not afford. Some of it could be used to enjoy postponed luxuries; the rest of it would be invested.

Roseanne, who was bright and well educated, knew as little about investing as her husband did; neither of them had ever given it much thought. She, however, had time to investigate and learn ways to use the money wisely; Charles did not. But dependence had become a pattern for her. Without considering any other alternatives, she turned over the inherited money to her husband and let him make the decisions about its use, since he was head of the house. Roseanne's generous decision was motivated by her desire to maintain the status quo of her dependency. Charles had always handled the money before, and she was reluctant to suggest that she might take the initiative and learn how best to invest it. She kept her ideas to herself, even when several of her husband's ventures failed. She told herself that she should trust him.

Roseanne related bitterly several years later in therapy that her husband's poor judgment has caused her inheritance to dwindle to nothing. They had had serious arguments as she watched her resources go down the drain. She blamed Charles, not realizing that if she had handled her dependency differently, things might have turned out more to her liking. She had not needed to depend upon him to invest her inheritance. She could have risked taking some action on her own, and it was foolish not to have done so. In giving up her rights because she hoped to avoid conflict, she laid the groundwork for the resentment that arose later. What her dependency had destroyed was their relationship.

We cannot realistically expect to have intimate relationships in which there is no resentment or anger. But such occasions can be very threatening to a woman who is dependent, especially if she is the recipient of negative messages. Negative feedback is usually interpreted by dependent women much more seriously than it is intended. When they are given the simple message, "You are so anxious that it is affecting our relationship," they hear a serious threat. They interpret the words to mean, "You are not good, and it is only a matter of time until I cast you aside."

Sometimes, in order to avoid painful feedback, dependent women give out cues that they are so fragile that it is not safe for others to react honestly to them. Their attitude suggests that negative feedback would cause them to feel wiped out. These controlling messages inhibit other persons from communicating honestly with them. This assures them that they will be safe from seeing how others view them. When others no longer give feedback to defensive women it is because they have decided, "I can't tell her anything because she gets so upset."

It is easy to explain why negative feedback seems so painful to women who are in dependent relationships. They feel they are sentenced to a life without choices and cannot change the things they do not like. They have made a fragile peace with life in order to survive, and see criticism as a form of rejection. In therapy we help these women to gain the interior strength to listen to feedback, which can be the starting point of growth. By seeing themselves as others see them they can determine whether they want to change and move out of dependency.

"There are some payoffs."

The paradox of dependency would not be so devastating if women could not be blinded by the rewards it offers. The payoff that women enjoy most often is freedom from responsibility. A life free of responsibility seems attractive; it provides security, it removes the necessity to risk, it allows others to make difficult decisions, and it relies upon others to be accountable for what happens. Such reinforcements disincline a woman to say, "No, I'd rather do it myself."

One of the compelling rewards of dependency is that when women marry they acquire the social and economic positions of their husbands. When a woman marries a man of prestige, even if she was born "on the other side of the tracks," she is automatically elevated to her husband's status. This has moved many women onto a level of economic success and social prominence they could never have achieved on their own. There is nothing objectionable about these rewards if they do not cost a woman too dearly. We are not suggesting that there is anything wrong with enjoying this aspect of marriage, nor that all wives who share their husbands' status are suffering from dependency. It is when women must sacrifice themselves to continue to enjoy the rewards that the paradox of dependency operates.

In resolving this paradox, women must look at the price they pay for the rewards they are getting. The payoffs have a way of backfiring. Continued dependence generates feelings of helplessness, which generate anger, which often turns into depression.

Women who have enjoyed status and prestige while married face a difficult adjustment if their marriage ends in divorce. One of the more poignant problems that we see in our clients is the loss of status suffered when a woman gets a divorce. Usually her life-style changes drastically while her husband's, for the most part, remains unchanged. It is difficult for a woman to make the transition to single life with less social acceptance and resources than she has ever known. She is likely to be depressed.

Some women have looked long and hard at the financial security they had in their marriages and have balanced the rewards of dependency against its alternatives. Some of these have decided that peace of mind in a humble apartment would preserve their integrity, whereas life in a mansion with a husband was destroying their sense of value as well as their zest for living. Others have stayed married, settling for a thimbleful of life, afraid to tell the world that they have a bucket they would like to see brimming with successes if they only had the confidence to risk accomplishing it. Timid women have held back, resisting taking risks, stilling an inner voice that could tell them that growth comes through struggle. And passive women have given away their power to have any impact on life, preferring to sit back and rationalize their inactivity by saying, "At least no one can blame *me*."

In working with dependent clients, we find that

when feelings of helplessness result in depression women become immobilized; there is usually unexpressed anger involved. A dependent woman may not allow herself to recognize angry feelings when she is treated shabbily. This fits in well with her reluctance to jeopardize the uneasy alliance that sustains her.

Women in therapy can release their anger at what has happened in the past. This frees their energies to be directed toward evaluating what is currently happening in their lives. Distress from past events cannot be discounted. But it can be discharged and put in proper perspective so that it no longer contaminates the present. Women can then find ways to make the present and the future what they would like it to be for themselves. Even dependent women have resources of strength and power that amaze them once they recognize and harness them.

Although they are not functional payoffs, obesity and alcoholism provide their own peculiar rewards and frequently can be traced to dependency. In unmarried women they are often generated by an unfulfilled need for someone to depend on. If the person upon whom a married woman depends is unreliable or disappointing, it may seem to her that there is no hope in the relationship and no place else to go. Anger, then, is added to disappointment. Food and alcohol can act to assuage loneliness, anger, and disappointment.

It is often highly talented women who report to us in therapy that they overeat or drink too much because they are bound in narrow dependent alliances and feel frustrated at having no satisfying outlets to challenge their abilities. Such women are usually married to men who insist that their wives stifle any desire for accomplishments that might upset the Jane-Tarzan status of their household. Resisting such domination and breaking out of dependency can frighten women; to do so would risk the only security they know.

Mandy was a young woman who did well at everything she attempted. Until she got married. There seemed little to do then in a small house without children. Living far from a bus line and having no car, she had little opportunity to get out and tackle the world.

Frustrated, she found herself gaining weight, which she attributed to boredom. To pass the time, she started oil painting. After a few months of self-teaching, she sold several pictures and was commissioned to do more. Instead of praising her success, her husband objected loudly when she enrolled for classes or spent money for supplies. She assuaged her disappointment and dulled her ambitions with sweets.

Rachel was another Mandy. She weighed 220 pounds when we first saw her. She, too, was a talented woman who sold the first short story she submitted for publication. Her husband ridiculed the small payment she received. He scoffed at her plan to schedule a regular time each day for writing. He seemed always to have compelling plans that interfered with her schedule. She gave up and swallowed her dreams along with mountains of calorie-rich food.

Neither Mandy nor Rachel challenged her husband's reactions to her creative efforts. Each was afraid of the confrontation; what if, when the truth of her need to express herself creatively was known, her husband adamantly opposed her? What if the final result would be a parting of the ways? She would then have to take charge of her life, and both women truly believed they could not handle life alone. Dependency, although destructive, had become a habit.

In fact, being overweight accomplished a dual purpose for Mandy and Rachel. While it relieved some of their frustration, it also descreased any likelihood that they would attract other men. Not doing so would protect them from having to confront the inadequacies in their marriages; there was no chance of comparing how other men might react to their ambitions with the ways in which their husbands did. It was more comfortable not to take chances. Destructive, too.

"I'm afraid I'll lose what is mine."

Although jealousy is not limited to women, the paradox of dependency makes women vulnerable to its ravages. Jealous women have usually experienced earlier paradoxes. Beginning with low self-esteem, they attempt to bolster their sense of self-worth by affiliating themselves with someone else. Having done so, they become dependent upon that person and feel threatened that someone might steal their loved one. No wonder dependency becomes the breeding ground of jealousy when a woman feels insecure. She is afraid she cannot hold onto her source of support, without which she cannot stand alone. Not trusting herself as worthy of loyalty, she clutches tightly while furtively searching for the enemy who would whisk away her chosen one. The accusations and distraught behavior that characterize jealousy have pushed many already imperfect relationships to the breaking point.

Jealousy in a relationship may involve children, parents, or friends. But for women in intimate alliances with men it usually involves other women. Dependent women tend to be cautious with all women. Since they see men as more important than women for survival, they focus on men and see most women as competition. When women are jealous of other women, they turn against each other.

Only a dependent woman would say, as did one of our clients, "I can't even go out to dinner with my husband because I'm afraid he will look at another woman." Another said, "I have always been okay when I was the only woman in the room, but if a beautiful woman walked in I was miserable." Some women feel threatened in the company of any competent woman.

A jealous woman tends to blame "the other woman," rather than her partner. This seems to be because it is safer to blame a woman whom she does not know than her partner, whom she feels she needs. To blame him would put a great strain on the affiliative ties and would risk losing all. But by blaming "the other woman," a woman sets her partner up to defend her rival, thereby causing herself to look even worse in his eyes. Furthermore, this prevents focusing on the real problems: his behavior, her jealousy and her fear that she may lose him to another woman.

Typical of jealous women were three of our clients.

109

All of them came to recognize in therapy that their anxiety was sharpened because of their dependency.

Jacqueline was a raven-haired beauty in her late twenties whom anyone would have imagined to be leading a full, happy life. During the day she did. She worked in an office and enjoyed her work and her coworkers. But at night she was miserable. Her free time was spent worrying about her boyfriend and checking up on him, driving by his apartment to see if he was home, and telephoning him late at night to assure herself that no one was with him.

For five years she had been devoted to Nick, a musician. His evening work hours and contacts with the public were constant threats to her. She was plagued by the thought that he might find someone more desirable than she. Later, after she had come for therapy and resolved her jealous feelings, she was able to say, "It seems so foolish now. I let myself be totally dependent on Nick even though he had made me no promises in the five years we dated. As soon as I took back my independence and started to go out with other men, I didn't feel jealous of him anymore."

Marilyn, who had been married for twenty-four jealous years, showed up for therapy with cuts and bruises on her legs and arms. She had clung crazily to the car when her angry husband Edward drove away from the house after one of her accusatory attacks. Jealousy had been a part of their life together from their earliest days. In identifying its pattern, Marilyn said, "Edward has been my whole world, from the first date we ever had. Since I have no family and his job moves us around a lot, I've never made many friends. He is all I have. Yet I have never felt secure. I've never been sure that he didn't cheat on me; as a matter of fact, I believe he has. I've found myself checking up on him when he travels by calling the hotel to see if he is registered alone. I even find excuses to drop into his office just to make sure that everyone knows he is very much married. Most of our fights come from my questioning him about women."

Virginia, too, was dependent upon a man: an attorney, married to someone else. After eight years of having Virginia as his back-street wife, he had finally gotten the divorce he had promised for so long. Only he did not marry her. Instead, he told her it would hurt the children too much to see him marry "the woman who broke up the family." She was appalled and furious. "It was he who seduced me into an affair, saying that his wife had rejected him. And I waited night after night for our few stolen minutes together. I had to be always available, which meant that I had to cut off all my friends. Now I find I have no friends and I'm jealous of his ex-wife; he is nicer to her than he is to me. When I criticize her, he defends her. Now I'm the villain and she's the nice guy. How do you like that?"

Jealousy need not be only of other women. Dependent women can feel jealous of time spent away from them. A woman who feels helpless without a man has a lot of time to churn with anxiety when her man chooses to develop gratifying or necessary interests that do not include her. It is as if she needs his constant presence as validation of her worth.

Women often feel angry because the men in their lives spend more time at work than with them. They take little pleasure in their men's autonomy and interpret it as disinterest. This is a frequent source of resentment, and it results when the capacity for an affiliative relationship is seen as a dependent need.

A more constructive approach is for women to appreciate their capacity to be interdependent, to share with their partners while leaving both of them free to order independent priorities in their lives. This results in a totally different kind of relationship, one in which both partners aim for the actualization of their potential. Such thinking defies the paradox of dependency. It results in mutual respect and the end of dominance in relationships.

"What happened to my autonomy?"

In being dependent, women lose the autonomy they need to gain the respect of other people. Even little children sense insecurity and vacillation when it is present in their mothers. Children do not respect, and do take advantage of, mothers who are not courageous enough to stand firmly and act with confidence, to say no when appropriate, and to uphold their convictions. Husbands of such women blame their wives for being weak and allowing their children to walk over them.

We see a far different picture in mothers we know who are not dependent. Children of these effective mothers admire and respect them. And these mothers provide good models for their children to follow. Research studies have established that daughters of mothers who were well adjusted, effective in their personal lives, and efficient in their family relationships hope to grow up to be like their mothers.

Women who are not autonomous, but look to someone else for emotional and financial security, miss many opportunities for self-determination. A negative response of any sort is enough to discourage them. They just give up.

This is what happened to Mary Jo, who described herself as just not caring anymore. Over the years she had made tentative efforts to feel competent but, needing validation from others to feel good, was usually disappointed. Analyzing it herself she said.

As a bride I was excited about decorating our new home. But I was never sure of my abilities, so I looked to Robert for reassurance that the choices I made were good. I remember the cool response he gave to our first sofa, which I loved. He didn't care for the draperies or paint, either. I interpreted his remarks to mean he thought I was inadequate. So I just gave up and now he picks out the furniture we buy.

It was the same thing with the children. I put myself out to cook nice meals. No one seemed to appreciate them. I sewed their clothes, and they complained that other children got to buy theirs. Now I don't do much at all. That's why I'm here for therapy. I've given up on home, but where do I go from here? I'm only thirty-seven, and I may live as long as my grandmother. who died at ninety.

Fortunately, it was possible for Mary Jo to gain back her autonomy. She had only to base her opinions of herself on her own achievements and not depend upon others for validation. She was a bright woman who could do it. Tasting small successes whetted her appetite for more, and each one propelled her to the next level of competence and confidence.

Not all women are so lucky. Some are like Vera. After twenty years of what she considered a reasonably contented life, her husband unceremoniously walked out on their marriage. His actions demonstrated a well-known fact: When dependent women lose their luster, their spouses often look elsewhere and switch their affection to more vibrant women.

Vera had to deal with the emptiness she felt; she had lost not only the person she loved, but also the man without whom she did not believe she could survive. She had depended totally upon him. Their children were teenagers and more than a match for her. She needed his help. After a divorce, life would be different. She would have to move to an apartment with the children. Without any special training, she faced either an unskilled job or a long period of preparation for a job. Autonomy seemed like a faraway dream; survival was closer to where she was.

Dependent women often come to us suffering from marriages that are painful to everyone involved. They are unable to accept the situations they are suffering, but are afraid to look at alternatives. They close their eyes to reality, ignore the signs, hoping they will go away. The process of destruction proceeds at a steady pace, whether or not it is noticed. As therapists, we help women deal with this denial and move through the stages of therapeutic growth, from denial to self-actualization.

The transition from feeling helpless to feeling competent is a particular challenge to client and therapist. It is a widely held misconception that when a woman moves out of dependency, she must swing all the way over to complete independence. Understandably, this has been a threat to both women and men. It suggests

113

that not needing others so much means not needing them at all. This is not true.

Interdependence is important to women. Generally they know that they do want to be related to someone. There are very few people who enjoy isolation. We view growth out of dependence for women as moving toward a state of effectiveness, where they can enjoy self-direction and accomplishments while retaining their capacity for relatedness. As one of our clients put it, "Marriage should be holding hands loosely."

Moving out of dependency does not have to mean the end of a relationship. All that is ended is an unhealthy reliance upon another, which destroys personal effectiveness as it adds pressure to please in order to stay safe. It involves changing from *needing* to *wanting* that person. In a love relationship it says to the other, "I no longer need you. Now you can know that I stay with you because I want you."

To change from needing a person to wanting that person in an undemanding way opens up both persons to self-fulfilling experiences and improves their self-esteem and ability to function. Between parents and children, this results in an ability to share as peers in their adult years. No longer needing each other, they can risk the expression of feelings and can accept differences with a safety not felt in the child-parent relationship.

Between husbands and wives, wanting and not needing each other removes the fear of divorce that renders a submissive spouse powerless. Marriage is then a center for growth, for stretching out to new experiences with a comfortable feeling that it is commitment, not the need to survive, that holds the relationship together.

In other relationships wanting, rather than needing each other replaces controlling and guilt-producing behaviors with the quality of true friendship. Friends enjoy, but can live without, that telephone call. Letters are written out of love, not because someone depends upon them. And time spent together is because both want to, not because one is afraid the other will be broken-hearted if they do not.

With our women clients, we emphasize the difference between need and want. If a client says, "I need someone and cannot survive without that person," she is expressing a compulsion and a lack of choice, which adds anxiety to the relationship. The result is a paradox that produces destructive pressure. In contrast, if she can say, "I choose to be with that other person, not because I have no other choice, but because I want to be," she is expressing a serenity that comes from freedom. She can say, "I am no longer dependent."

CHAPTER VI

Emotionality

"I can be emotional, but I mustn't upset anyone."

Women are defined as emotional; they are rewarded at times for feeling free to express themselves. However, only positive feelings are allowed; negative feelings are discouraged. The paradox is that although women are told they are emotional and cannot help being that way, they have been charged with responsibility for how others react when they express their feelings. They feel guilty if they express emotions to which others react with discomfort. The fact is that this discomfort reflects the inability of others to handle their own feelings and is not the responsibility of the woman who is expressing herself.

Jennifer called late one afternoon to request an appointment to discuss her feelings about her job, a middle-level government post. When she came for her appointment, she told of being reprimanded for not attending a meeting on her day off, despite the fact that she had not been notified ahead of time. When she told her supervisor that she felt angry and imposed upon, he shouted at her, "You have no right to feel angry, and you have no right to make me angry."

The truth of the situation seemed to be that Jennifer's boss was uncomfortable with her assertiveness. Unable to admit his mistake, he became aggressive and intimidating. He was punishing Jennifer because she was emotional, but not in the expected way; she infuriated her boss by saying that she was angry about an unfair situation.

Jennifer was caught in an untenable position. Her boss thought he had the right to blow up, whereas she had no right to even *feel* angry, let alone express it. In his judgment, she was to blame for the anger he felt. Jennifer was in a painful double-bind; in trying to correct an injustice, she had elicited another reprimand. If she did nothing, she felt powerless and even angrier than she had initially. If she tried again to discuss the conflict with her boss, she ran the risk of being punished even more.

No-win situations like the one Jennifer experienced are familiar to women. Because other people react negatively when women speak up directly to defend themselves or to state their thoughts and feelings, women often back down and say nothing. Jennifer's problem exemplifies the crippling paradox of emotionality: "Because you are a woman, you *are* emotional, but you can expect to be punished if I don't like what you say."

Women receive many contradictory messages about their emotionality. Indeed they are defined as emotional, the connotation being that this is not an ideal way to be, but something they really cannot help. Emotionality is patronized and tolerated, as if being emotional is a rather endearing and childish affliction for some reason beyond a woman's control. Since they cannot help themselves, women are "allowed" to have feelings. Paradoxically, when they do express their feelings, they get mixed messages that seem to say that, although they may not be responsible for their own emotionality, they are responsible for the way others react to it. If someone is angry, women tend to feel it is their fault; if someone is critical, they think they are to blame; if someone is disappointed, they feel they have let that person down; if someone is unhappy, they feel guilty.

Women's social development has encouraged them to acquire patterns and to make choices that are potentially destructive to their emotional well-being. They have been taught to see themselves as subservient to men, to act submissively with men, and to seek attachments to men in order to avoid feeling empty and lonely. They have been expected to depend upon men for emotional and financial security. In exchange for this "security," they are to be emotional and to communicate their feelings in such a way that they flesh out the happiness of others. Women are taught that their negative feelings are so distressing to others that they must suppress them entirely or express them in acceptably indirect ways.

A woman's response to another person's unhappiness is to worry. "Please tell me what have I done," she pleads, searching for a way to mend the rift. Caught in the paradox of being emotional without upsetting anyone, she assumes the impossible task of keeping someone else, everyone else, happy.

Males in our society are rewarded highly for being competitive and aggressive. They have been encouraged to take their place at the helm. In many ways, being masculine has meant that men have channeled their emotionality into sexuality, competition, and aggression. They tend to have difficulty verbalizing their emotions and frequently deny feelings of tension and anger. This denial can lead eventually to not feeling much of anything. Men's emotional responses then are shifted below the surface of their awareness, with sexual encounters substituting for intimacy.

Little boys are told not to cry and to stop snivelling when they are hurt, to be a man and to fight back when pals take advantage of them, and to stop being a sissy and to speak up when they feel afraid. In this way, boys are taught that fear, vulnerability, and weakness are unacceptable and must be suppressed or disowned.

Strength, dominance, and rationality are seen as masculine characteristics; emotions that men find anxiety-producing have been projected onto and invested in women. In this process, weakness, dependency, subservience, and emotionality have become part of being feminine. Thus we find that males are defined as strong, females as weak; males as dominant, females as subservient; males as *rational*, females as emotional. For the most part, positive characteristics have been reserved for men; negative characteristics have been assigned to women. And behavior patterns are expected to reflect this artificial and inaccurate characterization of female and male.

Fully functioning individuals, however, use their physical, intellectual, and emotional capabilities as an integrated whole. In accepting the definition of themselves as emotional beings, women have tended to ignore intellectual and physical development, focusing instead on their feelings and their relationships with loved ones. On the other hand, the inability of men to own and handle their emotions has created the paradox of emotionality that holds women responsible for men's emotional comfort.

"I shouldn't feel this way."

Women have been taught to judge their emotions as good or bad, worthy or unworthy, loving or hateful. Society has told women to be loving and nurturing, to be tender, understanding, compassionate, and generous. Difficulties occur when women do not fit these expectations. Thinking "I shouldn't feel this way" is a mental echo of the exhortations of others that negative feelings make people uncomfortable. The effect of this message is that women believe that they are bad whenever they detect a few rotten apples in their barrel of feelings.

The truth is that feelings are neither good nor bad. Emotions are autonomic, physiological reactions to experience. If I run out of gas, I may feel helpless or frustrated; if I am overworked, I am apt to feel harassed; if my house is burglarized, I am likely to feel enraged. I do not have to blame myself for these feelings. I am judged by the way I act on my feelings, not by what I feel. Unfortunately, for most women this knowledge is overruled by feelings of responsibility and guilt when their emotions elicit unpleasant reactions in other people; women have learned as children that they can be emotional only as long as they do not upset anyone.

The paradoxes of conflict and emotionality work hand in hand to encourage suppression of negative emotions. Expressing anger openly and directly leads to conflict, and angry women are viewed as ugly and unfeminine. A woman's angry feelings are generally mixed in with feelings of anxiety, guilt, and fear of physical punishment or rejection. Angry women may be placated with flowers or candy, patronized with, "Settle down, now," or told, "You look so cute when you're angry." They may be avoided completely, yelled at, or even beaten. Given these reactions, it is not surprising that women try to muffle their anger. Not feeling anything or communicating indirectly seems preferable to suffering the consequences of open confrontation.

Since women are told that they are responsible for keeping everybody happy and they are to blame if their unladylike, nasty feelings create unhappiness or disapproval, other people act as though they have the right to tell women how they should feel. Because they feel powerless, believe they are inferior to others, and often doubt themselves, women either agree with people or fail to speak up when they disagree. This reinforces the notion that one has a right to tell women, "You shouldn't feel that way."

Believing this command, untold numbers of women have obediently become emotional contortionists, trying to be themselves while acting out what they are expected to be to keep others comfortable. Some women learn not to feel anything, others act out their emotions instead of being emotional, while many just cut off the unacceptable, "nasty" side of their emotional self. Many women try to adjust to the paradox of emotionality by becoming nonassertive. They commonly disguise their own remotely felt rage and rebellion with acquiescent facades. Others betray the twisting knots of their emotions in indirect ways when their "nasties" peek out from behind their social masks: frowns accompanying smiles, catastrophizing to abort action, or self-blame to excuse the irresponsibility of others.

"Women are supposed to be emotional, but I'm not."

Karlene came to therapy because she was shattered when her boyfriend Chad told her that as far as he was concerned they had no common interests or any depth of intimacy. "I don't even know what he's talking about," she said. "As far as I'm concerned, we mean everything to each other."

Karlene controlled her emotions with Spartan discipline. The pattern was established in childhood when Karlene's mother and father were divorced. Her father was a wealthy farmer, distant, disapproving, and uninvolved with his children. He had kept his farm holdings in his parents' name throughout his marriage to avoid having to divide his property with his wife should they ever divorce.

Karlene's mother was an outgoing, attractive woman who looked to men to give her the sense of self-esteem that had been poisoned by her marriage. As an adult, Karlene remembered her mother as happy and uninhibited, working at two menial jobs to try to make ends meet, since her father paid only minimal child support. Karlene tried to keep everyone happy at home and took care of her two little sisters. Beyond that, she could recall very few events and nothing of what she had felt during those years, except that she remembered seeing her mother laughing and flirting with the men she brought home.

When Karlene was a teenager, role-reversals complicated her journey to adulthood. Her mother became her competitor. Any boy Karlene went with immediately became her mother's challenge, and her mother was almost always successful at winning the boy over. Karlene became her mother's peer and her sisters' mother. She described herself as always being on the sidelines, watching what went on and doing what had to be done. Eventually her mother assumed the adolescent role, focusing on clothes, parties, and dates, and trying to keep work from interfering with her fun, while Karlene became the uncomplaining, dependable, hard-working "parent."

During this time Karlene's father saw his daughters infrequently and he always had a young, beautiful woman in his life. Whenever the children visited him, the woman would assume the mother role and Karlene's father would remain as unapproachable as ever. The only time Karlene remembered expressing any of her feelings was when one of her father's girlfriends said that Karlene was so quiet she must be unhappy.

It was so seldom that anyone ever paid any attention to me that I burst into tears. Her remark seemed so caring that I thought I could trust her, I guess. Anyhow, I told her that I felt unimportant and ugly and I wished my father would talk to me and listen to me now and then. I didn't dream that she'd tell him what I said. She did though, and the next night, at dinnertime, he started in on me. He kept saying that I was just like my mother, wanting him to talk and wanting to be listened to all the time, never satisfied no matter what he did. I remember I just sat there without saying a word. From then on I felt throttled and never risked opening up to anyone. Not that anyone ever cared, except Chad,

she ended bitterly.

Chad wanted intimacy and spontaneity, while Karlene had no conception of how to put those concepts into action. As a child, her role had been to keep her family happy and to not make demands on her parents. The pain of their rejection had been too severe. Not allowed at that time to say what she felt, she had learned not to feel at all. As an adult, she was completely cut off from her emotional self. She did kind, thoughtful things for Chad, but her behavior seemed frozen and automatic rather than a spontaneous expression of positive feelings. Karlene had resolved the paradox of emotionality by losing her personality and becoming perfunctory, never dipping beneath the surface of life.

Therapy for Karlene was a slow process that involved reclaiming her emotional being. At first she forced herself to speak in emotional terms. When Chad said to her, "I love you," Karlene made herself look at him, smile, and say, "I feel happy when you say that."

At first, Karlene expressed her emotions in broad categories, such as, "I feel mad," or "I feel happy." Gradually, as seeds buried in a garden respond to water and sun, her feelings came to the surface and she could identify what they were. Her concentrated effort was rewarded. One day Karlene reported to her therapist, "Today I feel so free. I said 'I love you' to Chad for the first time. He didn't even say it first, and you know what? I don't even know if he said 'I love you' back. It doesn't matter. I just felt it and wanted to say it, and I didn't need to hear his answer."

Karlene had discovered one of the secrets of intimacy. The ability to distinguish between and to express different feelings and the subtleties of the same feeling adds depth to one's emotional well-being and one's relationships. To be able to say, "I feel cut off," or "I feel disillusioned," conveys much more specific information than saying, "I feel angry." To say, "I feel light-hearted," or "I feel rewarded," are more specific than just saying, "I feel happy." Being able to differentiate between feelings and to express them more and more accurately adds color to otherwise carefully laundered, flat-white conversations. One feels freer, more relaxed, more expressive, and more in charge, open to experience one's own feelings as well as someone else's, and looks forward to the shared communication of them.

For Annette, the attempt to resolve the paradox of emotionality took a different turn than it did for Karlene. She was a thin, tense woman of thirty. She wore gold chains, which she twisted busily while she spoke in clipped, businesslike tones. She came to therapy after abruptly filing for divorce because her husband expressed casual interest in another woman. There was a mix-up in the initial appointment time, and Annette was furious. Unable to express her anger directly, she was tempted not to proceed with therapy. She was shocked to discover when she and her therapist talked over the mix-up that this was the same diversionary tactic she had used to handle distress throughout her life. She had habitually exploded like a firecracker, impulsively allowing her feelings to determine what she did. So that she would not have to worry about making people feel uncomfortable because of her negative feelings, she acted them out and then slammed the door on the consequences.

Annette remembered dropping out of college rather than telling a professor he had been unjust. She cut off a friendship instead of saying how hurt she had felt about a misunderstanding. She frequently filled her trash barrel with valuable things that she threw away in reaction to negative feelings that she could not seem to get rid of directly. Throwing away her marriage was an extension of this pattern. Annette's efforts not to upset anyone with her hurt and anger had crippled her, too.

"How in the world could anyone be described as too loving?"

When women focus on emotionality in a positive way, they feel highly rewarded, for others find it very pleasant to be with someone who is happy, loving, and affectionate. It is satisfying to express love through serving other persons, facilitating their growth and their achievements and filling nurturing roles. Some women have become so attuned to focusing on others that they have lost touch with their own feelings and desires. To their bewilderment, they may be accused of being too nice, too loving, and too generous.

For instance, Sally described herself as too nice, for it seemed to her that she had become a doormat. Her family seemed to accept the things she did without even a "thank you," as though she did them for her own pleasure. Pat said she must be too loving, for her seventeen-year-old son insisted that she smothered him because she kept his dinner warm when he worked late at his after-school job and expected him to share confidences with her while he ate. Rhoda thought she prob-

123

ably was too generous, because her daughter-in-law had forbidden her to give presents to her grandchildren except at Christmas and on their birthdays. As a matter of fact, these women only seemed too nice, too loving, and too generous because they were caught in the double-bind of emotionality. They had learned long before that their negative feelings were unacceptable and so being nice became their vocation. Their intent was to keep themselves from being cut off from those they loved, but because these women expressed only positive feelings, others were annoyed by their seeming refusal to deal with the realities of life. The people close to them, knowing that they themselves felt both positive and negative feelings, felt manipulated and tended to distrust the loving messages and kindnesses they received.

Women who suppress their negative feelings reduce the risks of incurring another person's displeasure; by expressing only their happy side, there is no danger that they will betray themselves. But the long-standing pattern of denying their nasty feelings stifles one-half of their emotional expressiveness and eventually cuts it off entirely.

It is essential for increased awareness and personal growth that women acknowledge the full range of their feelings. Those with which they feel uncomfortable are as important as the comfortable ones. Effective people pay attention to all of their feelings. Denying or suppressing emotions cuts out information that is essential for integrated behavior in an individual and honest relationships with others.

One of us remembers Avis, a friend she had as a young woman. We used to double date and had several friends in common; we had many happy times together. Then we married and each of us established a home. It soon became obvious that Avis's marriage was not happy. Nevertheless, she was careful to say only good things about everyone, especially her husband. She continued to act as if everything were beautiful. Her cheerfulness came to signal a barrier that was not to be violated. After a while, our relationship seemed stilted and superficial. It was distressing to see

124

a friend suffering and be unable to talk with her about it, or even to say, "I'm sorry about the misery you're going through." When her divorce was final, Avis's only remark—said cheerfully, of course—was, "I'm glad that's over."

Perhaps she did not trust our friendship enough to discuss anything unpleasant, but it seems more likely that she was the same with everyone. She was a victim, a woman caught in the paradox of emotionality. The person she became was an artificial, superficial woman who created distance and discomfort in those around her and shut herself off from support and personal growth.

"Sometimes the pressure cooker blows."

In their attempt to resolve the paradox of emotionality, nonassertive women like Sally, Pat, Rhoda, and Avis throttled their "nasties" almost completely. Other nonassertive women have learned that when they state negative feelings openly, others frequently feel criticized, hurt, and uncomfortable, and may respond with defensiveness or anger. These women try to resolve the paradox of being emotional without upsetting anyone by failing to speak up when they feel misunderstood. They let someone else talk while they listen. They back down quickly when challenged. They avoid disturbing or hurting anyone, and they worry about what other people think.

These women are aware that they have negative feelings and know that they feel unable to express them. What happens? They come to feel imposed upon and unimportant; they try so hard to please, yet other people seem to take them for granted. They stockpile their anger and use it as ammunition for blow-ups over small incidents at inappropriate times.

Being out of control during such explosions creates further humiliation, anxiety, and guilt, which does nothing to help a nonassertive woman feel good about herself. It imprisons her further in the paradox that asks her to control her emotions to free others from discomfort.

Wendy reported in therapy that she could not understand why she lost her temper with the school nurse who called to say her son was sick and had to be picked up and taken home. Thinking about the incident, Wendy said with surprise, "I was really angry at my husband, not the nurse. I asked him this morning whether he thought Teddy was well enough to go to school. He just rushed out the door, looking annoyed, and said, 'How should I know? You're his mother,' as if that made me an expert on childhood illness." Wendy added with some bitterness, "Come to think of it, he does that a lot. He's never around, and doesn't take an interest in Teddy. Whenever there's any problem, he leaves and I have to handle it."

Wendy was quiet for a long moment and then said thoughtfully, "I wasn't mad at that nurse at all. I'm really mad at my husband for neglecting me as well as Teddy. I have never been able to tell him, though, because he gets so hostile when I try to talk to him about how I feel that I just try not to think about it at all. Then every once in a while something happens and I blow up, and I think at first I'm overreacting."

Wendy, like most nonassertive women, paid a heavy price because of the paradox of emotionality. Unable to express her feelings directly, she displaced her frustration and anger on innocent people or dissipated it by blowing up over little incidents. She ended up feeling guilty and resolved to try even harder to suppress her negative feelings. She kept thinking, "It's terrible to feel this way. I've got to learn not to overreact. I won't feel so guilty if I just stop being emotional."

After learning about the tricks that unexpressed emotions played on her, Wendy said, "I realize now that it isn't a question of overreacting; I'm just reacting in the wrong direction. I'm letting loose with all the nasty feelings I've been storing up. The trouble is, I'm usually letting loose at the wrong person."

"I'll let people know how I feel somehow."

Being unable to discuss negative emotions directly, most women find countless indirect ways to do so. It is as if they say, "Since everyone says women are emotional, I will get my feelings out somehow," perhaps because not to do so results in feeling powerless, shut down, defeated, or sick. One of the most destructive of these roundabout expressions is passive-aggressive behavior, a covert act intended to force the other person to act overtly and take the blame for anything that happens. It is punishing, guilt-inducing, and manipulative, an attempt to communicate distress while avoiding the possibility that the person will respond with punishment or destructive conflict.

Angie was twenty-five when she stopped driving a car because her husband refused to spend any time with her. By requiring him to take her to the grocery store and the laundry, she forced him to do something that he refused to do when she spoke to him openly about it. Karen was habitually late for dates; she was unable to tell her boyfriend that she did not like going to visit his friends every time they went out. By forcing him to wait, she expressed her anger in this indirect way.

Not answering when spoken to, spending money in retaliation when they see others being extravagant, not going to bed until after their partners are asleep or going to sleep before their partners come to bed are examples of passive-aggressive ways of expressing emotions rather than communicating them directly for fear that others will become upset.

Sabotaging someone's plans is another way of expressing feelings that cannot be said openly. Billy crammed her schedule full of activities so that she had no time to entertain her in-laws when they came to town. They were people she disliked, and she had no intention of spending time with them. Letty, rather than tell her boss that she was feeling very pressured by a large, unexpected order, unaccountably forgot how to fix her jammed typewriter ribbon. She took a rest period while waiting for the repairman. Pam, who worked as a waitress during the dinner-hour rush, felt annoyed with customers who wanted quick service. She acted out her feelings by deliberately moving slowly, while pretending she was working hard to accommodate them.

Some women, caught in the double-bind of being emotional without upsetting anyone, resort to the use of "womanly wiles." They may flirt with strangers to make their boyfriends jealous, they may sweet talk their partners out of silent withdrawals, and they operate on the principle that flattery will get them anything they want.

Other women express negative emotions with body language, while being verbally pleasant. For example, a woman might frown when she says yes or smile sweetly when saying no. Such incongruences are usually obvious to other persons and fool only the woman who is giving the conflicting message. Another woman might smile constantly as she talks, regardless of what she is feeling, but especially when she is angry. At best she is seen as discounting whatever she is saying and conveying the message that she is not to be taken seriously; at worst she is seen as insincere, manipulative, and even hypocritical.

Although a woman may be accused of being manipulative when she cries, of using tears to get her own way, this is seldom the case. Crying is often an indirect way of expressing anger. Tears also accompany depression as an expression of grief over the loss of someone dear or a valued part of one's own self. When a woman feels trapped and unable to express herself because others are in control and she is afraid of their displeasure, tears provide relief and convey a watered-down version of the difficulty of her dilemma. Even though women are told they are emotional, they apologize for their tears, feeling ashamed and vulnerable and very much aware that the person they are with may be embarrassed and upset. Once again, being emotional means be happy and do not disturb anyone.

A woman might try to resolve the contradiction inherent in "I can be emotional, but I mustn't upset anyone" by becoming a happy-go-lucky person who never lets anything bother her. By taking everything with a smile, she makes light of the weighty burden of others' unhappiness and does not feel responsible for it.

Being afraid of expressing feelings openly, a woman may catastrophize. That is, she predicts that a disaster will happen if she says what she is really thinking and feeling. She tells herself, "If I tell my friend what I think, she will never talk to me again," or "If I tell my boss I'm angry, I'll be fired," or, "If I say anything negative, I'll be rejected." By predicting that something terrible will follow if she says what she feels, she scares herself into a stomach-churning silence.

The indirect ways that women use to try to resolve their emotional conflicts are punishing to them. For some women, long-suppressed emotions finally surface, unnamed, in psychosomatic illnesses. The final irony seems to be that other people can accept a woman's illness more readily than they can accept her negative feelings. Illness often elicits the responses of appreciation and caring that were not forthcoming when she was well. Becoming sick is a self-punishing, circuitous way to resolve the paradox of emotionality.

Overeating, too, is self-punishing, an indirect expression of unacceptable emotions. Instead of speaking up, women swallow their anxiety and frustration. Their bodies reflect the unattractiveness of the emotions they have harbored.

Sometimes a woman who fears what will happen if she criticizes others becomes self-critical. Helen was such a woman. She felt guilty whenever she had an unpleasant thought about anyone. To relieve her guilt, she punished herself with a put-down. When she complained about her students being inattentive, she said, "Of course, I drew pictures and never paid attention all tha way through school. I can't expect the kids to do more than I did myself." When she felt angry with her brother for breaking her stereo, she said, "I wrecked my brother's car once because I was such a terrible driver, so I shouldn't complain about this." By rationalizing away all of her angry feelings, she tried to resolve the paradox. Helen was, like many women, much more critical of herself than she was of others, or than they were of her. For Helen, too, this attempt at resolution of the conflict meant that she protected someone else at her own expense.

"I'm an angry person."

When hurt cannot be communicated directly to the person involved, there is a tendency to project it as anger. Instead of being self-punishing, an angry woman punishes whomever seems to be the generator of her painful emotions. This appears to her to be the only way out of the paradox of emotionality.

Barbara was a high-school senior, vibrant with fury when we first saw her for therapy. "I have to talk to someone or I'll explode," she cried. "I'm so mad at my parents. This is the year I'm to be the editor of the school paper and homecoming queen, and they say we're moving. It's supposed to be a big promotion for my father so I haven't told him what he's doing to me. I'm going to wait until we get moved, and then I'll just pack my bags and come back. I don't care how many times I have to do it." In her anger at her father, Barbara did not realize that she was expecting him to read her mind.

Barbara was a victim of the myth that states, "If he really loves me, he will know what I want without my having to ask. Since he doesn't give me what I want, then he must not love me." Barbara learned in therapy that this mythical nonsense allowed her to be irresponsible to herself as well as to her father and guaranteed that their problems would continue.

Another way of trying to solve the problem of being emotional without causing anyone else unhappiness is to discharge negative feelings through dysfunctional bitching, that is, telling a third party what is really bothering one, rather than speaking directly to the person toward whom one feels angry.

Glenda's status as a sheltered only daughter of a small-town family practitioner had not prepared her for marriage to Todd. He was a lusty, outspoken man whose anger seemed as explosive as a summer thundercloud and blew over just as quickly. Glena was a quiet, rather shy woman whose sweetness served initially as a backdrop for Todd's brashness.

In her ten years of marriage, Glenda had experienced cycles of distress caused mostly by unavoidable events and circumstances. Feeling guilty and punished by the threat of Todd's outrage whenever she told him that she was unhappy, Glenda developed a pattern of bitterly complaining about him. She inflicted her dysfunctional bitching upon family, friends, and acquaintances as a way of getting recognition from other people of just how bad her life was. Understandably, they did not give Glenda the kind of support that would have helped her to be more direct with her feelings. Instead, finding her behavior extremely unpleasant, they began to avoid her. She felt shunned and alienated and, at the same time, blamed herself for feeling bitter and negative toward everyone. These were qualities she certainly did not admire in herself, but she felt unable to change them. She saw herself becoming the proverbial shrew. In her efforts to avoid being punished for her negative feelings, Glenda's sweetness turned sour.

Glenda's complaining pattern was dysfunctional because in expressing her thoughts to other persons rather than directly to Todd, she denied him the opportunity to respond differently than he had in the past. Furthermore, about the time Glenda and he had patched up each argument, her family and friends were solidly lined up in her camp. Then he felt resentful toward Glenda for airing their personal business in public, and the vicious battle began again.

There are many functional ways of communicating unpleasant feelings. In fact, doing so seems essential to clearing out the tangled underbrush of unhappiness so that positive feelings can grow and flower. If one cannot speak directly to the person concerned, but has a good confidant who can listen with empathy without giving advice or taking sides, discussion with her or him can calm and clarify ragged feelings. As Todd and Glenda's experience shows, however, this is a big challenge most friends would do well to avoid. Friends want to help, but they tend to give sympathy and take sides, adding fuel to the conflagration. They are likely to give advice based on their own experience, which probably does not apply to anyone else.

One does not always have to express feelings out

loud. One can write them down in a notebook and keep the book to refer to later to see if the feelings have changed, or one can destroy the notes. One can hit a tennis ball or pound a pillow. One can turn up the car radio and shout at the top of one's lungs while driving, or one can sing in the shower. One can also discharge the "nasties" in therapy. A therapist who is objective will not punish or blame a client or think poorly of those a client is angry with. A woman can be emotional in such a way that no one is inadvertently or needlessly hurt. This is a functional way to resolve the paradox of emotionality.

"I've finally given up."

Betsy and Matt came for therapy together. They described their marriage of ten years as well laundered, pleasant most of the time, but without any excitement, emotional closeness, sexual intimacy, or communication. Both had dated others, hoping in this way to revitalize their sex life. Failing in this, they had decided that Matt would move out. Betsy felt she had done everything possible to try to make the marriage work.

In therapy Betsy described the marriage.

When we first got married, I worked. Then I had the two kids and stayed home. I felt prematurely old and discontented. We never had any money to do things. Matt's a nice guy, but he isn't very stimulating. I like lots of parties, excitement, and laughter, and he likes to watch television and play with the kids.

I didn't know anything about sex, and I guess I thought Matt did, but he was one big disappointment for me. He seemed interested only in his own pleasure. I was tired all the time with the kids and felt turned off in general. I turned him down frequently when he wanted sex, and I felt terribly guilty. A couple of years ago I read some books about sexuality and thought how foolish I had been. I felt there might be hope for us. I talked to Matt and said I'd like for us to start over. He said he

132

wasn't the least bit interested. I was really hurt and angry. It seemed to me that when I finally did what he always said he wanted me to do, he rejected me just to get even. Anyhow, that's when we decided to see other people.

Matt described himself as a nice, unemotional, distant, and undemanding man who believed that he had always done his share in their marriage. He saw Betsy as immmature and inefficient. She always seemed ready to play with the children and friends—and with him, if he only would—even though the house was usually a mess and meals were haphazard. He believed in having fun, like camping trips and going out for pizzas, but only when all the work was done and everything was organized, including whatever Betsy had not accomplished. Matt's fears of emotional commitment to a woman he considered unpredictable and childish were expressed as sexual incompatibility and lack of involvement.

Once Matt moved to an apartment, Betsy felt free and happy. For the first time in her life she had a competent and adult attitude about herself. She was brimming with confidence; she could take care of whatever problems came along. In contrast to Betsy, Matt was so distraught that he became physically ill. He lived daily with the pain of previously buried anxieties, which wracked him when he was alone. He could no longer deny that he had become very dependent upon Betsy over the years, and his aloofness had been a protection against getting too close.

It is not important what or who started the emotional chasm that separated Betsy and Matt. As children, both of them had developed patterns for expressing their emotionality and protecting themselves from hurt, rejection, and abandonment. Betsy had become a happy-go-lucky, pleasing child, and Matt had become dependable, goal-oriented, and serious. When they married and misunderstandings developed, these patterns served as defenses that drove them further apart. Betsy felt overwhelmed and defeated trying to interact with a man who apparently resented her but

133

would not discuss their conflicts with her. She also felt guilty, because she knew she would feel angry and hurt if she were Matt; this made it very difficult for Betsy to finally say she wanted a divorce. Matt, faced with the loss of the only emotional support and affiliative bond he had, decided he was ready to try to jump the gulf created by their problems. At that point, however, Betsy was not ready to reconcile.

Over the next eighteen months, first one, then the other was interested in trying to narrow the gap between them. This pattern had operated while they lived together to create emotional distance, and it served the same function during their separation. As long as Betsy was trying her best to elicit Matt's affection, he could stay aloof and feel comfortable, because his fears of losing her were allayed. Whenever she declared her unwillingness to continue what for her was an empty, bleached-out marriage, however, he was unable to contain his fears and scrambled after her to reestablish the status quo. Like two chess players, they chased each other back and forth across the board, working very hard to avoid a checkmate but accomplishing nothing else.

This is a common situation in many marriages. Men, ashamed of having emotions that seem weak and feminine, deny such feelings. Women, locked into partnerships with such men, feel trapped, hurt, and empty. When they finally feel strong enough to unlock the trap, women are astonished and bitterly angry to find their partners belatedly willing to sit down and listen, to discuss the issues, and to nondefensively involve themselves in exchanges of thoughts and feelings. Unfortunately, this long-dormant interest often comes too late; the women have given up.

"I feel so upset."

The word upset is often used as a substitute for the word *angry* by women who need to avoid directly expressing what they are feeling. The effect of saying, "I feel upset," is to elicit help, whereas "I feel angry" might elicit a defensive or punishing response.

Ann, a public relations specialist for a large manufacturing company, came to therapy because of difficulties she was experiencing at work. During her therapy session she described how upset she felt when her boss refused to make decisions and failed to follow through on her suggestions for improving customer relations. In therapy Ann repeatedly referred to herself as upset, and when she did so she became visibly more and more agitated. Her therapist asked her to describe how she felt, right then, being upset, and Ann said, "Harassed, weak, ineffective. Right now, talking about it, I feel just exactly the same as I feel at work."

Ann's therapist asked her to talk about her work again, using the words "I feel angry," instead of "I feel upset." As Ann did this, her voice sounded stronger and more energetic. She was astonished to learn that she really was feeling angry at her boss. Using the word *upset* reflected her inability to express her anger directly for fear of displeasing him. This self-deception distorted her feelings and neutralized her ability to deal with unpleasant situations. Rather than acting competently, as she was capable of doing, she elicited help.

During the following week, Ann found that she had been substituting *upset* for *angry* in almost all of her interpersonal relationships. The help elicited by being upset was not, however, what Ann was seeking from people. What she did want was cooperation, understanding, and caring, and sometimes a change in behavior. When Ann began saying explicitly what she was feeling, people responded to her differently. More important, her timidity was quickly replaced with self-confidence.

Anger, like *upset* is often a cover-up for feelings that are even more painful than the anger itself. The word becomes an umbrella under which women put many of their negative feelings, like disappointment, disillusionment, rejection, frustration, disapproval, and especially hurt. Feeling angry serves as a protection against experiencing the severe pain of hurt and rejection, much as an umbrella protects one from a heavy rainstorm. Because the hurt seems unbearable, all of one's distress is put under the anger umbrella and, in doing so, one keeps from awareness the complexities of what one is experiencing. All negative emotions are labeled as anger and one evaluates oneself as bad.

It is difficult to differentiate all of the feelings lumped under an anger umbrella. Caught in the conflict between feeling responsible for everyone's happiness and not being able to upset anyone, women turn their unexpressed negative emotions inward and use them against themselves. These feelings are then experienced as depression.

In an effort to help them sort out these emotions, we frequently ask our clients to draw pictures of their anger. Beneath the calm exterior of one woman's depression she saw her anger as a tornado, whirling around and around, powerful enough to destroy everything in its path. Another woman drew her anger as a smooth surface with a great big fissure. Under the surface molten lava bubbled and boiled, waiting to spill out and destroy everything in its path. Both women realized that beneath their fury were feelings that were even more painful than the rage itself, feelings of abandonment, low self-esteem, and despair.

Both of these clients felt their anger dissipate as they identified these deeply buried emotions. Being aware of exactly what they were feeling gave them the power to connect with others in a way that could not be misunderstood. They were no longer simply angry women. At times they *did* feel irate; at other times they felt astonished, resentful, annoyed, disillusioned, confused, distrustful, or bewildered. Their happy side was also free to surface undiffused. No one needed to wonder what they were feeling; they were able to communicate clearly themselves.

"I've got a lot of garbage I've been carrying around."

Much of the work of therapy involves the discharge of anger, pain, and grief associated with what used to be. Unfortunately, it is not possible simply to stow away the past as if it had never happened. It is not true that a woman's past has nothing to do with what is happening and what she is feeling in the present. Until she has discharged the pain of her past, she will react in present time with the restimulation of the feelings that were associated with past events. Some clients think that understanding what has caused their distress should be all that is necessary to remove it. They are dismayed to find that the pain of almost forgotten incidents needs to be gone over several times, so that emotions associated with the past can be resolved. If a woman's husband has been unfaithful to her, she likely will not be able to trust him again until she has worked through her feeling of being betrayed. When children have been mistreated by their parents, it may be impossible for them to trust authority figures until they have expressed their terror. A woman who has been repeatedly and severely criticized may find it impossible to feel comfortable in close relationships until she has dealt with her feelings of inadequacy.

The pain of the past is real and has a severe impact on women's lives. They do not have to carry that pain with them for the rest of their lives, whether or not they were responsible for what happened. Expressing feelings of hurt, grief, rage, and blame in therapy allows them to discharge past distress so that they can live in the present and plan and change for the future.

When women express feelings from the past and eventually discharge them, they are freed from the guilt associated with having negative emotions, feeling bad about themselves, and thinking unpleasant thoughts. At the same time, they are able to let others be responsible for their own feelings just as women are responsible for the emotions they experience.

We help our clients explore the past when there is a connection between present feelings and old distress. Dysfunctional behavior usually reflects patterns that were developed at an early age, or perhaps in a time of trauma. These patterns may have been helpful then as distractors or attempts to muffle their pain, but they are no longer useful tools for resolving the painful paradox of emotionality.

Fran jeopardized her marriage because of patterns she acquired in childhood to handle her own emotionality. She was a smart, self-contained woman who learned early that discretion paid off when any emotional tug-of-war threatened. As a child, when her parents had stormy disagreements, she left the house. If her brothers and sisters tumbled in fisticuffs, she went to her room and shut the door. At school, jibes and jeers were no problem; she retreated to the safety of her classroom. In any battle where physical strength or emotional stamina seemed balanced against her, Fran's tactic was immediate withdrawal to a position well guarded against feeling any emotion at all.

Fran was so unnerved by any outburst of her husband's anger that she developed ways to avoid him, too. When Fran and Jim were in a therapy session together, she mentioned that whenever he fixed things around the house, she found errands to run. She did not want to be there for his inevitable cursing when things failed to go smoothly. Although Jim did get angry easily, he was surprised that Fran was threatened by his eruptions. He had felt hurt and rejected; it had seemed to him that she always avoided being at home when he was there.

One of the bonuses that came from Fran and Jim's therapy together was that once he understood the source of Fran's avoidance pattern, he felt motivated to try to control his feelings. He did not want his anger to frighten her. Although this was difficult for him to do, he believed that it was well worth the effort to improve their relationship, and he was proud of his own growth in self-control. Fran responded with a willingness to change avoidance to approach; she stopped retreating the minute the emotionality paradox reared its head, and her self-containment slowly gave way to risk-taking.

Many women are distressed when they try to express their feelings, only to receive a curt "That's your problem," by which other persons disclaim any help in examining their feelings. An individual's behavior does elicit feelings in others, and they have a right to express these feelings. Not to do so cuts off the give and take of valuable information and the growth-enhancing, supportive interactions that are needed to encourage intimacy and positive mutuality in relationships.

Margaret was in group therapy because, as she described it, "I'm so easily dismissed. No one seems to take me seriously, even though I'm reasonably competent as an interior designer and I'm an open, trusting person. I tell people my feelings and expect them to reciprocate, but instead I seem to get blank stares and uncomfortable silence."

When Margaret talked about this puzzling problem in her group, the other women pointed out with gentle-tough caring several examples of the way she appeared to them to be acting like a little child, which almost guaranteed her not being taken seriously. She hung her head when she talked, giggled when people were earnestly discussing issues, and said, "I don't know," whenever she was asked for an opinion. Although Margaret did not like what her group members said to her, she did appreciate their honesty. In conveying to her how they felt about her behavior, they were also giving her the message that they thought she could handle her own feelings and that she was responsible for how she felt.

Burdened with the task of being responsible for everyone's happiness, many women believe that other people would be wounded if they expressed negative feelings, that the sensitivity of others would be offended. They see themselves as being considerate when they hold back. Because they find it so difficult to own and to express their own feelings, they think that other people cannot handle emotions either.

A woman who tells herself that she is protecting a man's ego when she fails to tell him what she likes and what she expects of him sexually is actually avoiding discussing sex because of her own discomfort with the subject. Saying that her mother would be hurt if she told her that she had other plans and cannot go to her mother's house for Sunday dinner is a way for a woman to avoid feeling like an ungrateful daughter. A third woman, believing that her friend would feel rejected if she told her she wants to vacation alone, sidesteps having to disappoint someone she thinks is depending upon her.

It is a shock for women to hear that this attitude is very patronizing, that one only talks down to people who are seen as inferior. The message given covertly in an attempt to protect someone is that he or she is weaker or less capable than one would like that person to be. This attitude is irresponsible to the other person and to one's own self; opportunities for involvement that could be mutually enhancing are passed up. This sets the stage for withdrawal and creates distance between people.

It may be that more emotional pain is accumulated in women because of unexpressed positive emotions than because of stored-up unhappy and critical feelings. If a relationship is important to a woman, she has to take risks, even if it means giving someone messages about which she feels uncomfortable, despite their benevolence.

Not that a woman has to express all of her feelings. At times she may choose not to do so, for it is at that time enough just to be aware of what she feels and thinks, or to know that everybody has done his or her best. If your roommate has had a hard day at work, you may choose not to tell her how angry you are that she forgot to clean the bathroom that morning. If you feel impatient because a clerk is very slow in waiting on you and you discover that it is his first day at work, you may decide to react with tolerance. If a sudden rain comes up and the barbecue is not hot enough when you are ready to cook the steaks, you may choose to say nothing. If you have lost weight and your birthday gift is one size too big, you may act appreciative anyhow. When children do their best, but their efforts are not up to your standards, you may go ahead and tell them how delighted you are with what they *have* done. The important thing is that you are able to choose whether or not you will express your feelings, without feeling guilty and being afraid of rejection and without feeling responsible if the other person is defensive.

When women understand that others' feelings belong

to them and that they are not responsible for them, they can listen without feeling hurt, attacked, threatened, or guilty. They can empathize and explore differences between people as they arise. They can keep relationships spontaneous and current, free of stored-up resentment and hurt. They can be emotional without worrying about upsetting anyone.

Once women have resolved the paradox of emotionality, they know that they are intellectual and physical as well as emotional. They can be emotional when they choose to be. They assume responsibility not for *having* feelings, but for how they *act* in response to their feelings. Being emotional is not a liability. It is a strength, a capacity, a positive aspect of one's personhood. Becoming aware of what she is feeling and deciding how she chooses to act on her feelings is a woman's first step in solving the next paradox, perception.

CHAPTER VII

Perception

> "I don't see it the way you do, so I must be wrong."

Men have described how the world is. Because they are subordinate to men, women are supposed to agree with them. But women's perceptions tell them that things are different; their reality is not as it is defined by men. Women are comfortable and confident in how they perceive things until they are challenged. When that happens they tend to back off and assume they are wrong. The paradox for women has been that when they cannot trust their own perceptions, they do not know how to act. The challenge, "How dare you see it the way I don't?" is enough to immobilize most women.

Underlying many of a woman's fears when she begins therapy is the terrifying question, "I'm going crazy, aren't I?" Anna was such a woman. She sat down and said, "I have a lovely home, a wonderful husband, and three beautiful children, yet I'm not happy. I don't know what is the matter with me." Tears welled up in her eyes and spilled over, tears of relief as she sensed that she had found a safe place to express the frightening possibility that she was "losing her mind." Anna was caught in the paradox of perception. Because she perceived things differently than she was "supposed" to, she assumed that she was wrong, so much so that she must be crazy.

Perception can be defined as awareness gained through the senses. In general, men trust their perceptions, whereas women are full of self-doubt. Men, being dominant, have defined how the world is and how it should be in ways that reinforce their perceptions and their power. The message that men give to women is that they should be satisfied with the subservient roles men have decided are good for them. Women are expected to see the world as it is perceived by men. Furthermore, they are supposed to be happy because they are allowed to be what they were born to be: wives, mothers, and helpmates.

Anna's husband Al was a competitive, aggressive, and successful businessman. He usually maintained a tight grip on his frustrations and anger. He used alcohol to relax, however, and when he drank he often became verbally abusive and insensitive to other people. Al was so afraid of his own weaknesses and the possibility of losing control that he denied any inconsistencies between what he wanted to be and the way he was. He insisted that all men drank some and let loose now and then. He saw Anna as overly sensitive. He assured her that there was nothing for her to worry about; he would never allow himself to have a drinking problem, let alone to become an alcoholic. He could give up drinking any time he wanted to.

Like most people, Al had an image of himself that he wanted to maintain. He reserved for himself what he regarded as positive masculine qualities, such as strength, competitiveness, courage, dominance, and intelligence. He assigned to Anna the qualities he denied in himself: fear, timidity, unreliability, and weakness. Whenever Anna tentatively brought up her perception of his behavior when he drank, he told her, in a polite way, of course, that she was crazy. Al's strong rebuttal, combined with Anna's own doubts about her perception of the situation, made her question what she thought to be true.

A person's awareness of her or his sensory experience is very complex and subject to many variables and inconsistencies. Since perceptions are based on each individual's history of personal experiences and his or her interpretation of these experiences, the potential for disagreement and confusion is great. Law enforcement agencies know that not all witnesses to an accident or crime will tell the same story; the event is seen and interpreted differently by different persons. One who does not understand this may think that some of the witnesses are lying.

Anna saw Al's behavior when he drank as being out of control. She thought his intention was to punish her and others because he could not express his anger in direct ways. Al, unable to accept that he had a drinking problem, did not agree. He triggered Anna's self-doubts when he became defensive and tried to convince her that she was wrong. Anna's conflict arose because she, like most women, doubted herself when Al challenged her. It was an easy step, then, for her to accept his label, and to feel "crazy," and blame herself because she did not see the problem the way he did.

Anna's dilemma is one with which countless women are familiar. When women act on their own perceptions and they differ from another person's, that person is likely to respond to them as if they are criticizing, questioning the person's authority, or threatening to usurp the other's power. Women are told they should not feel or think the way they do. The same people they are expected to depend upon and look to for validation, feedback, approval, and confirmation when they are uncertain respond in ways that lower self-esteem and reinforce their feelings of self-doubt. Women often end up feeling punished for independent thought and action. In this way they are taught not to trust themselves or their own perceptions.

There is a progression of the paradoxes that lead to women's lack of trust in their perceptions. They have been assigned caretaker functions that are viewed as unimportant. They have learned to see themselves as inferior and to feel bad about themselves because of this. They are encouraged to look to other people to make them feel whole; and, in order to feel secure, they become dependent upon those people. Women are described as emotional, yet they are expected to have only positive feelings. It is no wonder that they do not trust their own thoughts and feelings and are frequently immobilized by self-doubt. The paradox is that, when a woman accepts another person's negative evaluations of her, she accepts inferiority and submissiveness, but when she rejects that evaluation, she confirms that what that person knows about her is true.

Anna believed that she had two choices: She could agree with Al that she was crazy or she could continue to disagree with him and tell him that he *did* have a drinking problem whether he knew it or not. Either response on her part would be interpreted by Al as confirmation that he was right and she was wrong, so both of these outcomes meant that she would be ineffective in changing the situation or his perception of it and her.

Neither alternative was satisfactory to Anna, despite her self-doubts. She came for therapy to try to resolve the immobilizing struggle in which she was caught. She explored the inconsistent messages she had received all her life, messages that said anger was a bad thing, even though it was important for her to speak up honestly; that she must be seen and not heard; that she was to be a happy, obedient follower.

With the support of her therapist, Anna learned to value herself and to sort out from other people's perceptions of her those that seemed accurate and those that did not. She learned to use feedback to confirm and expand her own awareness of herself and others.

When messages did not fit, she was able to reject the information without feeling hurt or criticized.

At first, though, Anna continued to try to get confirmation of her belief that Al was prealcoholic. If her therapist, her family doctor, or some authority figure would only confirm her suspicions, then her self-doubts would be resolved.

Instead of discussing who was right and who was wrong, her therapist focused on Anna's discomfort when Al drank. Whether or not his drinking was a problem for Al, it was for Anna. Their perceptions could be quite different and still be accurate for each of them, depending on their individual experiences, strengths, and weaknesses. As she learned to trust her own viewpoint, Anna could see that Al was a master of self-deception. He was drinking more and more frequently and in greater amounts; his temper invariably flared when the liquor flowed. Living with the uproar of his excesses was no longer possible for her.

As therapy continued, Anna explored other alternatives than the two she had considered. "I've even thought of getting sick," she said in one session with a rueful laugh. "If I become weaker than he is, then he'd have to be the one to shape up." Even as she said it, Anna realized that this was not necessarily true and that it would not be wise to take such a risk. Getting sick was too big a price to pay. Another alternative she considered was to become a nag about Al's drinking, like a parent constantly scolding a naughty child. This, too, was unacceptable to her. She wanted a husband, not a child, and putting herself in a parent role with Al seemed sure to elicit even more of his temper tantrums.

For someone who feels confident about what he or she knows, the resolution of Anna's conflict seems simple. "Just stand up to him and tell him that you don't have to take the garbage he dumps on you," is the advice often given by well-meaning friends. For Anna, though, getting constant messages from Al that she was crazy because she disagreed with him was very threatening. If she challenged him, he might become angrier. Then what would happen? "He'll divorce me," she catastrophized in answer to her own question.

145

Anna could not consider leaving Al, because she believed that she was responsible for his drinking. "After all," she said, "I've read that when men drink, usually it is condoned or even encouraged in some sick way by the wife." She felt guilty and wondered what part she had contributed to the whole mess. She believed that it was up to her to find a happy solution.

On the other hand, Anna knew that Al was successful and confident when sober. She told herself that surely he knew what he was doing. "Besides," she said, "what if my assessment of his drinking is wrong? What right do I have to tell him what to do and how he should act, just because I don't like what he is doing? He has a right to live his own life. I can either shut up and put up with it, or I can leave him."

Anna went over and over the problem in her mind for months, seesawing back and forth, while her doubts increased to the point that she was immobilized. Not until she learned to trust her perceptions was she able to check them out for accuracy and then to take action. Until she felt somewhat confident about what she knew, she was unable to act. Once she did trust herself it became very important to her to do what she thought was best.

The alternative Anna decided upon was to tell Al what she saw and felt. She believed that she had the right to bring up issues that were important to her no matter how he might respond. She was prepared to take the worst consequences she could imagine, complete rejection and divorce, even though she hoped for the best. Anna learned to focus on the conditions of her relationship with Al that were bad, instead of condemning him as bad and portraying herself as good. She was able to talk to him about how she felt when he drank and about the otherwise positive feelings she had concerning their life together.

When Anna behaved differently toward him, Al responded differently. He felt less defensive and began to respect Anna for speaking up. He was able to examine objectively the validity of his own perceptions, and he admitted that they were inaccurate. Al had a positive self-concept and he wanted to change his behavior so

146

that it was congruent with his perception of himself. He loved Anna and valued their marriage. He agreed to stop drinking for a week in order to show Anna that he was not dependent upon alcohol. To his chagrin he discovered that not drinking was very difficult for him.

Several months later Anna called her therapist to tell her how happy she was. "I hope all the misery is behind us. I'm sure glad I didn't give up."

"He just keeps at it until I give in."

Thinking she is going crazy is only one of the consequences for a woman of being locked into the perception paradox. Many times a woman is bullied until she gives in and admits that her viewpoint is wrong and someone else's is right. When she remains unconvinced of the "error" of her personal mosaic of the world and refuses to cave in, those who have assumed an authoritative stance may respond with emotional or even physical abuse. In such situations many women feel compelled to bow at least outwardly to their partners as experts, and assume novice status. Contradictory perceptions demand explanation, however; self-doubt and inconsistency create guilt and lack of trust in oneself, which surface despite attempts to ignore their messages.

It is a common experience for women to suffer when they disagree with another person's evaluation of a situation. One of our clients, Debbie, described a fight she had with her husband Greg. Debbie had been talking to her friend Allie on the telephone, explaining that she preferred to give an upcoming party alone instead of together, as Allie had suggested. Debbie knew she had spoken kindly and assertively but Greg, hearing the end of the conversation, told her she had been rude and abrupt. Debbie replied, "No, I wasn't. I simply said that I like entertaining and enjoy preparing for a party. I also want to invite several people Allie doesn't know. Even if Allie wasn't pleased, I acted within my rights."

The next day Greg came home and said that Allie's husband had asked whether or not Debbie wanted to see Allie anymore. Debbie was surprised, but felt fine about her evaluation of what had happened until Greg continued to go over it. He insisted that Debbie had been rude to Allie and that he was right. He would not accept as accurate her perception of the telephone call, even though he had not even been involved. It made no difference what she said. Finally, unable to get Greg to leave her alone, Debbie blew up and said, "Get off my back! I won't discuss ridiculous trivia." Greg was furious, yelled at her, pushed her against the wall, and threw a clock across the room. Then he asked, "How does it feel to get a taste of your own medicine?"

Greg believed he knew what was going on and was furious because Debbie trusted her perceptions and not his. His behavior shouted, "How dare you think differently than I do? I have a right to tell you how you should see things; you should agree with me and look at the world the way I do. Your perceptions are wrong, and I'll devil you until you agree that you're wrong and I'm right."

Being in such situations elicits feelings of rage and helplessness in women. For the most part they do not want to make big issues out of small things. Nevertheless, when a woman gives in to such bullying, she feels that she has let herself down; when she defends herself, she often is punished. No matter what she does, she loses.

"I even have to fight the people I go to for help."

Our clients report that the uproar Debbie experienced with Greg occurs over big issues, too. Frequently they have to fight the battle of perception with professional people upon whom they depend for help and advice. Cleo remembered the time when her daughter, less than a year old, had been very ill. She took the child to the pediatrician and told him the baby's symptoms. He sent them home with a little reassurance. The baby continued to get worse. Cleo took the baby back to his office several times during the next two weeks, but he still failed to take the situation seriously. Once he told Cleo she was overreacting. On the eleventh day, Cleo felt totally whipped. She had done all she could to call attention to her child's symptoms, and all her efforts had been discounted. She sat in the doctor's examining room while he checked the baby, feeling desperate and helpless, with no place else to turn. At that point the doctor called in his associate and said, "I have never seen a child deteriorate so rapidly. She needs attention right now." For Cleo, this validation of her perception would have been rewarding if it had come before her child had been allowed to suffer needlessly for so long.

Jolynne reported checking her six-year-old's teeth and seeing what looked like a cavity. When the dentist examined the boy, he said, "This tooth has already been filled." He refused to believe Jolynne when she said that her son had never before been to a dentist. "Imagine," Jolynne said, "standing there arguing with the dentist while Johnnie was in the chair. That man yelled at me, and said, 'I know a filling when I see one, and that's a filling!' I was so mad I just sputtered. I couldn't even talk, and I felt completely helpless. Finally, the dentist picked at the tooth with a tool, and a piece of metal fell out. Apparently Johnnie had chewed on a toy and a bit of lead had lodged in his tooth. And you know, that man didn't even apologize to us."

Bonnie told of the time that both of her eyes had been operated on. The pain diminished rapidly in her right eye, while the left eye hurt more and more. After ten days, she requested an emergency appointment, spent forty-five minutes driving to the surgeon's office, and then waited one hour in such intense pain that she could hardly keep from crying. When the doctor examined the eye, he cut short her effort to tell him of her pain. He told Bonnie brusquely that everything was fine and her being "upset" was only making it worse. He gave her a new prescription and told her to let the eye heal for another week and then come back. During that time, the agony continued. When she saw the doctor the following week, he told her that he could understand why she was having so much pain. Apparently her left eye had been infected while she was still in the hospital and was not healing as it should.

Geraldine's husband Ken was a teacher on an Indian reservation. She had been ill for several months, often confined to her bed for a week at a time. The visiting physician referred her to a specialist in a city about 100 miles from her home. Ken refused to take her, saying he was too busy, and she would have to ask someone else for the favor. At that point Geraldine knew that her marriage was over. She sought out a psychiatrist as soon as she was well again to help her to make the transition from marriage to single life. After several visits, the psychiatrist requested that Ken come in for consultation. Once again he refused, saying he did not have time to make the trip. When Geraldine repeated this to her therapist, he exclaimed, "Well, I guess then you'd better start looking at reality and learn to adjust to your marriage. Ken is not going to change, so you have to accept him as he is. After all, what in the world could you do, divorced with two children, living alone?"

Cleo, Jolynne, Bonnie, and Geraldine had all trusted their own perceptions of what they were experiencing, yet they were not believed by the people on whom they had to depend for help. They were subjected to emotional and, for some of the people involved, physical punishment because they spoke up and were not believed. These women felt appropriately angry, yet they were powerless. They all knew they were not overreacting, but in every instance they were treated as if they were. They were supposed to resolve the paradox of perception by saying, "Since I don't see this the way you do, I must be wrong."

"I know more about this than I realized I did."

Feeling isolated and lacking the support of others, many women have felt too insecure to act on what they know and have developed indirect ways of resolving the immobility associated with the paradox of perception. For Corrine, this meant that she constantly wondered what her boss would think or say about how she

150

did her work and how he would probably like her to do it. Not trusting her own perceptions about work she actually was very capable of completing, she felt anxious and not in charge of herself.

Corrine went back to her office immediately after the therapy session in which she discussed her indecisiveness. During the first hour back at her desk, she counted five times that she thought of asking her boss a question or for his opinion about a project she was working on. Each time she had such a thought, she deliberated whether or not it was necessary to check with him. During the following week, only once did she find that she actually had to ask a question in order to continue her work. This proved that in looking to someone else for confirmation about what she thought, Corrine had permitted self-doubt to render her almost incapable of making even the simplest decisions. She had customarily checked out her perceptions even before they were questioned by anyone else, rather than make judgments and run the risk of making a mistake.

Corrine's boss commented two weeks later that he was pleased with her newfound willingness to assume responsibility for her job, and told her that he had been irritated by her timid behavior. He had accurately interpreted it as uncertainty and was annoyed by her need for continual reassurance.

When women trust their perceptions, they are more likely to be able to communicate them in such a way that others can think objectively about what they are saying. For example, a mother may have unexplained, uneasy feelings that a prospective marriage is not right for her child. If she says, "This isn't right for you," her perceptions are probably going to be rejected and she is likely to be accused of meddling. If she says, "These are just my perceptions. I would like to share them with you and see what you think about them," her child is more likely to trust her as an additional source of information. A young adult can feel comfortable measuring a mother's perceptions against his or her own in making a choice.

"It's my body, after all."

Body cues, too, are good indicators that women can use to learn about themselves and to feel comfortable with their own perceptions. In general, however, women have not been taught to pay attention to such cues or to see them as positive. Instead, they tend to ignore body cues or take pills to get rid of them.

When Anne began to pay attention to what her body was telling her, she discovered that she often had a feeling that she was sleepwalking through life. She realized that these shut-down feelings were associated with fear, and she asked herself, "What am I afraid of? What am I unwilling to perceive about what is happening in my life?" Anne discovered that she had an overpowering urge to sleep whenever she was involved in important decision-making processes that continued over a period of time. If she escaped from the situation by sleeping, there would be no opportunity to make a mistake. "Knowing this, now I can look at the issues and decide what mistakes I want to avoid," Anne said, "instead of escaping in sleep."

Sex is another area where women have not trusted their own perceptions enough to act on them. Jo was speaking for countless women we know when she said in group therapy:

I always thought that something was wrong with our sex life, that something was missing. Whenever I tried to talk about it, though, Michael told me that I was cold or frigid and that I'd have to work it out. After a while I believed him. I'd never had sex with anyone else, and it didn't seem to matter that he hadn't either. He became the authority because he was the man. When he wasn't pleased by our lovemaking, I felt like a failure as a woman and felt guilty because I'd let him down. Eventually, I believed that I didn't deserve to be married to him or anyone else. I finally got a divorce just so I could get out of feeling so guilty, and let him off the hook, so to speak. Now I know that both of us needed to examine our perceptions. We didn't know anything about sex and didn't take any steps to learn anything about it either.

Dawn continued the discussion:

> I had the same experience, except that Ben was the one who filed for divorce. He said he refused to put up with my "coldness" anymore. He refused to even consider how unpleasant sex was for me because it was so painful. I tried to tell him that he always started intercourse before I was ready and if I had more time, I thought it wouldn't hurt so much. That's what the books I read said. They were right, too. I've had sex with other men, and I enjoy it now.

Dawn felt a great deal of bitterness because she had been unable to convince Ben that she was right about much of anything, let alone her own body. "He just wouldn't read anything about sex. He just kept saying 'No book is going to tell me how to have sex with my own wife.' I know now that he had lots of problems with sex, and by putting them all on me he didn't have to even look at them."

Women's timidity in insisting that the messages of their bodies are valid extends beyond their sexual relationships to relationships with others whose expertise is rarely questioned. Women have a history of being intimidated by doctors, in part because they defer to their medical superiority and in part because doctors do not listen to what their female patients say. Women have legitimate questions to ask about their bodies and their health, but they fear, often justifiably, that their doctors would be annoyed if they did ask. Women frequently go away from medical appointments believing that they have let themselves down because they did not say what they had planned. Often when they do speak up, women receive patronizing responses like, "Let me worry about that. I'm the doctor. All you have to worry about is getting well."

Sometimes a woman has to rush to ask her questions because the doctor is on his way out the door. Receiving brusque answers, she feels that she should not be

153

taking so much time. All too often she is told to shape up, settle down, and make the best of things. Then she is given a prescription and told to call if she is not well within a few days. In these situations, a woman's perception that she is not important and that her questions are annoying is confirmed.

Frequently it even seems that speaking up is perceived by the doctor as a challenge to his expertise or authority. Gina had such an experience. She was feeling very pressured about financial problems. She was a freelance photographer and had not sold any work for several weeks. Finally she was commissioned to do a job another photographer had been unable to finish on time. Unfortunately, Gina got a bad cold when she was a week away from completing the work. She went to her physician for medication, hoping she would feel well enough to stay on the job.

As Gina took the prescription slip, she said, almost as an aside, "I sure hope this will do some good." The doctor answered angrily, "If you don't think I can help you you're free to go to another doctor anytime," and stomped out of the room. Until then Gina had seen her doctor as kind and concerned. "Boy, was I wrong!" she said, and resolved to take his advice and find someone else.

"My perceptions were wrong."

Sometimes it is a great relief to discover that one's perceptions about a situation are incorrect. Karrie had always explained her quietness by saying that she was just a reserved, rather unfriendly person, interested in academic pursuits instead of people. In therapy, she explored her perception of herself more closely. She realized that she avoided people because she feared that if they got to know her they might not like her any better than she liked herself.

Fearful of rejection, Karrie created barriers to keep people away. "It's easy to always carry a book around and stick my nose in it," she said. "The sad part is that sometimes I'm not even aware of what I'm reading because I'm so conscious of the other people around me and worried that they might notice me. I guess I'm really lonely; I'm not an unfriendly person at all!"

Being afraid of people was something Karrie could deal with, while perceiving herself as "unfriendly, reserved, and academic" became "that's the way I am" and seemed unchangeable. As Karrie stripped away at her reserve, the delights of friendships reassured her that her harsh evaluation of herself was not true.

Holly, too, felt tremendous relief in discovering that her perceptions were not true. She had accepted responsibility for the fact that her marriage had ended in divorce, dwelling on all the mistakes she had made. In reviewing the problems in the relationship and how she had tried to resolve them, she saw that if she were in a similar marriage with the same experience, knowledge, and feelings she had in her first marriage, she would probably do exactly the same thing. Only the crystal clear vision of looking back showed her ways she could have behaved differently. Knowing this allowed Holly to say that no one was to blame; she could let go of her regrets.

Dorene's experience was different. "I guess I was wrong about him," she sighed as she told her story to her therapist. "I needed a strong, considerate man at the time I met Alex, so I just proceeded to see in him all the qualities I wanted him to have." Unfortunately, Alex disappointed her. She was full of self-doubt as she struggled with the contradictions between what she wished he would be and what he actually was.

Alex's behavior was inconsistent with Dorene's "need" to be with a strong person. He was nonassertive with his former wife, then blew up at Dorene. He ate Dorene's food and slept in her bed, then left without a word about when he would be back. Dorene would resolve not to see him again, but when Alex rang her doorbell with a box of candy or flowers, fanciful illusions banished unpalatable truth.

Like many of the women who come to us for therapy, Dorene was reacting rather than acting in her own behalf. She waited for Alex to take the lead, and when he acted contrary to her expectations she tried to

155

deny the evidence that he was childish and thoughtless. Dorene's reactions resulted from her training, which said that women are supposed to let men take the lead and be the decision-makers. One of the problems with this is that women must wait for men to lead before they can fill the follower role. Their choices are thereby limited by the needs and wants of others.

Not trusting her own perceptions, Dorene rejected what she sensed but did not want to know. Once she explored what she wanted instead of what she believed she needed, she was able to clarify her thoughts and dance to her own tune.

"I've got the guilties."

Barbara was twenty-three when she came for therapy. She had year-old twins and two little boys, three and five. "I get so frustrated I could just scream," she sobbed. "I never have any time for myself, let alone for my husband. The work is endless. I get the house cleaned up, and one of them is busy making another mess. It seems as if one of the boys is always sick. I'm exhausted from being up half the night. I think there's something wrong with me; I should be able to cope better. They didn't ask to be born. They are just kids and I shouldn't even be talking this way!" Her perception of herself was that she was a failure, when in fact she was doing a difficult job very well.

Jenny came for therapy saying, "I shouldn't hate my mother. It isn't her fault she's sick and all alone. But she drives me crazy! I feel guilty every time I leave the house." Maxine explained, "I was so anxious to have a roommate, and now I hate it. I have no privacy, and she's so messy. We used to be best friends! I'm ashamed that I feel this way." Sally was imprisoned in compliance. "I thought he was the strong, silent type, and once we got married everything would be fine. Now I know he's not strong at all. He's silent because he doesn't have anything to say. But it's not his fault I made a mistake. I just have to accept life the way it is!"

156

All of these women came to therapy berating themselves and seeing themselves as bad. As they examined the reality of their lives, they saw that their perceptions were accurate, but that their conclusions were wiping out their options. Conditions in their lives were bad. However, they were not bad people. In therapy they learned to stop focusing on questions like, "What have I done wrong?" and "What's wrong with me?" They stopped saying, "I shouldn't be thinking this way," as they saw that they had the power to change themselves and redesign their lives.

Barbara started a cooperative nursery in her neighborhood, which gave her relief from the pressure cooker of all-day parenting. Jenny found a residential retirement home where two of her mother's friends lived, and she helped her mother to get settled there. Maxine decided that she could find a more compatible roommate more easily than she could find a new best friend. Her roommate agreed that she would rather move than lose Maxine's friendship. Sally discovered that when she expressed her self-doubts directly to her husband he could talk after all.

Women feel guilty when arguments end with, "You always have to have the last word!" When someone says, "You always have to have things your way!" women find it difficult to stick up for themselves, even when they know that their perceptions are accurate. They find themselves apologizing for things for which they really do not feel responsible in an effort to restore harmony. They cave in just to avoid arguments. Feelings of "why bother" erode their confidence in their perceptions and increase feelings of immobility.

Jennine reported such an experience. Her boss accused her of failing to complete a report on time. She said that she had finished her work on the report and sent it to the printer on schedule. Her boss replied angrily that he did not believe her. He had already called the printer, and the foreman said he had received the report just two days before, so Jennine must be covering up. The boss then said that the issue was closed and she was not to be so lax in the future. He refused

157

to discuss the matter further. When Jennine responded that in the future she would deliver all work to the printer in person and get a signed and dated receipt, he slammed his hand on the desk and said, "You always have to have the last word, don't you?"

Describing the scene to her therapist later, Jennine said that actually it had been the first time she had ever tried to defend herself with her boss. She was pleased with how she had handled the confrontation and would continue to be assertive. In the past, she had felt that she let herself down whenever she was intimidated by him. Now, even though he had been very aggressive, she did not feel punished, because she knew what had happened and could rely upon her own interpretation of the power struggle. Jennine had resolved the paradox of perception.

When our clients give tentative interpretations of events, we are likely to respond with, "Given the reality of your situation, what you are saying seems very appropriate." This encourages clients to learn to pay attention to their perceptions, to express their opinions and feelings, to take action, and to feel in charge of themselves. In doing so, women elicit new information which they can use to confirm or adjust their perceptions. In this way, the guilt associated with the conflicts of self-doubt is banished.

"I don't trust myself."

Candy's self-doubts originated with the double messages her parents gave her and were reflected in her inability to complete things she started. Her parents had told her that she could do anything she wanted to do because she was much smarter than other children. Then they proceeded to do everything for her. If she started a homework project, they soon took over and finished it. When she began swimming lessons, her mother went with her, then demonstrated all the strokes at home in their family pool so Candy could practice them. Her parents picked out her clothes, her friends, and her dates. They told her how she should fix her hair and what to read. In their fear that she would not be a perfect and happy reflection of their parenting, her mother and father convinced Candy that she could not trust herself to do anything at all. When she went away to college, she was accompanied by this spectre. She dropped a course whenever it appeared that she might not get a top grade. Trying to find something she could be sure of succeeding at, she flitted from one major to another.

Candy married a man who wanted a wife to facilitate his career. Almost immediately afterwards she could not decide whether she wanted to stay married or to have a career. She enrolled in school and spent hours agonizing over whether or not she should look for a job. She dropped the courses and got involved in a volunteer project, then began investigating other college programs.

In her therapy sessions, Candy presented a fragmented self-portrait. She focused on the paradoxical messages that had dominated her life. She understood the conflict she had experienced in trying to please her parents. Rather than run the risk of being less than perfect, she had failed to achieve any goal. Yet she had to keep setting goals and striving to achieve something in order to prove she was perfect. Her parents, in their misguided attempts to help, had robbed Candy of the opportunity to learn about herself. Her capabilities and her limitations remained untested. She did not feel secure in the things she knew and had no idea of how to find out what she did not know. Not being able to trust her perceptions, Candy's pattern became one of continuous mobility, which in her case was as limiting as immobility is for other women.

Candy's experience with the paradox of perception was sad, but not unusual. Adults who do not trust their own perceptions often depend upon their parents or other authorities to tell them how they should see the world. Because they were subordinate as children, they are comfortable with the pattern of accepting a parental view of how things should be. Parental value systems, ideals, and goals—parents' ways of perceiving the world—are thus transferred from one generation to another without thought or question. To question often means to invite conflict; not to question often means to become rigid and stagnant while the rest of the world changes.

Because women are expected to be subservient and obedient, first to their parents and then to their husbands, it is especially hard for them to challenge parental viewpoints and values and to act on their own perceptions. The result is that they end up with another case of the guilties, trying to live in the world of the past and the present and not feeling comfortable in either of them.

For Inez, the conflict was especially difficult to resolve because she came from a close, extended family of opinionated, strong men and women. Two sets of grandparents felt free to give her directives on how she should view herself and what she had to do to please them, namely, get married and raise happy children. Her parents were just as specific although a little more flexible: get marrried and be happy, or go to collage and be successful in a career.

Inez, at twenty-two, was not interested in either of these choices. "I don't want to get married," she told her therapist.

I'm having too much fun. But I don't have any career in mind, either. I'm just not interested in going to college. I've never been good in school, and I think I'm happy for now being a salesclerk, working nine to six and having fun the rest of the time. I've got fifty years to settle down. Just because they established their goals early, they want me to do so. I'm sure disappointing a lot of people because I won't get married or do something terrific. Maybe I should just find some nice guy to marry me. Then they'll all be happy, and I wouldn't have to feel so guilty.

Mothers of teenagers are vulnerable to coming down with the guilties. They see their children wobbling down a doubtful path, whereas the adolescents see themselves as adventuring along the main road to a challenging future. Teenagers often see their mothers as overprotective, nagging, critical, untrusting. They use persuasive statements like, "Everyone else gets to . . ."; "You're the only mother who won't let me . . ."; and "I know what I'm doing," to plead their case for freedom and autonomy. Not trusting their own perceptions, women often are afraid to establish rules and the consequences of breaking the rules. Mothers fear that their children may become angry and act out in order to punish them, not caring that in doing so they, too, may suffer. The uneasy feeling that her perceptions might be wrong and that her children's requests might be reasonable curdles a mother's confidence.

"I've really needed someone to talk to."

Television's close-knit family, the Waltons, is a representation of life that many families today have never known. As our society became more industrialized, the nuclear family became the stage for playing out clearly defined roles. Women were denied the support systems of the extended families and concerned, cooperative neighborhoods that "The Waltons" portrays. They experienced isolation and heavy responsibility, while men continued to enjoy their traditional support systems, their colleagues and fellow workers. As has often been the case, women themselves were unaware of the conflict they were experiencing and they failed to recognize the extreme sense of loss they felt. They only knew they felt locked into the sameness of their days and destined to wither in isolation.

Invested with the role of keeping others happy while remaining cut off from traditional support systems, women suffered in silence, smiling to mask feelings of quiet desperation. They had no way of knowing that many other women felt as oppressed and depressed as they did. One of the most positive experiences of group therapy for many women is learning that their thoughts and feelings are shared by other women who also saw themselves as uniquely isolated and troubled.

"Then there's nothing wrong with me?" someone in group will ask anxiously when other women confirm her perceptions. Then she may turn to another woman and add, "It's one thing to hear my therapist say I'm okay, but when you say just exactly what I've been saying to myself, then I think, 'Hey, if you see it the way I do, I can't be all wrong.'"

When what women perceive is based on erroneous assumptions, they create much of their own distress. Group therapy provides an opportunity for them to learn how their assumptions are reflected in their behavior, much as an extended family did when grandmothers, grandfathers, aunts, uncles, and cousins could be counted to say how they saw things.

Francie had always considered herself less intelligent than her husband Jack. Only a week before she began therapy, Jack had told her that he thought she was much smarter than he was, and certainly the smartest woman he knew. One of the things he admired most about her was her intelligence and sense of humor. Francie was shocked to think that any two people could live together for so long and have such different perceptions. As she thought about their years together, however, she recognized that in many instances she had played down her own capabilities. By operating as if her erroneous perceptions about her intelligence were true, Francie had denied herself opportunities to develop her own potential. Believing that Jack was smart and ambitious, Francie had directed her efforts toward promoting his career.

Jack offhand comment about his perception of Francie's intelligence came at a time in her life when she was ready to examine many of the decisions she had made about herself. Her children were grown, and it was no longer necessary for her to be a full-time homemaker. She realized that she had felt safe in her role as facilitator of Jack's career. Other options seemed both exciting and frightening. One of the questions to be answered now was whether or not she was willing to test out her newfound concept of herself as an intelligent woman. She came to therapy because she knew she had paid a heavy price in acting on misperceptions.

Agnes, too, had suffered because of her erroneous

162

perceptions. Her husband's construction work had been intermittent for twelve years, and so had been his drinking. In group therapy she mentioned that she thought there might be a connection between Steve's drinking and his feelings about being out of work. She had said this to him from time to time over the years, but he had insisted that it was not lack of work that triggered his drinking bouts.

Abusive when he drank, Steve sat around all day, grubby and growling. Agnes had served a long apprenticeship in keeping quiet. She had accepted Steve's denial that he was depressed and drinking because of unemployment. It was easier to doubt herself and back down than to confront Steve's angry outbursts. When she thought back over the years, however, Agnes could no longer deny the credibility of her perception.

The women in Agnes's therapy group urged her to trust her own perceptions. Once she trusted that her view was correct, she felt she had a right to speak up. She knew she did not have to put up with a grouchy bear.

For women, relying on their own perceptions is a new and exhilarating experience. They are used to the confusion that comes from thinking, "I know what I think, but when you ask me I don't know anymore." Learning that they can depend upon their own senses for accurate information about themselves builds a one-way bridge across the chasm separating self-doubt and effectiveness. Trusting themselves leads to feeling confident and being able to act on the basis of what they think and feel. Women can become involved in life; they can initiate as well as respond. They can check out their perceptions and then use the feedback they get to confirm, reject, alter, and expand these perceptions. Trusting their perceptions is necessary if women are to resolve the paradox of conflict, which is discussed in the following chapter.

CHAPTER VIII

Conflict

"I have to resolve differences without facing the issues."

It is not an accident that women are called peacemakers. They have been charged with creating harmony, making everyone happy, and preserving tranquility. They are told to be feminine, yet never to act with anger or directness, as men might do. The paradox is that women are charged with doing the impossible; conflict cannot be resolved without addressing the issues, and women are not psychologically prepared for conflict. They have learned and have been encouraged to use indirect ways to handle things, thereby perpetuating the paradox.

Visualize for a moment the complexities of mediating a contract dispute between tough, demanding union negotiators and a powerful manufacturing conglomerate. Complicated issues must be discussed and compromise resolutions hammered out. Imagine telling the opposing forces that they must achieve peace without discussing the issues they are fighting about.

Picture another conflict, a common, everyday interaction the implications of which are unrecognized. Once one is aware of what these struggles mean, however, they take on an unmistakable significance. Two little children, Bess and Carl, are playing with a top when the handle of the plunger falls off. Carl says that Bess broke the top. Bess can approach this conflict in many ways without challenging Carl's accusation. She can put up with the situation, sticking the handle back on each time as if it were supposed to fall off. She can stop using the handle and risk hurting her hand when she presses on the metal post. She can walk away or go and get another toy. She can find an adult to stick up for her, or she can sit and cry until someone comes to rescue her. She can get angry and stomp on the top, throw it across the room, or hit Carl with it.

Although she is only four years old, Bess has already become a victim of the paradox of conflict. Believing that she must do something so Carl will not be angry with her, but unable to speak up, she foregoes confronting the issue directly. She rummages around in her toy chest and pulls out a Jack-in-the-box. Carl smiles happily, and Bess sits down on the floor next to the broken top, holding her breath with anticipation as Carl turns the handle on the box, and squealing with glee each time Jack pops out.

This conflict between Bess and Carl was an opportunity for learning, and both of them did so. Bess learned that she could avoid a fight with Carl by not answering him directly and finding some distraction pleasing to him. Carl learned that he could accuse Bess without having to worry about her reactions; in fact, she promptly rewarded him.

The ridiculous mandate of the paradox of conflict, which presses a woman to resolve differences without addressing the issues, has been put on women's shoulders like a hooded black cloak that muffles her voice, obliterates her form, disguises her style, and threatens to trip her no matter how slowly and carefully she moves.

Disagreements usually are not over factual material, about which one person is right and the other is wrong and proof is readily available. Instead, most disagreements arise over feelings, beliefs, and ideas, issues in which one individual has just as much right to say, "This is the way I see things," as the other has to say, "My viewpoint is very different." Most conflicts arise because one person has difficulty accepting that others may think differently, may have opposing points of view, may not feel the same, or may do things in a different way than he or she does. Indeed, the statement, "Conflict can be a positive opportunity for growth and

165

change," often elicits sharp argument. Many people firmly reject the idea that conflict can be positive in any way.

This is not surprising, for we all learn about conflict as small children, a time when we feel particularly powerless. When a little girl sees conflict, especially when her caretakers are involved, she feels anxious and helpless, as she almost always is. Often she thinks she may have been responsible in some way and tries to stop the disagreement with crying, sweetness, and affection, or by playing the clown. If verbal and physical abuse are part of the conflict, she undoubtedly feels terror-stricken and immobilized.

Conflict is inevitable in dominant-submissive relationships because inequality creates dissonance and tension, which almost always demand resolution in some way. With direct confrontation, the dominant person tends to feel attacked and responds with silent withdrawal, with insistence that there is no conflict, or with demands for a return to the status quo. If the conflict is not resolved through these means and confrontation continues, women may receive some concessions. What more commonly happens is that they are labelled troublemakers, bitches, or nags. They may be threatened with physical, emotional, or financial sanctions. Many times these threats erupt into violence and women become the victims of physical abuse. In varying degrees, women are commonly punished when they attempt to resolve differences directly.

Other issues originating in male-female gamesmanship help to perpetuate conflict. Only women's positive emotions are acceptable, for they have been taught that it is "unfeminine" and "castrating" to express hostility. To do so elicits an angry reaction in return, and women then feel they have failed in their role as peacemaker. Furthermore, being financially and emotionally dependent means that they risk losing their security if their partners are not pleased with them. Women are hereby caught in a vicious double-bind. On the one hand, they must not engage in direct conflict or they will be punished, and on the other, they *are* likely to be punished in some way or another if they fail to keep

166

other people happy. Yet any time two or more people interact, dissonance will inevitably arise; however, dissension occurs with greater frequency and more virulence in unequal relationships.

Faced with a situation in which they cannot win, women tend to respond to the paradox of resolving conflict without facing the issues in three ways: first, by *giving* up; second, by *shutting* up; and third, by *putting* up with inequities.

Giving up as a solution seems to involve two choices. One is that women can lower their aspirations, let go of their hopes and dreams for intimacy and love with their families or partner, and get out of the situations they find intolerable. The second alternative is to give up much of their warm and loving self and become openly angry, critical, and bitter. Both of these solutions demand a heavy toll from everyone involved.

Because this cost is so immediate and so great, more women choose the second solution, shutting up, in an effort to resolve the conflict paradox. Instead of communicating directly, they learn indirect tactics to carry out their responsibilities to others and to attempt to meet their own wants.

The paradox of conflict decrees that women are supposed to do the impossible, for the third choice, putting up with whatever fate dishes out, *is* an impossible task unless a woman sacrifices her spirit and becomes numb, merely going through the motions of living. Another way of putting up with fate is to become a Pollyanna and to live in a pretend everything-is-perfect and keep-everybody-happy world. Very few women are able or want to sustain such pretense.

"I learned all about conflict as a child."

Youngsters are taught about conflict in ways that can shadow their entire lives. Discussing in group therapy their fear of confrontation, several women spoke of how childhood memories of anger and violence still haunted them. Dora was twenty-seven. At sixteen she had chosen to work as a maid for a wealthy family as a way to escape from her father's home.

167

Dora's fear of uncontrolled fury came from the times when she was little and her drunken father had put her in the back seat of his big Cadillac, where she bounced around screaming, "Daddy, stop!" as he roared over the hills and washes of dusty country roads, yelling at her to shut up.

Although Jenny was an adult woman who handled crises daily in her job as an emergency room nurse, she shook all over at the slightest disagreement, whether or not she was involved in the problem. Her agitation was the same as she had felt as a child, watching her two older brothers fighting, threatening to kill each other. She had no reason then not to believe them.

Although she tried to act friendly and forced herself to become involved socially, Debbie had great difficulty establishing close relationships. Her parents had long avoided any dissension by being cold and rejecting with each other and with her. Their pattern rubbed off on Debbie; she, too, avoided conflict in this way.

In group, Marcy maintained a friendly, superficial smile, much as she did during working hours as a loan officer in a large bank. At heart, though, she was distrustful of women, remembering how her sick mother had criticized her and screamed at her from her bedroom.

Florence was forty-two years old and had worked on an assembly line for twelve years with countless women, but she had never learned to get along with any of her coworkers; she became aggressive whenever difficulties came up. As a child she had had to take care of her unruly younger brothers and sisters. When they did not obey her, she slapped them and ordered them around to keep them in line, knowing that her parents would blame her if anything went wrong. She fell back on this method as an adult whenever human foibles threatened her responsibility pattern.

Carmen controlled conflicts with a nice-gal pose in keeping with her hard-won Volunteer of the Year award. She became placating and cheerful in order not to be like her angry, guilt-inducing parents. She was sure that if she felt any anger, she would become as destructive as they had been.

All of these women learned when they were children that conflict involves danger, violence, rejection, distrust, aggression, or anger. As adults, they tried to avoid dissension because conflict and the restimulation of feelings from the past associated with anger and hostility were extremely painful to them.

Belinda came for therapy embroiled in one crisis after another. Her distress was readily apparent from her first appointment. She came, disheveled and anxious, and said breathlessly, "I went past this building three times. The first time, I missed the office sign, so I drove around the block. The next time, I wasn't watching and drove right on by the entrance. The last go-around, there was a truck right behind me, and I was afraid he'd hit me if I slowed down." These difficulties were typical of Belinda's approach to life. She felt so helpless and anxious that she was always in a state of agitation. In her efforts to escape the paradoxical imperative of conflict, she seemed to manufacture a new dilemma in order to exit from each unresolved one.

Belinda told a poignant story of the event that triggered this unfortunate choice of solutions to the paradox of conflict. Her father was a weak, ineffective, and silent man who was afraid of his wife. Her most vivid childhood memory revolved around an incident when she was eight years old. Her mother complained that Belinda had not given her a birthday present. Actually, Belinda had spent all of her money on a frilly nightgown she thought her mother would love. But her older sister had forgotten to buy a gift and had put her name on Belinda's package. No one believed Belinda's explanation, and her sister remained silent when Belinda begged her to tell their mother the truth.

Throughout this traumatic scene, Belinda's father sat heavy with his silence, then later came to her room and loudly spanked her for ruining her mother's birthday party. From that time on Belinda had nightmares about terrifying situations; in the dreams her father became kind, loving, and strong, and stuck up for her when she was attacked or rescued her when she was in danger. This childhood exposure to conflict traumatized Belinda's development as surely as a late spring frost kills tender lilac buds.

Belinda married Marvin because he was strong, thoughtful, and caring. She believed that at last she had found her perfect father. Their first child arrived before they had been married a year, while he was traveling extensively in a new job. Belinda went to the hospital alone, angry and terror-stricken because Marvin was not there to take care of her. While she was still in the hospital, the baby developed a lung infection and Belinda became hysterical. Marvin was called home. He arrived on the day the baby was pronounced well and released from the hospital. The first crisis had passed.

Belinda became pregnant again almost immediately. Marvin plugged away single-mindedly at his work, then gambled their pitifully small savings to start his own business. Creditors and bills were a constant source of tension. Marvin assured her that he would take care of things, but to Belinda his promises were empty: it seemed that he was doing nothing.

Belinda began to have anxiety attacks, then turned to Marvin to calm her down, hoping that he would be the strong man she wanted, fearful he would fail her. She called him at work on any pretext, asking him to solve whatever problem overtaxed her uneasy, fretful calm. He responded patiently with his by now well-rehearsed recipes for conflict resolution. She rejected them one by one. Her anger at his "ineffectiveness" created yet another bout with anxiety.

Only when she understood the paradox of conflict did Belinda accept the fact that Marvin could not rescue her from herself, any more than her father had rescued her from her sister's viciousness. Belinda would have to focus on her own strength and power instead of demanding that Marvin be strong and powerful for her. Her childhood-generated conflicts resided within herself. So did adult-generated solutions.

"I don't know what to do."

Peggy began therapy steaming with anger on a hot

summer day. As she explained her frustration, she exemplified clearly the dilemma women experience in trying to deal with conflict.

"I know there's something wrong between us," Peggy said.

I'm not happy, and neither is my husband Les. We go around silent and glowering half the time. We talk about trivial things, and I'm so bored I could scream. But when I try to say anything important about us he shuts me out. I think I still love him, but it is well hidden beneath all this resentment. We hardly ever talk and nothing gets resolved. I really can't deal with anything, because all he says is that there wouldn't be any problem if I would only do such and such. I used to feel guilty and called myself a nagging bitch. Yet I know I'm right: there *is* something wrong. But when he won't talk about it, I feel shut out, hurt, and frustrated. Then I go away; I back off and feel helpless.

At that point Peggy burst into tears, then continued.

I don't know what to do. I get so frustrated, I just blow up. I don't want to become an angry, punishing person, yet I am. I hate myself for it. Other times I feel so defeated, I think I should just end it. There's no use knocking myself out for someone who refuses to get involved. Why in the world do I keep on hoping that Les will behave any differently? Sometimes I get so mad at myself. I'm just wasting my time and energy in this relationship and getting nowhere. I think of all the things I could do instead. I've just got to do something. I can't go on like this.

Peggy's frustration was fueled by sure-to-lose instructions to accomplish a miracle. She was to make her husband happy, to be happy herself, and to resolve any difficulties between them. This task was to be accomplished without his acknowledgement that there were any problems, without involvement on his part, and without interaction to clarify their difficulties. The paradox of conflict had sparked a chain reaction of frustration that threatened to end in an explosion.

Even though she felt unbearably frustrated by the situation, Peggy knew that she had several alternatives. She could continue to push for her husband's involvement, although this might mean that they would cross over a one-way bridge from love to hate. She could agree that he was right, that everything would be fine if she just shaped up and learned to adjust herself to meet his expectations. She could shut up and suffer in silence, possibly getting bitter, sick, or depressed. She could end her marriage and endure the slow, painful process of rebuilding her life. She could maintain the relationship and enjoy the good in it while learning to accept him just as he was, thus running the likely risk that without intimacy they would drift even further apart. Or she could talk to him assertively, stating very clearly the consequences that would follow if he continued to refuse to become involved in resolving their problems.

Peggy chose to be assertive as a way of freeing herself from the double-bind in which she was trapped. She was prepared to end her marriage rather than become a shrew or a martyr. Peggy understood that the ability to engage in constructive conflict was a strength. Dissension, although painful, could be an impetus for change and growth. Peggy had to call on her strength, for Les demanded comforts without commitment or involvement. Unable to meet his terms, Peggy had no choice but to seek a dissolution of their marriage.

Disagreement, as well as agreement, is an essential ingredient in healthy, mutually enhancing human interactions. The difficulty is not that disagreement should be eliminated from relationships, but that assertive communication skills should be added. Unhappily for Peggy and Les, these tools came too late to repair their marital breakdown.

An unrecognized fear of many women is that, if they ever do let go of their anger, they will lose control completely and the consequences will be catastrophic. Even when they become aware of this fear, women do not often verbalize it or let the knowledge surface undisguised in themselves. Instead, they feel ashamed of having angry thoughts and wary lest these feelings boil out. The anger camouflages itself as guilt, which serves to keep resentment and fury squashed down, except for occasional pressure-relieving outbursts.

One of the catastrophes that women fear if they do not control their anger is that more powerful persons will lash back with their own hostility. Destructive, angry reactions are frequently and repeatedly used to throttle conflict by scaring and controlling others. Anger is a central issue in conflict. In fact, this paradox is able to wreak its havoc because anger is so frightening to both men and women. Men have insisted that conflict with women must not exist, even when it does, and have maintained that it must be dealt with, if it does exist, indirectly. This demand is generated in large part because of men's fear of unleashing their own rage in interpersonal relationships. The paradox of conflict has been created to a great extent in an attempt to make women responsible for holding men's anger in check.

Cathy was an introspective, aware young woman who felt her individuality emerging as she made the transition from newlywed to adult. After two years of marrriage, Cathy began therapy to decide whether or not she want to stay married. Her husband Bill had a violent temper, and her growth and change threatened his need for maintaining dominance.

She described his childish temper tantrums in this way: "I made plans to go to a Sunday matinee with a girlfriend of mine last month. When I told Bill about it, I was appalled when he said, 'No wife of mine is going off to some movie unescorted!' He banged his fist down on the table. Another time I told him I wanted to take a psychology class at the junior college. He shook his fist at me and yelled that I'd better not get any big ideas in my empty head about *that*, as if I were going to do something outlandish or dangerous or subversive, even."

Every time Bill was abusive, Cathy dropped the issue. Giving up in response to his aggression only reinforced his behavior, for he continued to respond the same way every time she expressed any interest in taking independent action. In her paradoxical position of being expected to handle differences without facing the issues, Cathy was gradually giving up her aspirations for herself. As an alternative to this, she considered divorce. Giving up either herself or her hopes and dreams of what her marriage could be was not what she had expected in her life with Bill.

Once she understood how the paradox of conflict had worked in their marriage, Cathy was no longer able to tolerate her giving-up solution. It was difficult to overcome her fear of Bill's anger; the thought lurked within her that he might lose control and explode in violence and that she might suffer physical injury in addition to the emotional abuse to which she was subjected already. She knew, though, that she had no choice but to confront him; the prospect of living with her fears was intolerable.

Cathy faced Bill head on and said, "I refuse to be humiliated and cowed any longer by your threats. I want to talk calmly and reasonably about things. Unless we can live together without my being silenced by your anger, I'll lose the positive feelings I have for you. I don't want that to happen. Do you?" Bill confessed that his temper scared him, too, and that he needed to learn to be in charge of his feelings rather than using his emotions to control both of them.

For many women, the impossible task of resolving conflict is an extension of their training to assume responsibility for other people's emotions, including their anger. Mindful of their mandate to keep everybody happy, women have not learned that another person's anger is that person's own responsibility. Unable to separate themselves from someone else's dysfunctional behavior, women feel blameworthy and guilt-ridden for having created unhappiness and discord. Thinking they must have done something to cause the conflict, they also think they should do something to resolve it. Women fail to understand that others have the right to feel angry. If others lose control and express their emotions in an irrational or destructive way, that is something for which women need not assume responsibility.

174

Ted came to therapy with Eva only because she said she would divorce him if he did not. They were a couple comfortable with midlife, except for the hazards of the paradox of conflict. In her role as peacemaker in their large family, Eva had accepted most of the blame for any strife she and Ted experienced. He was quite happy to let Eva be the scapegoat; he spent two individual therapy sessions categorizing her faults. His chief complaint was that she was always upset; she was too emotional. Ted prided himself on being rational and, indeed, his emotions were hidden behind a verbal facade that covered up his little-boy feelings of inadequacy.

The one emotion that Ted was capable of expressing well was anger, although he denied feeling angry even when his words were clipped and his fists clenched. As long as Ted could focus on Eva's shortcomings, he could wear blinders about his own. Eva refused to cooperate any longer; she insisted that Ted face the strains in their relationship. The continued denial of his hostility became impossible when he blew up at their therapist's suggestion that conflict, if they faced its issues, could be positive and growth-enhancing, whereas assigning blame was unproductive and guilt-inducing.

Eva was present at this therapy session, and she was touched when Ted, following his explosion, burst into tears. He confessed that his deepest fear from the time they met had been that Eva was too good for him and would eventually leave him. He had decided when he asked her to marry him that he would make whatever time he did have with her as pleasant as possible. His plan had failed. Seeing Eva as above him, he had attempted to keep her attached to him by wearing down to his level. The imperatives of the conflict paradox required that Eva attempt to fit herself into this design.

Ted had feared, too, that getting involved in therapy would signal the end of the marriage. Like most women, Eva had been taught to seek help and to accept it. Like most men, Ted had not learned to do this.

It was a relief for Ted to see that therapy would enable them to resolve differences by raising the issues instead of burying them under verbiage, clenched fists, and blame.

Ted's fears are shared by many couples who come for therapy in a final effort to resolve "irreconcilable" differences. It is hard for some men and women to accept that the relationships they intensely want and hold dear may be terminated. As frightening as this possibility is, there is some satisfaction for them in knowing that whether or not they are able to resolve their conflicts, whether or not they stay together, they will both have done their very best. They can part with an understanding of each other, mutual respect, and ongoing friendship.

When a relationship ends with the death of one person, the mourning process generally involves four stages: denial, anger, grief, and acceptance. When emotional bonds are cut because of separation or divorce, an additional stage is necessary if both parties are to let go of past hurts and begin to build separate lives and experience positive individual growth. That step can be summed up in the word *understanding*—understanding of what each partner feels and thinks about what happened to their union, what went wrong with it, and how they might avoid conflict if they had to do it over again. This stage is essential; it fits somewhere between and overlaps with the stages of grief and acceptance. When an opportunity to reach this understanding is not available, the job of reconstructing one's self is usually slow and traumatic, with much backsliding into recrimination, guilt, and remorse.

"Either way I lose."

Karen came to therapy feeling heartbroken and devastated. "I always had two choices," she explained. "I could either accept our life together the way Gus wanted it to be, or I could get out."

Gus, Karen's husband of fifteen years, was pleasant and agreeable as long as everything was kept on a conflict-free level. He was the youngest son in a large family; perhaps this prepared him for his role of happily following Karen's lead in decision-making. Over the years, whenever she tried to get him involved in making plans or carrying them out, he either failed to follow through on his promises or took only half-hearted stabs at getting things done. If Karen had resigned her chores of budgeting their money, worrying about the bills, paying the taxes, speaking to insurance agents, and negotiating with repairmen, Gus would have attended to these necessities on a hit-or-miss basis.

Karen was an efficient and competent woman and, in general, handled these things well; occasionally she made mistakes. Although Gus did not say anything directly, he expressed his disappointment in obvious indirect ways, like mentioning that a friend had changed insurance companies because his was much cheaper than the policy Karen had just bought.

Eventually Karen realized that Gus had chosen the easy role. She made the decisions, ran the risk of making mistakes, and had to suffer the bruised ego of failure. Gus's contribution was to ignore, approve, or disapprove of whatever Karen did. Karen tried several times to talk to Gus about this unfair division of responsibility, but each time he withdrew into petulance. She interpreted his silence to mean, "'If you don't like it, get out, because I won't get involved."

This message struck home, for Karen's mother had behaved much the same way when Karen was a child. No matter what the occasion or who the recipient, when her mother was angry she pouted until someone did something to restore her sunny mood. Karen remembered well the tension her mother's wrath had created in the house. Feeling it, Karen had quickly referred to her mental checklist of all the things she had done or not done, in case there was something bad for which she was supposed to make amends. Being a child, it had not occurred to Karen that her mother's sulks were immature; most of the time Karen had blamed herself.

As an adult, Karen felt anxious and guilty about the

problems she had with Gus, even though she knew that it was their different approach to dealing with conflict that were creating the difficulty. "Gus has always tried to solve arguments and unpleasant issues by playing blindman's buff," Karen said.

Maybe if I could do the same thing, we would be able to get along just fine. The fact is, though, I can't stand the tension and silence of unresolved issues. I get more and more anxious until I feel sick. It seems so simple to me to sit down and talk things out. I can't understand people like my mother and Gus.

I feel so punished and angry at being in this situation that I constantly say things I don't mean. I don't even know exactly what I said the other day, I was so frustrated, but I remember telling him that our marriage was over unless he could stand to talk things out. Until now, Gus has been the one to threaten divorce, indirectly, with his put-up-or-shut-up attitude. I must have shocked him, because he told me that I had destroyed him finally with my criticism and pushing. He said that no matter what he did, it was never good enough. Then he called me a castrating bitch, and the truth is, I am.

Knowing that it was impossible to resolve conflicts without addressing the issues, Karen gave up her best self and became the kind of woman Gus seemed to fear the most. Gus refused to see that it was his unwillingness to deal with discord that maneuvered Karen into actions that displeased both of them.

The label "castrating bitch" is one of the most devastating indictments that can be hurled at a woman. It is a stereotype that encapsulates the aggressiveness and hostility women hate in themselves and the fear and rage men have for women. Curiously, there is no equivalent label that exemplifies men's hatred for themselves and women's fear and rage toward men, yet the arrows of destructiveness in relationships do bounce both ways. Both women and men are tragically demeaned and traumatized in their conflicts with each other. Women more often than men, however, are victimized, abused, and robbed of their personhood in their connections with men.

"I know all about roundabout tactics."

Barbara was approaching her thirtieth birthday when she began therapy, determined to repair her eroded self-esteem after ten years of a marriage that had just ended in divorce. Barbara's problems with the paradox of conflict were much the same as Karen's. She, too, had been unable to get her husband to face the issues. In tiptoeing around her personal marital landmines, however, she had developed her own offensive weapon: she used subtle manipulation. Caught in the paradox of conflict, Barbara quit trying to solve dilemmas with honesty; instead, she worked around her husband Fred, all the while encouraging him to think he was the boss. Fred was a busy, pessimistic man who responded to most problems by discussing how difficult they were, instead of how they might be solved. To get around his cynicism, which she scorned, Barbara posed as a subordinate, although in most situations she was not, for she skillfully engineered predetermined outcomes behind the scenes.

Barbara's game was to pretend to be dumb even though she knew she was not, reinforcing Fred's idea that he was the general and she was just a private. When they bought their house, for instance, she made arrangements with the agent for them to see several very expensive and very run-down places before they looked at the house she really wanted. Fred was a first-class patsy; he eagerly made the selection for which he had been programmed. In this way, Barbara not only won her objective, but bolstered Fred's ego as well.

Barbara's solution did not work well in the long run. She resented having to play dumb and became hostile as she carried out her strategies. Hoping Fred would confront her, she stopped trying very hard to fool him, but he seemed not to notice what she did. One day the truth popped into her head and would not go away:

She no longer respected him and she hated the woman she had become; their marriage was over. Barbara first resolved the impossibility of trying to maintain harmony without dealing with the issues by shutting up and using indirect methods to keep herself and Fred happy. When this failed, she tried another approach: giving up and getting out of her marriage.

Manipulative tactics for solving disagreements may well be the only weapons powerless women have when their distress about discord is ignored or scorned. Feeling unable to meet conflict head on, some women resort to snide remarks, complaints, coercion, and guilt-induction to force others into more agreeable behavior. Other women try to control people and situations so that conflict will be averted. In these indirect attempts to fill peacemaker roles, women may create even more conflict than they resolve. In addition, recognition that their devious methods are part of the problem creates guilt, commonly discharged as anger toward those they are closest to. Anger in turn generates even more guilt; this accumulation of emotional trash threatens to eclipse their personalities.

This shutting-up, manipulative pattern for solving the paradox of conflict is a sorry attempt to solve problems that others pretend do not exist. Giving up and getting out of a conflict-riddled relationship obliterates women's illusions about living happily ever after; shutting up and manipulating in order to survive destroys their once-proud images of themselves.

This happened to Robin, who had two preschoolers and a twelve-year-old, no education or work experience, and a husband who had just requested a divorce. Her survival strategy was devised out of necessity. She discussed in therapy her attorney's instructions for foiling any plans her husband might have for hiding their assets.

Even though I know there is no hope for our marriage, I have to pretend that I still trust him, but I feel like a thief. I talked one of his employees out of the key to his desk and got his bank statements, charge account records, income tax returns, and financial statements, then I made copies of them and put all the papers back and locked up the desk. I felt sick using such underhanded tactics when I would have liked to be open and honest about our assets. But I knew I had to do it. No one will be taking care of us from now on but me. There wasn't anything else I could do.

In the interest of maintaining harmony, women commonly extend their roles as peacemaker to the bedroom. They have sex when, if they were completely honest, they would prefer not to; it is easier than facing the consequences of refusal. Saying no to sex can create a defensive reaction in a man who interprets it as a personal rejection rather than a negative response to a request. Once again, shutting up and paying the price is chosen as a solution to the paradox of conflict.

Women are well aware that sex can disarm men, that sex can be used as an olive branch to seal an armistice or to smooth the way for making a request that might otherwise be denied. Women who know this and are reluctant to engage in direct conflict are thus encouraged to use sex to get concessions that seem unattainable otherwise.

Illness, too, can be used as a device to resolve conflict indirectly. Only a heel would not be kind and conciliatory when a woman is ill, and most people do not like to be seen as heels. If being sick is the only tactical maneuver that a woman has available to her to suspend hostilities and if this practice works, she will be inclined to get sick again because other means of conflict resolution are not available to her.

Guilt-induction is another indirect strategy for defusing conflict available to women who feel powerless. Opportunities to elicit guilt are available in all relationships; nonetheless, women who use the sins of others to resolve conflict are not admired figures. This defense against the paradox of conflict backfires, too. The end result of inducing guilt seems to be alienation and bitterness for the martyr and self-justification and resentment for her family and friends.

181

The underlying issue in many dysfunctional alliances centers around a struggle for power in the traditional sense of who has the control, who is the winner and who is the loser, who is the boss and who takes orders, who will determine what the rules for the relationship will be. This struggle for power surfaces in obvious as well as subtle ways designed to achieve victory without acknowledgment that there is any discord at all.

For instance, one woman refused to follow the budget her husband set up; she was not going to let him control her with "his" money. A busy secretary failed to keep a dentist appointment her mother made for her; she refused to be treated like a child in this way. A high-school student cancelled blind dates her best friend arranged; she would pick out her own dates. Another woman wasted time at work in indirect attempts to avoid being controlled. In devious ways like these women try to squirm out of the paradoxical position of having to resolve differences without facing the issues.

Maureen was a legal assistant who worked for a senior partner in a large law firm. She loved her work, but not her hard-driving, loud-talking, quick-tempered boss. She was challenged by the women in her therapy group to tell her boss how she felt about his daily blow-ups and put-downs. Maureen defended him, insisting that he was just that way and would never stop his bellowing, so it was useless for her to try to change him. Rationalizing away his tantrums reflected her fear of conflict; she felt powerless to speak up in her own behalf.

When she accepted the group's challenge and told her boss that she felt sick to her stomach and humiliated when he yelled at her, he replied, with unaccustomed calm, that he had yelled all his life and no one had ever objected before. He abruptly broke the habit, at least with Maureen.

Daring to confront her boss about his outbursts and holding a mirror up to him in which he could see his own behavior had a positive impact on Maureen's work. To her delight, she uncovered her own self-defeating but hidden pattern: by offering rationalizations

182

for her boss's behavior, she provided herself with a handy excuse for sidestepping conflict.

"I've got to make everyone happy."

Another method used by some women to stack the deck against themselves in the paradox-of-conflict game is to put up with whatever the dealer hands out. Some put on a poker face and become cold, although they once were warm and spontaneous; some become Pollyannas and pretend everything is aces; others play the peacemaker part, trying to keep everyone happy.

Victoria was thirty-five when she came for therapy. She clearly reflected the effects of playing out her please-everyone role. She carried a tremendous burden. Her elderly parents, both of whom were ill, lived nearby. Being an only child and feeling responsible for them, she tried to be available whenever they needed her and checked up on them almost daily. Her husband traveled frequently in his job and wanted her to go with him as his associates' wives did. Victoria would have liked to share with him the busy, exciting world he seemed so comfortable and happy in, but she felt duty-bound to be at home with their children.

Victoria felt pulled in three directions as she tried to take care of her parents, please her husband, and meet the needs of two demanding youngsters. Her aim was to create harmony for everybody. She assumed more and more control over her family as a pacification strategy designed to insure that every moment at home was serenely harmonious, that her parents' living arrangements and medical problems were conscientiously supervised, and that her children behaved correctly.

The strategy went awry. The more Victoria tried to control, the more conflict ensued and the more anxious she became. As the children grew older, their lives became more complex and separate from the family. They resented their mother's control and began to slip away. Victoria found herself restricting them with rules designed to make her job easier, and punishing them for their rebellion. Her husband interpreted her control as extending to him, too, and he became argumentative and distrustful of her. Meanwhile, as her parents became more confined by their infirmities, their reliance on Victoria increased.

At that point Victoria came for therapy because, she said, "I feel like scrambled eggs. I can't figure out why I behave the way I do or what I'm feeling, except that nothing seems to work the way it's supposed to." Victoria's attempts to resolve conflict by controlling her family were motivated by feelings of powerlessness. She learned in therapy that, for her, satisfaction would come, not from keeping her family safely happy, but in helping them to become fully functioning adults.

Jodie, like Victoria, tried to play the paradox-of-conflict game by putting up with the hand she was dealt. She married Kip when she was a junior in high school. He was older, and she felt very adult in her decision, especially since she was encouraged by her sister, the only family she had. Jodie knew that Kip had a bad temper, but he had never been angry with her. She interpreted his sexual demands as passion and felt very desired. After the wedding, Kip's sexual demands increased, but his skill did not. Jodie believed him when he said it was her fault and that his desires were cooling because she was sexually inexperienced and unexciting. Jodie decided that she would have to make the best of things.

Kip lost his reluctance to expose her to his violent side. He complained bitterly about her cooking, her housekeeping, her looks, her school work, as well as her lack of interest in sex. The tenderness and affection he had shown Jodie turned to querulous demands. Their sexual encounters centered on his instant gratification.

Jodie did not know how to resolve their conflicts, and Kip seemed unwilling to help. In desperation, she went to her sister and begged for permission to live with her. Her sister, fixed firmly in her own value system, said a wife's job was to stick by her husband, no matter what. Another time, when Kip had locked her out of the house with no money, Jodie went to a neighbor's home. The woman was sympathetic, but her husband worked with Kip and was afraid he would lose

184

his job if they became involved. Feeling physically as well as emotionally defeated, Jodie was a tragic victim of the paradox of conflict. Putting up with her lot did not give Jodie a happy ending.

"It's so hard to be assertive."

Because women have been encouraged to develop strong romantic atttachments, they are especially vulnerable when their intimate alliances are threatened. The paradox of conflict dictates a cautious *modus operandi* when it comes to love; actions and words must be carefully guarded when discord threatens. Most women are not psychologically prepared for conflict. The exhortations of female role expectations have encouraged them to be passive, submissive, and dependent. They have been taught that it is jarringly unfeminine to be direct or strong on interpersonal battlegrounds, and they have not learned to see conflict as a positive thing.

These factors have shaped women for nonassertiveness. They think it is impossible for them to have open confrontations without becoming aggressive; this thought is repugnant to women. And aggressiveness, of course, is seen as masculine behavior that women do not want to adopt. They do not like themselves when they become belligerent. They know that hostility is not a way to resolve conflict that bodes well for lasting love.

Both nonassertive and aggressive approaches to interpersonal problem-solving are demeaning and self-defeating for women. They undermine self-enhancement and self-responsibility; the focus is on the actions and reactions of others, instead of on women's effectiveness. Such tactics only perpetuate nonassertive pacification procedures and aggressive one-upsmanship campaigns.

Most destructive conflicts start with a spark or two that set off a chain reaction. This was true for Amy. She came for therapy because she was tired of being caught in the middle. Her husband and three sons were in constant strife. Conflict had frightened her since childhood; she felt helpless to intervene, but was unwilling to leave the boys unprotected from their father. Like many women trying to appease opposing forces, she was left with an uncomfortable feeling of failure no matter what she did.

In therapy, Amy described herself.

I'm like a mouse caught in a rat trap. My husband Bert blames me for anything our three boys do that he disapproves of or dislikes. Unfortunately, Bert is a perfectionistic man, somewhat aloof and quick to criticize. He has little time or patience to give to his sons. I'm constantly defending the children to Bert, and Bert to the children when they come to me complaining about how unfair their father is. I'm pushed and pulled in the constant struggle going on between them. I feel nervous all the time about these smoldering conflicts; they flare up at the slightest spark of provocation. I also feel resentful and guilty that I'm supposed to be able to keep the peace in the family.

Amy found it difficult to trust her therapist's suggestion that neither Bert nor the boys required her to act as a go-between. Because she was unable to engage in conflict herself, she was unable to tolerate seeing conflict between others. Feeling helpless, she had assumed that the boys felt the same way.

With great trepidation, Amy began a campaign to withdraw from her position in the buffer zone and to teach her sons how to become involved in constructive problem-solving with their father. At first, the boys were bewildered and confused when she refused to sympathize with them or to protect them from him. She encouraged them to speak to him about their complaints, but they had little experience with directness. After awhile, finding that she meant what she said, they began to shift for themselves with Bert. To Amy's delight, they soon overcame their fears of meeting him head on. They could speak up and make requests. And, with the candor of children, they focused immediately on basics. Amy told her therapist of her five-year-old son saying to Bert, who had ignored the little boy's repeated question, "I don't think you should always like your book better than me." In the past, to save Bert from feeling guilty and to protect the child from feeling rejected, Amy would have diverted the boy's attention to something else as if nothing unpleasant had happened.

When Amy first stepped out of her role as troubleshooter, Bert continued to blame her every time the children misbehaved. Then one day she shot back, "Bert, I resent it when you tell me it's my fault when the boys are bad. You've been here with them from the day they were born, just as I have, so if we must assign blame, then I would like you to accept your share. I would much prefer, though, that you speak directly to them if they do something you don't like." Once Amy stepped out of the middle, she was able to identify and point out the issue in her conflict with Bert.

Bert followed through on her suggestion. After a time, the entire family seemed much happier and more relaxed. When Amy exchanged placating for communicating, she saw that the children were a match for their father. They needed to take the measure of each others' strengths and weaknesses. By putting herself in the middle of their conflicts, Amy had thought that she was protecting them. Instead, she had denied Bert and the boys the opportunity to know each other and to work out satisfactory solutions to disagreements that all families can expect to encounter.

Women have a right to communicate their thoughts and feelings. This is the way they test their perceptions and share them with others. When conflict creates discomfort and tension, they have a right to bring up problems and to expect that other people will be willing to discuss them and get involved in resolutions. If others do not see that there is a problem, then the next step is to decide what independent strategy can be pursued.

Many women catastrophize, that is, predict that some extraordinarily terrible consequence will follow if they ask others to engage in conflict resolution. They tell themselves that others will be angry, will feel rejected, will be hurt, and will never speak to them again, or that the relationship will be over and they will be alone the rest of their lives. All of their experiences with socialization and their sex-role expectations combine with catastrophizing to create one huge stumbling block to facing the issues.

Countless women have dissipated their strength and power by focusing on dissatisfying and dysfunctional relationships, rather than identifying their resources and making decisions to use them effectively. When women develop assertive communications skills, conflict is no longer something that must be avoided at all costs or engaged in aggressively as a last resort because indirect approaches have failed. Assertive women know that they *cannot* resolve differences *without* facing the issues.

Hazel proved to herself that what she thought was a conflict could be a positive experience. She was a travel agent in a busy agency. When she stopped thinking that if her boss valued her work he would voluntarily give her a raise, she was able to take steps to accomplish her goal. She prepared her resumé, detailing her education, experience, training, and skills. She thought about her salary requirements and the compensation her contributions to his firm warranted, then requested an appointment with her employer to discuss a raise. To her delight, he said he would be happy to boost her salary far beyond what she had hoped.

Edna, a busy young homemaker, stopped feeling angry with her mother for telling her how to raise her children when she said, "Mom, I know you love your grandchildren and want what's best for them just as I do. You did a good job raising me, and I would like you to trust me to do just as good a job with my children." Edna's mother replied that she would try to offer help instead of criticism in the future.

Betty, a department store clerk, overcame her shame of failure by telling a prospective employer exactly why she had been fired from her last job, what she had learned from the experience, and how she would prevent such a thing from happening again.

Joanne stopped being a doormat for her boyfriend and told him that they would have to spend time doing some of the things she enjoyed if he expected to continue to see her.

All of these women resolved problems by being assertive and facing disagreements directly. Both self-generated and other-generated conflict became opportunities for growth. Hazel increased her earning power significantly. Edna enlisted her mother as an ally. Betty discharged negative feelings and perhaps got a job. Joanne increased her self-esteem and improved a relationship.

"I never thought of myself as powerful."

Power as it is traditionally used is in itself a paradoxical issue that has created conflict. Women have not been taught to be powerful about themselves or their own lives, yet they are expected to assume control over those who are sick, weak, or dependent, especially children. It seems ironic that, feeling as powerless and inadequate as they do, women are charged with being accountable for rearing the next generation.

Probably one of the most significant changes we see in women as they learn to engage in conflict constructively is that they experience exhilarating feelings, which they identify as coming from an increased sense of strength and power as they reclaim their ability to act directly, openly, and honestly.

For us, power refers *not* to having control over others, but to being in charge of oneself and one's own destiny. Power is the ability to put one's strength to use. Our concept of strength is a sense of knowing what one wants and developing inner and outer resources to be able to get it. Strength also involves having confidence, knowing that one has rights and that one can act on them.

It is rewarding to us to hear a woman say, "The more I'm in charge of myself, the more I don't have to be in control of others. I can just let them be." When women think of power as being in charge of themselves, as having the capacity to be effective, they can succeed by learning how to be effective. They are able to show other people by example how to be effective too. They in turn can develop their own personal strength and power and the tools to approach conflict positively by insisting that issues be faced directly. This is a positive self- and other-enhancing solution for the paradox of conflict.

CHAPTER IX

Guilt

> "I'm responsible for everything and power-less to effect change."

Women are able to control very few of the things for which they feel responsible. Important decisions are made by others without consultation with them. Yet they feel guilty about other people's failures, other people's feelings, other people's choices, and about circumstances and situations not of their own making. The paradox lies in the notion that responsibility and power can exist independently of each other. They cannot. Yet, in our culture, when things don't work out and someone is sought to take the blame, women accept that responsibility.

Women feel guilty for a lot of reasons. The paradox of guilt for women comes from internalizing messages that say that even in areas where women have no power and no way to control the behavior of others they are still responsible for what happens.

Wilma, a hard-working woman of thirty who had risen from clerk to department manager, felt guilty when the mortgage company for which she worked went bankrupt. She knew that in her middle-level position, she had no control over company success or failure; yet she felt ashamed to leave her home and face neigh-

190

bors who might question her about the defunct company. Maybe they would judge her as harshly as she judged herself; she felt guilty by association.

Patty, who was working as a secretary and going to school nights, spread herself thin trying to fit everything she needed to do into her busy life. She felt guilty for the angry and hurt reaction of her boyfriend when she told him that she needed more time for herself. She thought she made him feel bad.

Lucille was a generous woman who had loaned money to a friend a year earlier. By any standards she had been overly patient, yet she felt somehow to blame when her friend, whom she had asked to repay the loan, acted offended. She wondered if perhaps she should have let it go a bit longer.

Suzanne, a busy lawyer whose practice drained her time and energy, was unhappy that she could not meet the multiple demands of her friends, parents, children, and spouse. If she telephoned them, they would say, "Hello, stranger, I didn't think I'd ever hear from you." If they called her, they would say, "You never call anymore, so I thought I'd better see if you're alive."

Shara, a college speech professor who took very seriously her opportunity to direct her students toward success, found that no matter how hard she tried some students did not earn passing grades. She felt accountable and wondered how she had failed them.

Ann Marie, who was engaged to Ron, was bothered that, whereas she showed her devotion to him in many small ways, he seemed to take her for granted. She asked herself if she had tried hard enough to build the relationship because he did not seem to love her as much as she loved him.

Maureen, worn out after eighteen years of living a traditional role in her marriage, felt uneasy about telling her husband that she needed more in her life than child-rearing and that she would like to negotiate some reversals in their roles.

Tamara, a mother of four children, handled the family finances. She struggled mightily to stretch too little money to meet too many needs. When there was no money left and the children needed shoes, she blamed herself.

Women who feel culpable in situations like these are experiencing the paradox of guilt. This involves psychologically destructive guilt feelings that come from accepting responsibility in areas where one has no power to control the events that take place. Women characteristically do this. This is easy to explain in terms of how they have been raised. Women have been taught to please others rather than themselves. They have learned that it is nobler to give than to receive and that it is a special mark of virtue to put oneself last. Their stereotyped roles reinforce their sense of responsibility. Women accept that they are born with the mandate to smooth out the rough spots and fill in the holes for everyone else's journeys.

Women who come for therapy are often acutely uneasy because they feel responsible for everything that goes badly in their lives and in the lives of those around them. Many of our clients feel that they are drowning in the sea of this responsibility. Although they may not have identified their feelings as guilt, when we ask them if they feel guilty, they usually realize that they do. When asked what they could have done to change the situations, they report sadly that the circumstances were out of their hands; they did the best they could. Their distress comes from guilt in the face of powerlessness.

When women assume responsibility at appropriate times they gain a sense of confidence and competence, which leads to the gratification of effective living. The paradox of guilt for women involves responsibility without power. Despite the fact that women are generally deprived of the power necessary to ensure success, they are still held responsible for failures. Thus, whereas they do not get praise for successes, they do get a generous dose of blame for failure, even though it is beyond their control.

"I didn't live up to my parents' expectations."

When parents have the opinion that something is

right for them, they assume without question that they know exactly what will make their daughters happy. A conflict results from this rigid stance. Much human potential has been channeled inappropriately because, in making personal choices, many young women have felt compelled to measure up to their parents' notion of what their daughters should be.

Having had reinforcement for delighting and satisfying others, a young woman must have courage to open her mind to an identity that may differ from what her parents had designated for her. The problem is complicated by the hidden agenda of many parents who, without openly saying so, want their children to achieve in areas that had once seemed desirable for themselves. Able to give their daughters opportunities that eluded them in their own youth, parents may feel deeply disappointed if their daughters do not enthusiastically welcome these "advantages."

Sandra often heard her parents say with vexation, "We didn't raise our daughter to be like that." They were referring to her freewheeling life-style, which dismayed them because they saw it as perilously close to corruption. They had made many financial sacrifices for her, confident that she would never disappoint them. And in the process, they had burdened her with a mortgaged future by saying, in effect, "We will give you the best of everything, but you must do your part by growing up to be the way we want you to be."

Because this bargain was never communicated openly, its concealed requirements set up Sandra to experience the paradox of guilt. As she said in therapy,

I always accepted the advantages they pressed upon me, because they so obviously wanted me to enjoy everything they had missed in their childhood. Yet, I know how displeased they are that I have become independent as a result of the wonderful experiences they have given me. If I hadn't had these experiences I might have stayed in the latched-tight coop they have always lived in. But they encouraged me to go out and taste broader fare than they ever knew. And now I want to enjoy the world they opened up to me. They are shocked and disappointed; I can't help feeling guilty, yet what am I to do?

Sandra had carried into adulthood her discomfort at redesigning her parents' plans. She did not recognize the paradox of guilt in operation. As an adult she had a right to be autonomous and to make her own decisions; if her choices pleased her but rankled her parents, she was not responsible for their feelings.

Having decided to live with a man to whom she was not married, Sandra developed an elaborately deceptive plan to conceal the fact. Even though she was in other respects comfortable with her life-style, she suffered from a nagging feeling that the devil would get his due because she had no right to choose different values from those of her parents, whom she loved.

Eventually, Sandra was able to discuss her life-style with her parents. Her feeling of guilt was matched by that of her mother, who earnestly believed Sandra was ruining her life by living with a man to whom she was not married. Sandra's mother, too, had suffered from the paradox of guilt; she believed a mother failed if she did not instill her own value system in her daughter. She was so hurt that she could not talk about it. She suffered in silence, bewildered and angry as she tried to hide this evidence of her failure from herself and others.

This paradoxical issue is one that our clients face frequently. We point out to them that they are powerless to control the behavior of other adults. To believe that they are responsible for doing so is to be stuck in a conflict with no power to move out of it. The resolution comes in trusting others to make their own decisions and accepting that what is cut to the measure of one person may bind or chafe another.

When a woman still acts like an obedient child when relating with her parents, she is comfortable with other authority figures only when she is interacting cautiously. This includes her therapist. We have had many clients who apparently say to themselves, "If I let you know that I am less than perfect, you will reject me too." Generally this need to be above reproach stems from having seen their parents as critical and demanding.

The secrets these women are afraid to reveal sound shameful only to themselves. After many weeks of hesitation, Mavis confessed the earth-shaking news that "I've frequently felt angry with you, but I was afraid that if I told you so you might not like me." Roberta said reluctantly, "I've always been ashamed to admit how much I would like to be a little girl again, able to climb up on someone's lap and be cuddled." Both of these women needed to step over the stumbling blocks that told them their therapist was another authority figure who would reject them if they revealed what they considered to be the holes in their personalities. Only by doing so could they resolve their guilt.

"It's a wife's role."

One area where women feel most responsible, yet least powerful, is in their role as wives. Nancy's husband Jack was a would-be musician. This occupation gave him an excuse to frequent nightclubs, where he got an occasional engagement. In fact, he lived more like a perpetual playboy than a wage earner. Every night was a party. Nancy could not share his nighttime activities; she had to get up early in the morning to go to work. She needed her job because her income paid for the essentials; his intermittent windfalls were supplemental. Jack called Nancy "Good Old Nan." She was great for maintaining his clothes, keeping his books, and entertaining whenever he chose to do so.

When Nancy came for therapy she felt guilty because she was attracted to other men. On a conscious level, she valued her marriage and had originally accepted her multiple roles willingly. On a deeper level, she resented the uneven load of responsibilities she carried; they made her more of a servant than an equal.

In therapy Nancy compared her role and her duties with those of her husband. She realized that she felt a smoldering hostility at the injustice that she was in the harness while he rode comfortably behind. She saw her heavy responsibilities as unfair and oppressive, whereas his life was mostly fun. Her sexual longings were a symptom of an unresolved anger that she had buried deeply. After dealing with her anger, she could see the paradox by which she was immobilized. She had no power over Jack's choice of an occupation; the choice was his. But she did not need to feel guilty in refusing to provide the wherewithal to make his irresponsibility possible.

Like Nancy, many women, in accepting their roles as wives, accept the responsibility for choices they do not make. Even when their husbands create problems by their choices, women feel guilty because they are unable to adjust with ease to the troubled situation. Unable to adjust, they see themselves as lacking, blame themselves, and feel guilty.

Richard flirted with pretty women at every opportunity, even when his wife Velma was with him. Velma was not only embarrassed by his flirting, but felt at fault because she let his actions bother her. She tried to quiet the rage that churned in her stomach by telling herself that the problem was her jealousy rather than his behavior.

Mike insisted that Laura get rid of her sexual "hang-ups." Her sense of responsibility for the success of their sex life increased when he threatened that unless she began to enjoy sex more he could, on an hour's notice, find a woman who would welcome his advances. Even when assured by her therapist that it was Mike who had the hang-ups, Laura could not still the nagging feeling that she would be at fault if he strayed.

Darryl could not resist the ego boost he felt when he bought a new car, which he did without discussion with Roseanne. This created recurrent family financial crunches. Roseanne struggled month after month to juggle the accounts to pay the most pressing creditors. She blamed herself when she got depressed over unpaid bills.

Tom was perverse and unpleasant on family outings and vacations. He yelled and threatened the children if they acted up in the car. Mary regularly provided things to entertain them while riding, hoping that Tom would stay in better spirits. She felt like a poor helpmate when she could not stay calm and keep the children from jangling his nerves.

Feeling solely responsible for keeping intolerable marriages together is another unfair burden accepted by women who have not escaped the paradox of guilt. Seeing themselves with this impossible task causes women to feel trapped, frustrated, and hopeless, with no alternatives and no means of bringing about change. They think they must single-handedly do something that is essentially a two-person job. Feeling powerless, they often ask us in therapy to tell them what they should do. Sometimes they are disappointed when we tell them that our function is not to give them directions, but to help them identify for themselves the alternatives available to them and to see that they carefully consider the cost and the consequences of each option. Following this, we support them as they act upon the options they have freely chosen.

Maureen, married, tired, and beaten down, was experiencing the double-bind of powerlessness and responsibility when we first saw her. She explained, "I know that Hank and I are both good people. But he will never talk about anything that troubles us. I know it is up to me to do all I can because we really love each other. I want to save our marriage."

No wonder Maureen accepted this responsibility; her life had been characterized by a series of paradoxical conflicts. Feeling inferior since childhood, Maureen had very low self-esteem. As a young girl she had looked forward to marriage to give her the sense of worth that an alcoholic father and a poor family life had not provided. She had affiliated herself with Hank because she saw him as a ray of hope for the future. She was a modern-day Cinderella who vowed to be totally cooperative with Hank in gratitude for his having rescued her in marriage. Married before she was out of high school, she dutifully fulfilled a traditional role for eighteen years. She had the questionable distinction of having three children in diapers before she was twenty.

Another child was born five years later. Dependent upon Hank both emotionally and materially, she could not risk losing him; unconsciously she geared herself to holding tight to him. She became totally absorbed in being a caregiver. Her husband and children saw her as she saw herself, immersed in their lives and welfare.

Although several of their children were difficult to raise, Maureen did not complain. She felt, as many women do, that it would not be safe to face her ambivalent feelings about her marriage. She shouldered her burden while denying her negative feelings. Maureen told herself that she had freely accepted this role when she married and had no right not to like it. It would upset their whole relationship if she told her husband that her priorities had changed, that now that she knew more about child-rearing she also knew she was fed up with it and would like to stretch out and try something more in life. Since Hank reacted so negatively to her suggestion that she might go back to school or get a part-time job, she dropped the subject.

Maureen's Prince Charming was now silent and uncommunicative. Even before their marriage, he had not talked a great deal, but she had interpreted his silence as strength. Little did she know then how differently she would feel a few years down the road when the only power she experienced in his silence was its ability to frustrate completely her efforts to communicate with him.

Because he seemed sure of himself and saw no need to change, she read this as a sign that she must do all the changing. She handled conflicts by backing away from the friction they generated, and accepted the impossible task of making everyone else happy. Of course, she could not do that. Guilt was the inevitable result, guilt about all the things she felt responsible for but had no power to control. One day Maureen felt totally overwhelmed and knew she had to look for help. After years of wearily juggling child and husband problems complicated by her feelings of inadequacy, she saw herself as having thoroughly muddled her life and the lives of those around her. Swamped with feelings of guilt, she sought therapy.

When she came to us Maureen felt helpless. She believed she had only two equally distasteful choices: to stay in her unsatisfactory marriage, which she considered herself responsible to keep going since she had committed herself to it, or to abandon her security, which she saw as the consequence if she were to give up on her marriage. Fortunately, in therapy she identified a third alternative: to stay within the marriage, where she was heavily invested, and to grow. This involved learning that she had rights and could exercise them, that her husband could tolerate her changing even if he did not welcome it, and that her entire family would benefit from her growth and change.

"He's the head of the family, but . . ."

Capable women who are married to less capable men experience the paradox of guilt while struggling to stay in a submissive role. Women wrestle with their ambivalent feelings when they are in positions in which they support, as "head of the family," men who do not fit the male stereotype of strength and capability. When wives accept the reins of leadership and take the initiative to make family decisions, they are often accused of usurping their husband's prerogatives. There are not many social rewards for women who are seen as robbing a man of his position as head of the family.

Valerie found this out. She was a competent woman, married to a man who probably chose her because she was strong and could compensate for his feelings of inadequacy. (Of course, he did not want to *be* inadequate; teamed up with his wife, they would make an effective pair!) Although such decisions are seldom made on a conscious level, people do have a strong tendency to select partners who will fill in the inadequacies they sense in themselves. A dominant person looks for a submissive person to complement his or her personality. A weak person looks for someone upon whom to lean.

Dick and Valerie had served each other well in this way. She had enjoyed feeling strong and competent, and he had needed her support. Together they discussed vocational plans for Dick since he had previously had only sporadic employment. He became a sales representative, a job in which the rewards were related directly to the amount of diligence and creative energy he put forth. Over the years Dick's employment did not work out well. He was not one to push himself to pursue a sale when there were more pleasant things to do.

Valerie fretted, telling herself that she would have done things differently if she had been supporting the family. She had a strong need for achievement and would have enjoyed the challenge of working in a young business. Faced with Dick's easygoing ways, she felt frustrated because they were always in an economic crunch. Nonetheless, Valerie was committed to the notion that Dick was to be the breadwinner for the family, and she supported him in that role. This meant she would not permit herself to act lest she undercut Dick's position. In spite of the fact that he was backing off from work and she was well educated and capable, she did not look for employment for herself. She tried to deny her disappointment, but it bubbled out at times regardless of how hard she tried to keep quiet. In time she was nudging him in subtle and unsubtle ways. The more she needled him to achieve, the more he resisted. He eventually saw her as overbearing and controlling.

Feeling powerless and left with no valid way to motivate him, Valerie began to nag. She expressed her fears that family needs would not be met and her feelings of powerlessness to do anything about it. When Dick resisted her, she extended her sense of responsibility to include the children's lives and activities. She needed to alleviate her anxiety that they would suffer from growing up in a financially unsuccessful home. Eventually. Valerie became the unliked member of the family, while the children saw their father as a nice man who did not get on their backs as their mother did.

Valerie came for therapy feeling, in her words, "hollow and hurting." Her husband had moved out and told the children that nothing would make him come back to a nagging wife. Valerie was torn by the bitterness of contradictory feelings that came as a result of Dick's limitations. She felt guilty that she was more competent than he because she believed he deserved her support, yet it was hard to bolster up someone who was so irresponsible about his obligations. She also felt self-righteous, unloved, rejected, and confused because of her family's reaction to her earnest efforts. She wondered how their marriage had gotten into this unhappy state. One thing she knew for sure was that she had tried very hard to strengthen her husband's role as breadwinner and provider of the good life for the rest of the family. To have them see her to blame for the problems that developed was not only an affront to her goodwill, it also tormented her with guilt.

Since she had been criticized by her family, Valerie expected rejection from her therapist as well. She was visibly relieved to learn that nagging is a behavior adopted by competent persons who find themselves in intolerable situations that they do not have the power to change. Valerie learned that if she could come to feel less responsible for things over which she had no control, she could resolve this paradox. She could concentrate on developing her own competencies rather than prodding her husband into action in order to have her achievement needs fulfilled by his success. By connecting her ambitions to her own power, she could make things happen herself and save herself the frustration that comes from backseat driving. This insight spurred her to focus on making plans for a career of her own. In doing this, she could be confident that she would work hard and please herself; at the same time she could let Dick be different. Once she stopped feeling responsible for sparking him into action, she no longer felt guilty when he was not successful. Besides, by becoming financially independent she could move out of the paradox of dependency; her survival would no longer depend upon his success.

Like Valerie, Lorraine was another client who needed to see her husband as head of the family. She was a young doctor when she married Roy, a man with no ambitions for a demanding professional career for

201

himself. He liked his nine-to-five civil service job, which allowed him time and energy for outside enjoyments. Lorraine advanced rapidly in her profession, and her earnings reflected this. Even so, she had always believed that a husband should take the lead in the family and expected that this would be so in their home. Lorraine promoted the notion that Roy was the family provider. She deferred to him for final decisions and authority. She shielded him from the fact that she was carrying burdens usually associated with a husband's role as well as those seen as belonging to a wife. She earned much more money than Roy did, and her income paid for new cars, vacations, and college tuition. All the same, Lorraine made light of her financial contributions, and the children were never aware of the disparity in their parents' incomes.

Over the years Lorraine felt the pressure of striving not to slight either her family or the many patients in her care. Of course, she was often exhausted by the end of the day. Roy began to see a fatigued Lorraine as uninteresting and socially withdrawn. He felt rejected when she enjoyed her one relaxation: reading the newspaper in order to unwind at the end of a long demanding day.

When Roy asked for a divorce after nearly three decades of marriage, Lorraine felt like a failure. She was overwhelmed with guilt feelings and began searching the past, adding up her shortcomings. She came to therapy thinking that she must have done something to cause the breakup and hoping to do something to avert it. In therapy she came to see how the paradox of guilt had hemmed her in, convincing her that she was responsible for the failure of her marriage when, in fact, she had been responsible for most of its successes. She said bitterly, "What a fool I've been. I have felt responsible for propping my husband up in his rightful place! I've minimized my professional contributions in order not to outshine him. I've knocked myself out trying to be subordinate to Roy, supporting the illusion that he was the head of the family. This meant also doing all the traditional mothering tasks so I wouldn't feel guilty about having a profession. I know now that I did have the power to do differently, but my guilt wouldn't let me."

"I hate myself when I nag."

Rosa, a young married woman with two children and a resistant husband, was typical of many young women we see in therapy. She felt guilty and readily blamed herself for being a nag. She saw that the name-calling, bitter quarrels between herself and her husband Jim were the result of her keeping after him to do tasks around the house. She felt bitter and rejected when he procrastinated about doing chores that would make her life more comfortable. The lawn was never mowed until she mentioned it several times; a leaking faucet dripped interminably. She had even had to wait six months to get the oven timer fixed. Every little task was met with his inattention.

Rosa had been pregnant when they married. Being pregnant was in itself enough to put her in a subservient position in relation to Jim. Frightened and apprehensive when she realized what she would have to face, she felt relieved and grateful that Jim was willing to marry her; she would not have to cope with her pregnancy alone. She felt powerless and was willing to be totally dependent upon him. It was easy for the young woman who had once been confident and spontaneous to slip into a passive sanctuary.

Both Rosa and Jim were very young, and neither of them realized the amount of growing up they needed to do before they could assume the responsibilities of marriage and a family. After the birth of their child, Jim spent a lot of time going out evenings with his buddies, reliving the days of being single, having the kind of fun that carefree young men usually have together. He established a pattern of spending money, drinking, and having fun. He expected to continue doing these things throughout his married life. Meanwhile, Rosa felt overworked and neglected when left at home. By the time they had two children and Jim's partying did not decrease, she felt bitter much of the time. When he ignored her requests that he fix things around the house, help with the children, and spend less money, she felt powerless to get him to change. Not knowing what else to do, Rosa began to nag.

In a joint therapy session, Rosa freely admitted that she nagged a lot and Jim said this was one of her behaviors that he most objected to. Neither had ever realized that she nagged bacause she felt powerless, and had felt so from the very beginning of their marriage. At issue here was a conflict involving several paradoxes: dependency, because she did not see that she could survive without him; conflict, since she could not risk open confrontation; and guilt because she felt that she should be nicer than she was. She attributed their marital problems to her unattractive habit of nagging and hated herself because she could not change.

Akin to nagging is complaining. Many of our clients feel guilty because they see themselves as complainers. Trapped, as Rosa was, in dependent situations they feel powerless to change, they blame themselves if they complain. In therapy they are relieved of their remorse when they understand that their socialization experiences are at the root of the problem. They have been conditioned to adjust to even the most odious situations, rather than to search for ways to take action for change. Not being able to adapt to unfair situations, they feel helpless and express their grievances by complaining. Seeing complaining as an unattractive habit, they do not like themselves when they grumble.

We have seen many women learn in therapy to identify unrecognized sources of strength and power in themselves that can be utilized to break their complaining pattern. If they begin to make things happen they can feel more in charge of what is going on in their lives. For example, Marge no longer needed to protest helplessly that the house badly needed repairs once she felt courageous enough to insist on a family budget that would allow her to hire workmen to fix things that were important to her. Rhonda stopped complaining to anyone who would listen that her husband would never travel after she found that she could plan and take trips without him. Maura no longer needed to express her dissatisfaction that the children's bedrooms were messy after deciding it was possible to close their doors and leave the mess for them. Rose stopped muttering about being imposed upon at work when she stood up tall and gave a clear message that she would not work extra hours without pay. All the women in these examples eliminated their need to complain by taking action and changing the situation themselves. They resolved conflicts by recognizing and acting on their rights without feeling guilty.

"I'll take the blame."

Couples often come to therapy believing that one of them must be at fault and should be blamed for the problems between them. In general, women seem to accept blame more readily than men since women have been taught to be responsible for keeping others happy.

Pearl, who could not face ending her twelve-year marriage, accepted this paradoxical guilt. She said, "I married on the rebound. I knew I didn't love my husband, but he offered security, which I'd never had in my stormy romance with my previous boyfriend. I knew before we were out of the church that I'd made a mistake. But he always has loved me and I hate to hurt him. I think I owe it to him to stay married."

In other cases, when a husband is a spendthrift or unfaithful or angry or short-tempered, a woman who accepts guilt easily can allow the facts to be turned around until she seems to be the cause of his shortcomings. She blames his unfaithfulness on her lack of interest in sex, his extravagance on her failure to speak up, and his temper on her real or imagined faults. Unfortunately, this has been reinforced by many marriage counselors who have urged women to adjust to men's wishes and needs. Women feel unsupported, then, by the very professional helpers they expected to trust. They are left to struggle in the quicksand of their guilt.

Lenora came for therapy because, she said, "Sex is a nightmare." She told us that when she went for marriage counseling with her husband some years before, she had censured herself for their sexual problems. She had been badly frightened and shamed as a child when her stepfather abused her sexually. She had never been able to enjoy sex with her husband and felt guilty because he was disappointed in her. We shuddered when she said that the marriage counselor had told her that it was appropriate for a wife to be "a lady in the living room and a whore in the bedroom," and that he believed this was not too much to expect of her since it was important to her husband. This communication did nothing to reduce her sense of guilt.

It is a new concept for many couples that mismatching is often at the root of problems between two otherwise fine people; neither one has to be a villain when they do not get along well. People who are mismatched and who married each other for the wrong reasons end up feeling depleted rather than enhanced by being with each other. They may feel guilty about their disappointment. This guilt often makes it difficult for them to see their problems clearly; the focus becomes who is right and who is wrong, rather than "what is there about our relationship that we would like to change, and what steps can we take to change it?"

Lucy came for therapy knowing that she and Jim had grown apart. She thought that someone must be culpable and searched within herself for explanations for their rift. They were not enemies, but they did not share common interests or goals and neither felt motivated to work toward a commitment to the other. They had been mismatched from the beginning. Lucy was twelve years younger than Jim. When she was seventeen and he was twenty-nine, the sophistication of an older man seemed irresistible to her. He drove a sportscar and took her to elegant restaurants while the high school crowd ate hamburgers at the drive-in. The gifts he gave her bedazzled Lucy and her classmates. It was a short trip from high school graduation to the altar.

In therapy seven years later, Lucy realized that she had married Jim for the wrong reasons. The twelve years' difference in their ages had ceased to be glamorous. At thirty-six, he had more paunch and less hair than she admired. He wanted to settle down, have the children they had once talked of, and spend his free time relaxing with his shoes off in front of the television set. Lucy was not ready for a quiet life; she wanted excitement and adventure rather than children and a large home. But Jim was a good man, and she hated to disappoint him. She felt guilty even to think of leaving him. Her remorse was reduced, however, when she said to herself, "There must be something more than this in life. I can't stand the thought of fifty more years of stagnation."

For Lucy and Jim, therapy provided support for the difficult process of ending their marriage. They both regretted that it held so little promise for them. An objective analysis convinced them that no amount of goodwill could put them on a mutually happy course again. Lucy was able to shed her guilt when she discovered with relief that their alienation was caused not by a defect in herself but by the fact that they had never had a sound relationship on which to build. They had been mismatched from the beginning of their life together, and they were truly incompatible.

Not all mismatched relationships have to end in divorce. Sometimes couples can go on to build a solid relationship even though they chose each other for the wrong reasons. This takes the cooperation of both partners. A woman alone cannot turn things around just because she feels guilty and is willing to do all in her power to improve things.

Linda and Joe's history sounded very much like that of Lucy and Jim, but there was an essential difference: there were strengths in their union on which they could build. They, too, had married when Linda was not yet out of her teens and Joe was fourteen years older. Through the years their growth had been divergent. In his position as an engineer, Joe moved up in the world and away from his family, while Linda was nearly overwhelmed trying to hold up under a job and the demands of a home and two children. Often angry and resentful of each other, they put up a front of amiability for the rest of the world while they grew further apart.

Linda and Joe considered divorce when they realized that their lives seemed empty. They rarely talked pleasantly with each other and enjoyed little time and few activities together. Over the years, most of their conversations had ended in arguments. Messages to each other were grossly misunderstood. Both were sensitive and easily offended by the other's remarks. To cool tempers, they had learned to swallow their feelings, say very little, and lead independent lives. They came to therapy to discuss their tentative decision to get a divorce before contacting a lawyer.

As we customarily do in therapy with clients who have marriage problems, we encouraged them to look at their relationship as having four parts. One part is the history they have together. In Linda and Joe's case this involved twelve years during which they had built up a large emotional investment of pleasure and pain. A second part was their children, whom they could not discount in their plans. Would they be better off with parents who were alienated while living together, or would they benefit if their parents were divorced? The third element of the alliance is the economic factor. This always takes serious thought, since money and material possessions figure largely in anyone's life-style and must be considered for the future. Linda and Joe had a home and some investments, but both would have to lower their living standards if they divorced. The fourth factor is the personal relationship, and it is the crux of the whole decision. Although the other three factors must be considered, it is the essential foundation upon which the whole alliance is built. Relationships can be a source of either growth or destructiveness. Growth-producing ones should be kept and improved when necessary; destructive ones should be abandoned as soon as their true nature is recognized.

As Linda and Joe examined their concerns it became apparent to both of them that there were many good qualities that they valued in each other. They decided they wanted to work on their marriage, even though it had started out badly. To their surprise, they found that their suppressed anger and resentment had

208

blocked many genuine feelings of love for each other. Once in therapy they learned to get rid of their negative feelings by discharging the distress connected with them. In therapy they told each other how angry and unsupported they had felt. Once they did this, the burden of their pushed-down feelings lifted and their resentment dissipated. Both were then free to choose if and how much they were willing to change to please each other. They began to do things together that were mutually enjoyable. Linda had never been athletic, but she learned to play tennis and went camping with Joe because he liked these sports. Joe started square dancing because that was Linda's choice and he wanted to please her. They learned that negotiation and compromise work better to resolve differences than do arguments and silence.

The important thing is that Linda and Joe both accepted responsibility to look at themselves and to turn their dysfunctional marriage around. This freed Linda from the paradox of guilt because, with Joe cooperating, she was not powerless to effect change. Many of the women we have seen in therapy are not so fortunate. They experience the paradox of feeling responsible when their relationships break up even though they are helpless to effect change because their partners are unwilling to work with them to resolve differences.

"I feel guilty about almost everything."

Women accept undeserved blame for many things besides difficulties in their relationships. Sadie told her therapist how guilty she had felt when she was helping a friend clean up her kitchen after a dinner party. Some of the silverware was left on a table on the patio. When her friend asked her if she knew where it was, Sadie became flustered and frantically searched for it. When it was found, she said with relief, "I was so afraid you thought I had taken it."

The absurdity of the situation had not occurred to Sadie. Of course her friend was not accusing her. Since Sadie had been unfairly blamed for mishaps many times as a child, she still felt guilty in any situation when things went wrong. Not feeling good about herself, she expected others to distrust her. Unfortunately, she had developed a pattern of defensiveness, which is an alienating response used often by women who feel guilty.

Some of our clients feel guilty because they are competent; others feel guilty because they are incompetent. Some feel guilty because they are dependent, others because they are independent. Feelings of discomfort, shame, embarrassment, and self-condemnation are all nuances of the guilt women feel. Sally felt uncomfortable because she was the most beautiful woman in her college class, while Marge felt ashamed because she envied women who were more beautiful than she. Laurie felt embarrassed because she was the initiator of sex, and Flo condemned herself because she never initiated sexually.

Paradoxical guilt involves feeling, "I am to blame because I am responsible." For most women, therapy includes sorting out feelings and determining whether they are based on realistic perceptions of responsibility or whether they are baggage that rightly belongs to another. If a client can see that she is experiencing the paradox of guilt, she has a chance to resolve it. She does not have to feel blameworthy about things she cannot change or things for which she was never responsible in the first place.

It is understandable that women blame themselves for how they feel, think, and act; they have been blamed by so many others. Our clients often feel ashamed when they need to express grief, disappointment, or sorrow. They feel guilty about having menopausal symptoms. They feel unworthy when they do not always feel loving toward their children. They feel inadequate when criticized by anyone who is important to them.

These feelings are reactions, and some reactive behavior serves a good purpose. One of our tasks as therapists is to help women recognize the difference between appropriate and inappropriate reactions, and not to be frightened out of one or into the other. It is appropriate to react with grief when a relationship is terminated through death or separation. Tears are a body's natural way of relieving grief, and no one need be ashamed of trying to heal the sadness.

Patricia sat in therapy, struggling to stifle the tears she still needed to shed over the loss of her child. Ever since the funeral she had been trying to accept the well-meaning advice of friends to get on with her life, their insistence that tears would not bring her daughter back. In the privacy of her backyard, at night in bed, and even while driving, her body reminded her of her need to grieve. The tears she was ashamed of poured down her cheeks. In therapy she learned that if she allowed herself to cry without feeling guilty, someday she would have wept enough and she would not feel the need to weep more. For other Patricias, the loss of a friend, a lover, a parent, a spouse, a job, or even a home when one moves to a new community may produce grief that can be healed only with tears.

Menopausal symptoms are not "all in the head"; they are related to real physical as well as emotional changes. Of course, women react to these changes. Unfortunately, until more is understood about women's physiology, adequate tools to give menopausal women the understanding and medical care they need are not available. In the meantime, as we do the best we can, they should not feel guilty!

Women's patience is also severely tried by exasperating experiences when children are difficult. Not to react in such cases leaves the undesirable alternative of suppressing or denying feelings. This can hardly be expected to benefit either mother or child.

Women can give themselves permission to stop blaming themselves for all things big and small. This creates a sense of freedom as they shrug off undeserved burdens. They can experience the return of zest and spontaneity when they free themselves from guilt-caused depression. They can enjoy a sense of self-direction as they determine what they are responsible for and where they will direct their energies.

"I'm responsible for whatever happpens to my children."

A popular psychological theory suggests that women are not complete until they bear children. Women are said to experience a vague emptiness unless they have this life-giving experience. We do not undervalue motherhood; we are both mothers, and our children have been enormously rewarding parts of our lives. We are sensitive, however, to the unfairness of our culture, which puts so much emphasis on bearing and nurturing children that a woman who chooses not to do so is viewed with disdain, disapproval, or, at the very least, pity. Successful career women and homemakers alike are more comfortably accepted by society in general if they have also "proved" their femininity through maternity. Having cooperated to this point they are easy targets for the guilt associated with mothering.

One manifestation of the paradox of guilt for mothers is that they are held more responsible than are fathers for their children's welfare. Mothers are blamed for the failures of their offspring, even when they have little power to control what happens to them.

There is a fine line between a nurturing, loving mother and an overly protective one. There are few guidelines to help busy women, caught up in the day-to-day care of children, home, and often an outside job, to determine whether they are being loving or smothering. They are expected to know intuitively. People feel free to criticize mothers and hold them responsible for all their children's problems.

During World War II, when many young men had emotional problems and were diagnosed as being dependent upon their mothers, the term *momism* was coined. Mothers were blamed for emotional immaturity in children who could not function well without them. Mothers were seen as retarding their children's emotional growth by smothering them with attention, making their decisions for them, and protecting them from challenges. This charge is still commonly leveled at mothers whose children's lives are not pristine examples of achievement, health, and happiness. It has rarely been pointed out, however, that in such cases mothers have had to do all the parenting because fathers neglected to do any. Mothers have not been, and still are not, credited with moving into the vacuum that fathers leave when accomplishments, fame, and success compete with their families for their time, and win. In such homes mothers are doing their best to do the job of both parents. Instead of being supported for doing a doubly difficult job, they have been blamed for exercising too much control over their children.

Women have been told that raising children is so important that they must not pass on their nurturing role to someone else, lest the twig be bent in the wrong direction. Clients tell us that they believe no one else could do as good a job with their children as they. They had heard vivid descriptions of nefarious things that could happen when children are left in day-care centers or at the homes of babysitters. They felt guilty if they were not able to be home whenever their children were there. One woman said,

> When I was sick, my guilt hurt as bad as my illness as I lay in the hospital recuperating. I was sure my little ones at home were suffering miserably, not able to understand why I had abandoned them. Yet as I look back now, I realize that if my kids had been in good nurseries they would have had other models to relate to, both adults and children. They would have learned new ways of doing things and would not have become so set in some of the dysfunctional patterns that they learned in our home. They would have had some of their rough edges rubbed off in learning to get along with strangers. And they would have had fewer lessons to learn later.

Mothers feel particularly guilty when children are born with handicaps, as if this were a reflection of some flaw in themselves. They feel at fault when their children are sick; as if a good mother would have been able to prevent the invasion of germs, viruses, and disease! To add to their feeling of responsibility and guilt, they get little support or assistance when their children are ill. A father rarely sits up at night with a sick child. He is excused because he has to go to work the next day. It does not matter that mother's day will be busy too.

Mothers of sick children report receiving little support from their pediatricians either. Doctors often say that no one understands a youngster's illness like his or her mother, yet mothers find that most doctors disregard their concern when they try to report their observations about their children. They may be tagged as anxious, overly concerned, or neurotic. One of us remembers speaking to the pediatrician with alarm when her son was very ill. He said, "Oh, you bragging mothers; every one of you wants her child to be sicker than the next!"

The paradoxical guilt felt by mothers who come to therapy is often associated with ambivalent feelings about their children. Loving their children, they find their resentful and hateful feelings incompatible with their image of what a good mother should be.

Susan was pregnant when she got married and did not realize that her exasperation with her baby was actually displaced resentment toward her husband, to whom she could not express it directly. Before their marriage he had pressured her persistently to have sex with him, even though she had wanted to wait. Finally she had given in. Her pregnancy was both embarrassing and difficult for her. It was not the way she had wanted to start her married life.

For other clients, too, motherhood was accompanied by ambivalent feelings that included guilt. Nana could not accept her honest annoyance at having to lose sleep every night because of the constant demands of caring for her child who suffered from cystic fibrosis. She felt that since she had been given the child to raise, she should have no negative feelings about the task. Teddy blamed herself for occasionally getting angry and exploding at her children. She could not condone her behavior because it seemed incompatible with her love for them. She did not realize that love and anger are not mutually exclusive and that every parent blows up

at times. Nancy felt crushed because her child was re-
tarded and thought she must somehow have been to
blame. Her guilt made it hard for her to treat him with
the firmness he needed. Lucinda felt lacking because
she was unable to give her son all the things he
wanted. His demands intensified her feelings of inadequacy and triggered her depression, for which she
blamed herself.

All of these mothers needed to face and express the
understandable resentment they felt in order to accept
their feelings as reasonable responses to difficult situations. Airing them keeps the feelings from festering and
growing more unmanageable, as repressed emotions do.
These mothers learned in therapy not to judge themselves by how they *felt* about their children, but by
how they *acted* toward them. For them this was a big
step toward the resolution of paradoxical guilt.

Among our clients who suffer from the paradox of
guilt are mothers who are older than average when
their children are born. These mothers, who lack the
vitality that they see in young mothers, literally sabotage themselves by trying too hard. If their children
seem inadequate in any way or if they misbehave, older
mothers put themselves out to make up the deficiency,
then tend to feel guilty and helpless when nothing
works. They may feel sorry for their children and try
to still their feelings of guilt by overindulgence or permissiveness. Even when they know that it is irrational,
they still blame themselves for not being younger.

Mothers learn in therapy to explore the amount of
time and energy they have poured into feeling responsible and guilty about their children, draining themselves
while helping no one. They learn to appreciate themselves and take pleasure in the good things they have
done for and with their children. With a little help,
mothers can usually find more to feel good about than
they recognized at first. As therapists, we explain their
parenting behavior in terms of alternatives. Usually
they have acted as they did because they saw the
choices they made as the best under the circumstances.
Often they found no other alternatives to the courses
they followed.

Helping mothers to focus on searching for more creative alternatives to use in child-rearing is an exciting and rewarding experience, because they are eager learners. In our experience, mothers we have worked with were genuinely concerned about being good parents. Sometimes all they needed was a little support as they found the way.

Given the grave responsibility of their roles, some mothers find it difficult to let children grow without excessive attention. We tell parents that sometimes young people need just to loaf. At times it is okay for them to lie on their backs, perhaps to the consternation of overly eager parents, until they are ready to move. In fact, this is an important part of a child's growth, although it may be very different from what a parent thinks a youngster should be doing. Too many mothers worry if their children are not always doing something constructive. We tell such mothers to trust their children's internal clocks. Suzy or Johnny may need to go to her or his room and close the door to shut out the noise, for reasons known only to the child. This does not mean that he or she is meditating about some horrible problem or is distressed and unhappy, nor that he or she will be forever without friends. The child may be gathering resources to use later to move in self-directed ways.

We urge mothers to take the details of their parenting responsibilities less seriously. Children should be encouraged to take charge of their own lives as much as is appropriate for their age. They need to see themselves as increasingly responsible for their own growth and direction. They need to make some mistakes and learn from them. Since a mother does not have the power to make a child self-directed, once she has served as a model and provided guidelines and support she has done her job and should step aside. This is the best way to deal with the paradox of guilt created by the mothering role.

When Isabel, the mother of a large family, came to therapy, she did not think this was possible. She could not stand herself for what she was doing to her children, but neither could she stand what they were doing

216

to her. As she said, "We can't go on. I wanted these kids, and now I can't stand them. They scream and yell at me all day, and I do the same thing. I feel that they are demanding the last pound of my flesh, and yet I never feel that I do enough for them."

Isabel had tried diligently to prevent her children from making mistakes and had carefully supervised everything from cutting out paper dolls to writing term papers. When she learned in therapy that this was preventing them from growing by stretching against their limitations, she began teaching them about responsibility and the power to exercise it. She started by giving them a small weekly allowance. At first it hurt her to see them spend it all the first or second day and feel deprived and unhappy the rest of the week. As time went on, she saw that they learned to plan ahead to make better use of their money.

She also bought alarm clocks for her older children so they could be responsible for getting up and getting to school on time. She no longer was in charge of their schedules. If their plans interfered with meals at home, it became their job to fix something for themselves to eat. She no longer feared instant malnutrition if they did not eat the balanced diet she provided at mealtimes.

Best of all, freed of responsibility for the myriad details of her children's lives, Isabel was able to listen to their disappointments and failures with an open, understanding ear. Since she did not feel guilty when they had unhappy experiences for which she was not accountable, she had a clear mind and could offer them support and encouragement without being overly involved emotionally. Previously, when she had felt responsible for their happiness, she had become distressed whenever they were hurt or unhappy. She felt angry for them, and sided with them, blaming others with whom they had difficulties. Her reactions had not taught them anything about handling problems, which everyone must expect in life. Her new behavior resolved the paradox of guilt for her, while it encouraged their sense of effectiveness and self-worth.

"Even when they're grown. . . ."

One of the unfortunate things that happens when women have assumed responsibility for the well-being of their families is that the duty becomes an ingrained habit. It is painfully hard, then, to stop feeling responsible when the children are grown. Such mothers worry about things over which they have no control in their adult children's lives. Decisions concerning marriage, children, education, jobs, religion, divorce, and finances are best made by adults for themselves. Often their mother's opinions about difficult choices are neither sought nor welcome. Yet mothers, recognizing their helplessness in dilemmas, are plagued by the distress they see their children endure. It is a devastating feeling, one of the harsher sentences of the paradox of guilt.

While her youngsters were growing, Jeannie, the mother of two daughters and a son, knew that she had few rights in her family, but she felt responsible for the welfare of the children and felt guilty when they suffered. Her husband George had been a harsh taskmaster, and Jeannie often had found herself standing between him and the children. He had given the orders; Jeannie had been responsible for seeing that they were carried out. Unable to modify George's demands, Jeannie's concern grew. And it stayed with her; she still worried about her children's well-being even after they were grown and no longer in the house. She came for therapy because she felt so bad that they were "making a mess of their lives."

It shocked Jeannie when she discovered in therapy that her tears for her grown children reflected the feelings of helplessness and guilt she had experienced when they were little, and that she was no longer responsible for smoothing out their lives for them. She had felt protective and sorry for them as youngsters when she saw her tyrannical husband's effect upon them. They had become withdrawn and timid and seemed to miss out on the good times of childhood. She had felt closer to them as her pity for them grew.

She still felt the same way, even though they were now adults.

In most homes the emotional tie between a woman and her family would have lessened as the children grew and assumed more and more responsibilities for themselves. But Jeannie saw her children as unprepared for adulthood and was still trying to do the things that she hoped would make their lives better. Like many other mothers Jeannie felt responsible for her grown children because she believed she had failed them when they were young.

Women often feel guilty when they have to compromise between what they would ideally like to be and what reality has dictated that they are. They harbor the notion that a woman should be able to rise above her human frailties and somehow achieve an impossible ideal. Our aim with women who are struggling in this way with the paradox of guilt is to encourage them to stop blaming themselves and to help them find a way out of their dilemma. For most women, this means moving out of a nonassertive position in which they try to avoid conflict and moving into a position of self-assertiveness, where they can express their feelings and act upon their rights while feeling comfortable doing so. It includes recognizing that much of the guilt women feel has been dumped on them by people who have something to gain when women feel guilty.

The paradox of guilt can be resolved by a direct, positive, and strong approach. Its solution involves learning to handle one's own business and developing a healthy detachment from everyone else's. This means refusing to accept responsibility for a burden that should rightfully be shouldered by someone else and refusing to accept blame for situations where one has no power to control events.

CHAPTER X

Myths

> *"I lose, especially when I win."*

Unrealistic hope has set the stage for women's disillusionment. Because they have believed many romantic notions about fairy-tale futures, women have given up aspirations and achievement goals that could provide real success. They have designed their lives to fit a mythical model in which Prince Charming and Cinderella live happily ever after. The paradox is that they lose even when they win; there is no way that achieving a goal based on fantasy and myth can result in a satisfying reality.

There is a children's ditty that goes, "If wishes were fishes, we'd have some fried; if wishes were horses, we'd all take a ride." It is implied in these lines that it is futile to waste our time wishing and that reality does not always accommodate our dreams. Throughout history, however, humankind has tried to alleviate the pain of reality and to explain the mysteries of the world in ways that would be emotionally satisfying and provide a guide for action. At times, logic and reason have been pushed aside and myths have been developed. The early classic myths of the Greeks and Romans were used to explain how the world began, what caused crops to grow, why the rain fell, and how the sun rose and set. Providing a framework for understanding the mysterious, these myths also supplied directions for action to avoid disaster.

Modern-day myths are the fantasies that fool us into thinking life is different than it really is. These myths become paradoxes for women when actions are based upon them, rather than upon reality.

For women, most paradoxical myths are related to affiliative relationships. Those considered in this chapter fall into four categories. First, myths that fulfill the longings in our hearts and say that things *are* the way we would *like them to be*. For women, paradoxical myths in this category replace reality with fanciful dreams that promise lifetimes of happiness in rewarding relationships. These include "Someday my prince will come"; "I don't have to prepare for my future"; and "After we are married, everything will be fine."

The second category contains myths that give easy explanations for complicated things. These are paradoxes that sound plausible, but are not based on facts. For women, the paradox arises because simple explanations of complex issues encourage them to distort their relationships with others and to deny their rights. They suggest that "Women are to be both idealized and feared"; "Women like a subordinate role"; and "Women must be mothers in order to be complete."

The third category includes myths that tell women how to behave. Paradoxically, when myths provide injunctions for women to follow, they serve the purposes of others and enhance them rather than ourselves. For women, behaving as one has been told usually means acting subservient to men and children. For instance, these myths say, "I see it the way I need to"; "Males are superior to females"; "Men are naturally more aggressive sexually than women"; and "Good mothers put children first."

The final category consists of myths that keep women from changing and growing. They lock women into the stereotypes of our culture with high-sounding but paradoxical phrases that have passed for truth, but are not true to women's experiences. Among them are phrases like "Complementary is equal"; "I will never be lonely again"; "It's a woman's nature"; and "Women are lucky."

For women, the paradox of myths is that they promise happiness, but the promises cannot be fulfilled. If women fashion their lives according to myths, they find, even when they achieve their dreams, that their cups are not brimful and running over; they are, rather, sieve-bottomed and empty. Women lose *especially* when they win.

"Someday my prince will come."

The single most frequent complaint we hear from married women in therapy is that they are disappointed in their marriages. If married life were only like the fantasy that entices young women to the altar, we would see fewer women in therapy distressed and bewildered when their love story becomes a charade. If every woman were a Cinderella and there were a real Prince Charming for every maiden, then the fairy tale would come true. Prince Charming would provide everlasting happiness along with his love and protection. The expectation that the two of them will get married and live happily ever after would not be such a fraudulent promise.

A trouble-free, blissful married life is what young girls expect. Experiencing the paradox of equality as they grow up invites a young woman to yearn for and expect to enjoy a passive role, dominated by a strong and fault-free husband who will anticipate her wishes, meet her needs, and provide a storybook future. Nursery tales, books, the media, friends, and family all emphasize the glory of romantic love and its culmination, of course, in marriage. Generally young girls are not told that marriage is serious business and that, in addition to love, it takes all the help that preparation, maturity, and realistic expectations can provide to make marriage mutually and permanently rewarding.

Although the fantasy of living happily ever after fulfills women's longing for beautiful lives, it does not measure up to reality. Most women marry and are bitterly disappointed when, just beyond the gates of wedlock, anticipations chafe against reality. They come eventually to therapy, either blaming themselves for failing or not yet recognizing the myth in which they are entangled. At that point they are often hoping to get out of their present marriage only to find another dream relationship with a new Prince Charming who will not let them down as the first one did.

Mary Jane is a good example. Her whole girlhood seemed to have been an odyssey of dreams moving her inexorably toward her wedding day. Finally, she found her prince. He was tall, handsome, affectionate, attentive, lots of fun, and had a promising future. Her parents, too, approved of him and entered enthusiastically into her wedding plans. She had dreamed since she had been a little girl of a white wedding gown, of sharing her happy planning with her bridesmaids, of all the other preparations for a big wedding, and of walking down a long aisle to meet her groom. Since she was the only daughter in the family, no effort or expense was spared to see that the celebration was impressive.

After twelve years of marriage, Mary Jane came for therapy; the dream had become a nightmare. She knew something was wrong, but she blamed herself for having failed, rather than seeing that she was the victim of the paradox of myths. She sought therapy thinking she wanted a divorce. Her ardent love for her husband had cooled and she grieved for the "wasted years" she had invested in her marriage. She felt guilty, believing that divorce would blight her children's lives.

Nothing in Mary Jane and Nick's married life had measured up to her expectations. Sex had not been especially rewarding, even from the first. As time went on, it became an increasingly unwelcome chore. Nick was no longer the validating, chivalrous partner of their courting days. He became critical and demanded that she carry out her role as he would like it done. Among other things, he expected her to answer to him for all the money she spent. He objected if she "neglected" the housework to do other things she thought were important. He dealt with the frustrations of his job by controlling his temper until he got home and then unleashing his anger on Mary Jane, the children, and even the pets.

In addition to her lack of harmony with Nick, Mary Jane had found that raising children, even though she loved them, was a lonesome chore without another adult as a cushion of comfort. The fantasy children she had looked forward to were far different from the real ones she bore and had to nurture. These got sick just as she was preparing for a long-awaited night out. They threw up at the wrong times in the wrong places. They had temper tantrums that she felt unprepared to handle. And they talked and talked and talked when all she wanted was a few minutes of quiet.

To top off Mary Jane's unhappiness, the old ambition she once had to finish college and work as an urban planner began to surface again. She thought longingly of the pleasure it would be to have a job where she could be with adults all day and busy herself with exciting projects without being criticized for neglecting her housework. The possibility of realizing this dream seemed hopelessly remote to Mary Jane, locked as she was into her role at home. It would require several more years of school, and that seemed impossible. Nick would object, and she would feel guilty leaving the children.

When she came to therapy, Mary Jane felt bitter, trapped, and helpless. She was also confused; she knew she could not go on as she was, but she did not see any acceptable alternative. She was experiencing one of the worst effects of mythical thinking: Her myth had become an imperative and had made her believe that she could not change.

It was necessary for Mary Jane to deal with several important issues in therapy in order to clarify her mythical thinking. First, she had to rid herself of the shame and guilt that made her feel she had spoiled her dream. She had to see that she was a victim who had accepted the unrealistic expectation that she would live happily ever after. She had been brought up to expect that once her world revolved around a man she would be magically taken care of. She needed to see that she had put aside, in favor of a traditional role, ambitions that could have given her a sense of self-esteem and autonomy, and that she could have combined these ambitions with the role of wife and mother.

Mary Jane had been cheated by a myth. The marriage she had looked forward to was a *fantasy*; the one she was in was *real*. Even the best of marriages would never have fit the unrealistic hopes she had. A wedding is not an event up to which everything leads and from which follows unending bliss. A wedding is only one step in a long process through which two people work to develop a mutually rewarding alliance.

There was no rapid cure for the disillusionment Mary Jane felt; all women are victimized by the same messages she had received. It was helpful for her to understand the different emotional socialization men and women undergo, which does not prepare them to live harmoniously together. Men have been taught that their feelings are not an adequate guide to action; women have been taught that the rewards of an intimate relationship are essentially emotional. No wonder problems arise when women and men, who are raised so differently, are joined together in marriage. They are not prepared for each other's diversity; it takes more than the illusion of a myth to resolve dissimilarities. And to divorce one husband in the expectation that a *real* Prince Charming awaits her only perpetuates a woman's distress.

Mary Jane might have avoided disillusionment if she and Nick had viewed marriage realistically before they got married. They could have identified what each wanted from the other, compromised when necessary, and accommodated the needs of both. There would have been no myth involved. They would have been prepared for the pinch of reality.

Mary Jane reacted with disbelief when her therapist suggested that she might have many loving feelings for Nick that had been held down over the years by the unexpressed feelings of anger she felt too guilty or too frightened to let come to the surface. Perhaps she would, after discharging the hurt and anger accumulated during the years of disillusionment, determine that there was nothing worth reestablishing in the relationship. Or perhaps, once the anger was gone, she would feel free to express her needs and reestablish her relationship with Nick on a new basis, one in which she was not submissive and he was not dominant. Along the way, she would have to learn how to resolve the many paradoxes from which she had suffered. After

225

doing so, if she decided upon a divorce, she would have rejected illusory thinking and would have a realistic picture of her future without her husband, along with new skills to help her cope in an admittedly difficult life. If she decided to stay married, she could negotiate openly with Nick, express all her feelings, and build on positive qualities that could enhance their future life together. Such a realistic approach would provide a way to resolve the Cinderella myth and replace fantasy with reality.

"I don't have to prepare for my future."

When marriage is seen as the primary goal in a woman's life, and when it is not viewed realistically, women focus on the event of getting married. They tend to neglect the development of outstanding talents that could provide both emotional and financial rewards whether they are married or not.

Many of our clients are women of great ability who have put aside opportunities for personal growth and public acclaim because the myth says you do not need skills to have a good life. In their youth, they labored under the illusion that all they needed was to grow up and stay marriageable, so that when the right man came along they would luck into a lifetime identity, basking in the rays of someone else's sun. Knowing that intellectual or artistic excellence might cost them social acceptability, they willingly sacrificed all other achievements and concentrated on developing affiliative attachments. This myth eventually exacted a tremendous price when, after their affiliative relationships failed, they found that they had developed no other talents upon which they could now rely.

Phyllis was a young woman who had exceptional artistic ability and received a great deal of recognition of her talent as a child. Yet she never considered art as a career. She did, however, dream of being a mother. Her marriage at eighteen produced two children and a progressively miserable life with her husband. At twenty-three, she found herself divorced, responsible for two children, lacking in salable skills, and sitting in a therapist's office trying to put together a sensible plan for her future. At that point, she had no time or money to develop her artistic talent. She was pressed by the needs of her growing family; her child-support payments were irregular, and she was employed full time on an assembly line. She was on a dead-end path with no comfort along the way.

When she came for therapy, she was withdrawn, afraid of people, disillusioned, overworked, and discouraged about her future. In therapy, she came to realize that the reactions she was experiencing could be expected in her situation. Like most women, she tended to blame herself for feeling bad, rather than seeing her feelings as normal reactions to destructive circumstances. For Phyllis, like *was* tough. Her dreams had been as hollow and as fragile as balloons. She felt bitter because she had unused talents that she now had no chance to develop. She saw belatedly that, while she was growing up and looking forward to being married, she could have been preparing for other fulfilling realities in life. Homemaking could have been only one role in her repertoire. She could have prepared herself to fill many roles had she not been deluded by mythical thinking.

After dealing with her regrets about the past, Phyllis was ready to work toward her future. She had two-thirds of her life left to live, and she could make plans to enjoy what she presently had in her life with her children while taking positive steps toward becoming an artist. At first, little steps were short-range goals, which rewarded her along the way to her long-range goal. When her children no longer needed so much of her time and effort, she could devote full time to the study of art. It would be a long time before her career was launched. Phyllis knew the sadness of having believed a myth that promised to fulfill the longings of her heart.

"After we are married, everything will be fine."

When Sharla came for therapy, she had been married only two years and her dreams were already tarnished with bitterness, loneliness, and unhappiness. Sharla and Floyd had married in their teens. They had been happy together in high school, sharing teenage experiences, most of which involved having fun together. Their innocent illusion was that marriage would only increase their joy. When it came to the day-to-day experiences of role-filling, however, they found themselves surprised and disillusioned.

Their first child was born within a year of their wedding, and Sharla knew little about either child care or homemaking. The unfamiliar tasks seemed to her repetitious and boring. She was not used to being without the stimulation of friends her own age. Needing emotional support, she waited eagerly for Floyd to come home at night to provide the companionship and love she craved. It was also hard to do without the comforts she had in her parents' home, where money had always been plentiful. On Floyd's salary they felt fortunate if there was enough money left after the bills were paid to buy ice-cream cones for a weekly treat.

They had not realized, either, that Floyd would be under a great deal of pressure in his first full-time job. He felt he had to do his best so he could advance and earn more money. When he came home at night, what he wanted was relief from the emotional strain of the day. He saw home as a place where he could have time to recoup his strength in order to face the challenges of the working world.

Sharla and Floyd had sidestepped all conflicts before they were married. Not wanting to risk losing their closeness, they had avoided facing any realities that might have caused difficulty, but would also have given them experience in resolving differences of opinion. Their mutual myth said, "After we are married, everything will be fine." Thus reassured that they had nothing to worry about beforehand, they reinforced themselves with another myth: "Our love is so powerful that it can overcome anything." Such mythical thinking denied the need to be realistic, to communicate negative thoughts and feelings, to identify and work out problems, to compromise and negotiate differences. When down-to-earth married life faced them with daily bumps and bruises, the paradox of the myth became apparent. They had tried to build a marriage on a cherished illusion, and now they had a few resources or strengths on which to build their relationship.

"Women are to be both idealized and feared."

Another function of paradoxical myths in women's lives is to explain things that are not easily understood. If a woman accepts mythical explanations, they become her beliefs and her actions are influenced by them. Since myths are fanciful and not bound by fact, however, they explain things in ways that are costly and confusing to women.

Among the myths that have influenced society's thinking is one that suggests that women are to be both idealized and feared, that they must be protected for their own and others' welfare. This myth was born in primitive times in response to women's mysterious reproductive capacities. In accordance with the myth, women were assigned a special protected place. This myth has carried into today's world, but being protected makes many women feel fenced in and presents insurmountable barriers to the development of self-oriented capacities.

Rita found this to be true when she applied for graduate school in physics. She knew she had as much ability as the male applicants, yet she was treated as if she were different from them. She was interviewed three times, whereas they were accepted or rejected after one interview. She was offended by the questions asked, which were variations on the theme, "What is a pretty girl like you taking a career seriously for?" Didn't she intend to marry and have children? Did she believe she could work in a male-dominated field without her sex being an issue? Did she believe a mother could do justice to her children and a job, too? Did she think she could contribute as much to science as could a male who would surely work for the rest of his life? After all, graduate school slots were scarce and they should not be wasted!

Although the questions were couched as concern for

her welfare, Rita resented the implication that she needed this solicitude. She knew the interviewers had no right to ask such questions; all the same, her fenced-in feeling kept her from confronting her questioners. She did want to get into school and did not want to antagonize the people who had the power to approve or deny her application. She resented their using the myth that she needed a protected place, but she was in no position to challenge it.

"Women like a subordinate role."

Another myth that explains things that are not easy to understand reflects how often myths ignore facts. Both women and men's thinking have been greatly influenced by the myth that women really like being socially subordinate to men, that there are more rewards in submission than in autonomy. This is an oversimplification and a generalization that does not fit most women's experiences. Clients who believe the myth that women are supposed to be subordinate have been socialized to believe it. Sophia did and acted accordingly until her experience showed her how false it was.

Sophia had taken a backseat to her brother when they were growing up. He went to college; she became a secretary and never questioned the injustice that her brother, as a surgeon, earned ten times as much as she did. After she married, her husband made the decisions; she deferred to him. She did not question this, either. She had a problem shared with many of the women we have discussed in previous paradoxes: she really felt inferior. She had never questioned her submissive role in which devotion to duty meant deferring to men.

When Sophia came for therapy, the bubble of female submissiveness had burst in the face of reality. Her husband had become ill, and she had to support the family. She could not earn half what her husband had when he was well. Her work days were longer than his had been, and she still went home to broom, mop, and bucket. Sophia was bitter that her years of submissiveness had left her unprepared for the leadership role she had to assume. No, she did not enjoy being subordinate at all!

The myth that women like subordination puts them into a double-bind when they have thrust upon them responsibilities that push them into working in a "man's world," whether they like to or not. It is often suggested that they will lose their femininity if they no longer use charm, manipulation, and persuasion to get along; yet if they do use these methods to succeed, they are accused of using feminine wiles instead of competing with men on an equal basis.

Twila, a young attorney, had gone to law school after a disastrous early marriage in which she learned how unpleasant it was for her to wheedle, flatter, and cajole her husband, hoping to nudge him toward treating her with equality and mutuality. After her divorce she accepted the responsibility of supporting herself and her young daughter and expected fair consideration in the business world. Her forthright expectations were naively unrealistic. She did not receive the same treatment as her male colleagues. The sexual innuendos made to her and the unchallenging assignments she regularly received seemed messages that she was treated differently because she was a woman. She was asked to serve the refreshments at a case conference. She was assigned family cases since, her employers believed, a woman would best know how to handle them. She was not chosen to handle a particular important case because it required a strong, hard-driving approach and it was believed that she would not look feminine handling it. Twila knew that she did not like being subordinate. Her problem was how to challenge the myth and how to convince others that it was not true.

"Women must be mothers in order to be complete."

Another explanatory myth that women find does not fit their experience is the one that says women can achieve wholeness only through the joys of child-raising. This myth has so permeated the fabric of our cul-

231

ture that many women are ashamed to admit that instead of feeling whole they feel fragmented by always being home with their children. And women who choose not to have any children know that they run the risk of being considered "abnormal."

When Natalie went back to school and left her two young children in a day-care center three mornings a week, she sensed the displeasure of her neighbors and her parents. The neighbors missed no opportunity to impress upon her the joys they experienced with their children, while grandma and grandpa brought the children presents, since "mother is away so much." The guilt-inducing messages worked, and Natalie felt frustrated; she knew she needed to move beyond the motherhood-is-all phase, but it was hard going with all that criticism.

One day in therapy she said angrily, "What's the matter with me? I'm blaming myself as if I were out gambling or carousing and neglecting my children, instead of doing something to make myself a better person, so we will all benefit. It isn't that I don't love them, but they don't need my constant attention, and school puts me in the adult world where I am stimulated intellectually. I want to get over feeling that I have no right to do things for myself." Plainly, the myth that she would be totally fulfilled by her children did not fit Natalie's experience.

It did not fit for Maura either. One of her big concerns in therapy was the way other people reacted to her decision not to have children. She knew she did not want a family, but felt constrained to keep this information to herself. Although she knew it was no one else's business, she had seen the look of disbelief on too many faces when she discussed her decision. It was as if her not wanting a family branded her as abnormal. She stopped explaining to people that she believed it was better for her not to have children than to have them to prove to others that she was "normal."

"I see it the way I need to."

The third function of myths, to tell us how to behave, works by defining rigid roles for both males and females. These stereotyped roles defy logical reasoning but invite strong emotional attachment. These myths provide imperatives for women, starting with the assumption that they should be submissive helpmates to men.

Gaining the courage to break out of a prescribed role is often the most difficult task a woman accomplishes in therapy. Once a woman accepts that things should be a certain way and weaves the myth into the fabric of her life, it may be necessary for her to deny obvious realities and substitute illusion to keep the fantasy alive. She may go through life seeing other people the way she needs to, rather than seeing them as they are. As she lives out the myth, her investment in it grows with the years, compounding the dysfunction in her relationships.

Paula had needed to see her husband as a leader and herself as a follower in order to fulfill her image of a good wife. She was thirty-two and had been married for nine years when she came for therapy. She could not say to herself or to her therapist that for the past seven years she had been struggling to be subordinate to her husband Jim in a business in which she was more competent than he. Because it was important to her to let Jim stay at least one step ahead of her, she had stifled her talent, creativity, and imagination, and taken care to walk in his shadow. It had finally caught up with her. She had started shaking so badly she could hardly work, and she did not know how to explain her anxiety.

Paula worked eight to twelve hours daily in their printing business. She had learned subtle ways not to outshine Jim; she proposed ideas that he could then believe were his own; she thought up new promotions and stood back while he presented them less well than she would have; she deferred to him as the owner of the business, although she was his partner. She told herself that her role was to be a helpmate.

Jim worked hard, but he lacked the imagination and drive that Paula possessed. She tried not to notice when he made remarks that showed he resented her competence. Not a decision-maker, he agonized over questions Paula would have decided quickly. But she held back. Both Jim and Paula thought it appropriate for him to be the boss.

In trying to live a role that did not fit her, Paula had been denying her own spontaneity. This led to the frustration she felt. She had been bound by the prescription of dominant male and subordinate female roles for all husbands and wives. In order to follow it Paula had denied her competence and restructured reality until she saw it the way she needed to. Since Jim had also accepted the myth of his superiority, his self-image was protected when he saw Paula as a follower. It was necessary for Paula to discover in therapy that it was okay for her to be competent, capable, and ambitious, to have goals of her own, and to make decisions herself. She was, in fact, patronizing Jim when she played down her own excellence.

In therapy Paula was able to admit that her creative, leadership, and executive capacities were superior to Jim's. She did not need to feel guilty about this, and neither did he. In trying to deny it, she had cheated herself out of actualizing much of her finest potential, and Jim had missed the pleasures that come from relating to a whole, spontaneous, capable person. Once she accepted this she could stop seeing him the way she needed to in order to maintain a stereotype.

With some therapeutic support and an opportunity to explore her motives, Paula was able to accept both herself and Jim as they really were. She and Jim did not have to work together. She could cast her own shadow. She went into a totally different field in which she could excel independently of Jim. As she experienced competence there, she gained a sound base on which to improve their marriage. Both Paula and Jim learned to become partners in the true sense of the word. They supported each other as equals in their personal endeavors. They came to appreciate their individual successes without either having to assume an inferior position. They demythologized their role relationships. They recognized that in advancing their own development they in no way limited each other's capacities. They also worked toward creating a rewarding personal relationship in which individual differences were seen as good and appropriate; stereotypes were no longer needed as definitions for how each of them should be.

"Males are superior to females."

The myth of male superiority (and female inferiority) is so pervasive that, until recent years, it was rarely questioned, even by women. Socially, politically, and economically, women stayed dutifully in their "rightful place," a few steps behind men. Current challenges by the women's movement have brought into focus the fallacy of this myth, but they have not eradicated it from people's thoughts. No matter what women do, they face a prejudgment of inferiority that is as subtle and pervasive as the air we breathe. This paradoxical myth cheats women in two ways. First, it keeps them from taking their place beside men as equals, and second, it encourages women to treat each other with less respect than they show men.

How many women would choose a woman doctor in preference to a male one? There is a deep-seated reluctance to trust one's life to a woman. It is not that women necessarily like male doctors better (frequently they do not), but they believe that men are more competent than women. Anyone who questions this should ask several women how they would select a doctor if they needed one while vacationing in a strange town. Would they pick a male or female doctor's name from the telephone book? If a woman doctor were recommended to them, would they question her credentials more than they might question a man's?

Myths die hard, and the myth of male superiority follows most professional women. No wonder female lawyers, dentists, and accountants have remarked that they will be happy to see the day when a competent woman can expect to be as successful professionally as a competent man. Based upon their experiences, some have added, "I'd also like to see mediocre women get as far in this world as mediocre men do."

235

Among the women we see in therapy, many are more intelligent than their husbands. Some are more logical, some make better business decisions, and some have greater common sense than the men they defer to. Women find themselves totally frustrated when they try to live the myth that men, being "superior" to women, are also the smart ones.

As Wilma said, "My husband has been gaining status, achieving success, and earning financial security while I have been seen as trivial. He has the impression that I spend my days sitting at home, eating chocolates, wasting time in coffee klatches, and having unlimited freedom. I know his life isn't all two-martini lunches and I do appreciate his efforts, but I'd like a chance to use my intelligence as he does. I would gladly change places with him, letting him carry my baggage while I handle his; that is, if I could earn the same salary he does."

Wilma knew that the myth of male superiority makes role reversals in families next to impossible; only the brave attempt them, since few women can command a salary equal to a man's. No wonder we have so few househusbands and so many women who never get a chance to test their equality with men.

"Men are naturally more aggressive sexually than women."

In our culture, many women still accept the myth that men should be the aggressors sexually. This has resulted in a twofold problem. First, women have had to suppress their own sexuality, and second, this myth fosters the belief that a woman's role in sex is to respond and cooperate, regardless of her feelings, because sex has been viewed as a man's right and a woman's duty.

It is not an accident that women are usually reluctant to discuss their own sexual experiences and inclinations. The myth operates so effectively that women who enjoy their own sexuality and are sexually assertive often feel that there is something seriously unfeminine about their behavior The myth that the man should always be the aggressor serves to perpetuate the notion that whatever he does sexually is appropriate and should be satisfying to a woman. The anguish for a woman is that this thinking leaves her no recourse in an unsatisfactory sexual relationship.

Marian believed that Paul would bring to their first sexual encounter the information, skills, and techniques that would result in perfect sexual harmony. Unfortunately, sex with Paul was not the bell-ringing, cymbal-clashing experience that she had anticipated. In fact, it was a two-ton letdown. During their six years of marriage, her early disappointments did not go away. Sex became a burden for her and the source of many arguments between them. Marian fully believed, until she began therapy, that Paul was responsible for letting her down.

Neither Marian nor Paul had recognized the myth that underlay their attitudes toward sexual pleasure. He felt inadequate and frustrated because he saw it as his task to please her and he did not seem to be able to do so. She felt that it would be unfeminine of her to tell him what she might enjoy. On some level, she was saying to herself, "If he loves me, he should know what I want and I shouldn't have to ask." And on some level, he was saying to himself, "If she loved me, I'd be able to turn her on."

Marian did not see herself as responsible for her disappointment. Believing the myth relieved her of all responsibility for her sexual pleasure. The result was that both she and Paul were losers, a common experience when people behave as paradoxical myths tell them to.

"Good mothers put children first."

There are dozens of myths that prescribe how women should behave in relation to their children. They involve the shoulds and the should nots that keep mothers worried that they might be neglecting their children; in adopting these dictates the mothers cheat themselves of their own rights.

For example, Norma thought she should stay home and not seek outside work; her children "needed" her

237

and would suffer under anyone else's care. When she had to take an outside job after a divorce, she pushed herself to the breaking point at home to make up for her time away from them. Diane did not believe that she could let Billy make mistakes—wasn't he hers to protect and guide? She anxiously watched what he wore, ate, read, and whom he played with. Noreen felt guilty because she was often sick and had to ask her children to cooperate with meals and laundry, which she considered her job. If they were rebellious and disrespectful, she tolerated their rudeness because of her guilt. Susan limited her activities to those that did not conflict with her children's schedule. She was always available to mother them when they got home from school.

All these mothers suffered from mythical precepts based on the belief that children should be put first. Their lives were controlled by subservience to their children. We are not suggesting that children do not need their mothers, nor that children be put last in a woman's plans. In accepting the responsibility of having children, women make an important commitment. Nurturing children *is* important to a woman, and it is a source of many rewards. Fathers, too, are rewarded by and enjoy their children, but no one suggests that these satisfactions are sufficient to fill a father's lifetime. The conflict for women comes when they limit their own self-actualization because the myth says that in caring for themselves they are neglecting their children.

Ironically, having a mother who has adopted this myth does not work well for a child either. Anxiety, overprotection, and overindulgence are characteristic behaviors of mothers who take seriously the nonsense that children must always come first. Children who are overindulged and overprotected are not better persons nor more fulfilled ones; rather, they may well be on the way to acquiring emotional problems.

Mildred spoke from experience when she said, after several months in therapy,

If I could live my life over again, I would do things differently. I wouldn't be dependent upon my children in my old age. I'm sixty-seven years old now; my husband has been dead for seventeen years. I've spent those years living a few months with one of my children, then moving on to spend time with the next. They and my grandchildren are my whole life, but I am not that important to them. I know they have their own lives to live, but that doesn't make mine less lonely. All the time they were growing up, I put them first. It would have been better if I had thought more about making myself independent so I wouldn't have to rely upon them now. We'd all be happier.

Mildred's story could be repeated by thousands of women who did not realize that raising their children would take only the middle third of their lives. In becoming absorbed by their children's concerns, they neglected the chance to develop the resources they would need for the rest of their lives. A healthy response to the myth, "Good mothers put children first," would be, "Children grow up, and good mothers prepare themselves for that."

"Complementary is equal."

Myths exact their final toll from women when they keep them from changing and growing. Through the use of high-sounding but empty phrases, error is promoted as truth and women are urged to believe "facts" which are contrary to what they experience as true. These supposed facts imply that women have an ordained place in society that cannot be improved by change.

"Complementary is equal" becomes a paradoxical myth when a person is told that the inferior position she holds is, in fact, equal to a superior position someone else enjoys. In practice, it has been used to justify putting women in inferior positions, then telling them piously, "You have nothing to complain about; we are a team." Women consistently confront this myth in their interactions with men.

Among our clients are women who have cut their

239

own education short in order to provide support for a man while he finished his own training. They are victims of the myth that says a woman does not need to develop her own talents and job skills; in the terms of this myth, after her man is educated he will take care of both of them, and the equal relationship will continue as it was before.

The problem is that things rarely turn out that way. In many cases, as a man grows intellectually he sees his wife as standing still. He may eventually feel he has outgrown her. In spite of his previous good intentions, he no longer sees his wife as his equal and may find other women whom he admires as more stimulating, more interested in the things he has learned. He may think his wife does not fit in with his new friends; he may even come to feel ashamed of her. This is chilling news to a wife who has based so much of her commitment on her conviction that things would not change.

Thinking in mythical terms disguises the fact that women and men can expect to grow when they continue their education, and sometimes they grow apart. If only one member of the relationship has an opportunity for growth, there must be a concerted effort on the part of both to ensure that one is not sacrificed to the other's development. As therapists, we see evidence that today some couples are facing this challenge realistically. They recognize that both deserve an opportunity to develop their potential; they see to it that plans are based on fact and not illusion so that both are able to grow. This is still not the norm, however, and women who experience this paradox are lulled into positions of inequality and subservience for their future.

Rae faced such a decision early in her marriage. She was a promising dramatist who had earned a scholarship to pursue her studies. She was in love with Steve, who had been accepted for law school in Texas. As tempting as a career was, Rae wanted to marry more. In order to do so, one of them had to work. They agreed that Steve would go to school while Rae took a job. since his career as a lawyer promised them the good life they had dreamed of having together. By the time Steve got through with his education, Rae's plans were put off again because they both thought it was time to have a family.

When Rae came to therapy twenty years later, she looked back wistfully at the career she "might have had." Steve was highly successful in his demanding practice. His daily experiences revolved around people whom he found much more stimulating than Rae. His time alone with her was not very rewarding for either of them. Perhaps because of his success, he had begun to believe he knew better than she did about almost everything, and he acted out that belief. It was not uncommon for him to ridicule her opinions in front of friends and to insist upon the final word at home. There was no question that "complementary is equal" had meant for Rae a subtle coercion toward staleness and resignation.

It was so threatening for Rae to risk changing and to stand up to Steve that she stayed in therapy only long enough to identify her myth. She quit searching after a few sessions. Rather than challenge Steve's dominance and forge steps toward equality with him, she decided she would have to live with sadness and make the best of it. Her potential and capacities truly had been sacrificed in the service of the myth that partners will gain by focusing on the enhancement of only one of them.

Robin also told herself that by taking a complementary role she would always be seen as Larry's equal. Her situation was different from Rae's. She wanted a home and a family from the beginning of her marriage. They were both in their freshman year of college when they decided to get married. She was willing to wait a few years for children; she quit school and got a job as a secretary while Larry earned his accounting degree. Even after the babies came along, Robin continued to work because Larry wanted to complete a higher degree. Their first exciting years stretched into comfortable familiarity for Robin. She continued to see their marriage as a love affair. She thought they were as close as when they were first married.

The myth backfired when, after fifteen years, Larry told Robin that he was no longer interested in her, that she no longer fulfilled his need for intellectual and sexual stimulation. He had been having carefully concealed affairs with other women and wanted to be able to do so openly. He wanted a divorce. Too crushed to fight, Robin agreed.

When Robin came for therapy two years later, she had regained her balance and was struggling to reconcile herself to a life with pale hope. She was bumping along, handling the problems of raising four children, juggling a part-time job, and getting an education so she could begin her career. She knew that had she not interrupted her education to contribute to her husband's development, she would have been well established in the career she was yet to launch.

"I'll never be lonely again."

One of the satisfactions that socialization promises women is children, and one of the myths connected with motherhood claims that children will protect a woman from loneliness. If children are to be rewarding. one must have realistic expectations of them. There will be good times and bad, disappointments and rewards. Children do not automatically keep a woman from feeling lonely. They do not have the capacity to make up for gaps left from poor relationships with other people and unfulfilled ambitions of one's own. And motherhood is a job that women work themselves out of as their children grow.

Georgine, Theresa, and Stella each experienced this myth in a different way. For each of them the experience of motherhood was different than she had expected it would be.

Georgine, who had been lonely and unsure of herself as a child, looked forward to marriage primarily because she wanted children. She believed that motherhood would affirm her importance and give her life meaning. Secretly she expected that her child would be perfect. as she herself was not. and would shine brilliantly with accomplishments which Georgine had once dreamed of for herself. When her little girl was born, Georgine was unprepared for the overwhelming responsibilities and the demands of an active child. Having reached her lifelong goal of being a mother, she believed that she was supposed to be happy, yet she wasn't. She felt severely depressed when she came for therapy, bewildered because life was still so empty and her days were lonely. Georgine had not realized that a child does not make an adult completely happy, nor can a child be expected to fulfill the unrealized dreams of her parents.

Theresa, on the other hand, so completely believed that her little daughter Linda should fill her otherwise empty life that she overidentified with the child. Every detail of Linda's life had been of major importance to Theresa. Finally, when she was twelve, Linda rebelled. She wanted her own friends, she did not want to go anywhere with her mother, and she resented her mother's curiosity about her telephone conversations with friends. She expressed her rebelliousness so rudely that Theresa was often left in tears. She had never thought it could be so heartbreaking to love a child so much and to feel so rejected.

Stella, at sixty-three, had still not gotten over her disappointment that her daughter's husband did not care for his in-laws and insisted on living in a distant city. This made a close relationship between Stella and her daugher Karen very difficult. They saw each other only yearly and exchanged occasional letters. Stella lamented that she had never thought one could raise a daughter and receive so little pleasure from the relationship in one's lonely later years.

"It's a woman's nature."

Women's "nature" has been used as an excuse to keep women in the home, giving, satisfying, and sustaining family relationships, and to prevent women from making choices about their own lives, reproductivity, and personal goals. Taking the myth at face value suggests that a woman who has other goals than staying home and nurturing children is somehow going against nature. Such thinking excuses society for not making changes that would keep pace with the realities of women who can see themselves as equal to men, or women who must work outside their homes.

The word *nature* reflects the philosophical essence of a species; it is not a sex-linked quality. Therefore, nothing can accurately be described as a "woman's nature." All women and all men have the same nature since they all belong to the same species. It is the bastardization of the concept of *human* nature that has spawned the myth that there is such a thing as "woman's nature."

Whenever a woman hears, "It's a woman's nature," she can expect that the phrase will be followed by some remark intended to keep her subservient, and that someone else will gain by her servitude. Based flimsily on the fact that women conceive and bear children, the myth that women have a special nature programs them to care for children for the rest of their lives and to respond to all the nurturant demands of society. Women are to be other-directed caregivers, relating to the needs of others rather than to their own.

"Women are lucky."

Women are also told by another myth that is intended to keep them from changing that they are lucky to be women and that men don't have it so good. The women we know are not inclined to debate this issue. There *are* wonderful things about being women: yet the paradox arises when women are expected to accept injustices because it would be unseemly for anyone lucky enough to be a woman to complain.

Our clients have reported to us that they do not feel lucky as long as the following are true:

• Even when the law ensures that women will get equal pay for equal work, they cannot get those "equal" jobs. They fill the lower paid, less prestigious jobs in every field.

• Women who are employed earn only fifty-eight cents for every dollar earned by men.

• Day-care facilities for children of working mothers are inadequate, expensive, or even nonexistent.

244

● Women's illnesses are taken less seriously than men's; women are often labeled neurotic, given tranquilizers, or passed on to another practitioner.

● There is more money for research in almost every other area of health than there is in the area of women's reproductive systems.

● Women are still being told by their husbands that it is okay if they take an outside job as long as they do not neglect their duties at home.

● Men control government, business, education, and most of the money in this country, and they use their power in these areas to keep women from gaining equality with them.

● In many states women cannot even sell their own property without their husbands' consent.

● A divorced or single woman who is head of a household cannot get the same credit a man can, in spite of laws prohibiting discrimination.

● Women are left with the major personal and financial responsibility for children after a divorce, although their earning capacity is rarely equal to that of most fathers.

● Rape is the only crime of violence for which the victim is frequently put "on trial" in the courtroom and required to prove that she did not invite the crime.

This partial list can be supplemented by every woman who has been told that she is lucky to be a woman and that, if she were to strive to move into a position of equality with men, she would destroy her favored position.

In resolving the conflict that mythical thinking has caused in their lives, our clients are encouraged to examine carefully the paradoxical notions they have taken for granted and then acted upon. Are they truth or mythology? Myths collapse when challenged; it is when one believes them without question that they are perpetuated.

CHAPTER XI

Models

"My models are not to follow."

Modeling is a most influential source of a child's learning. Children learn to be like the significant adults whose behavior has impressed them. Lucky is the woman who has had positive models whom she admired in her early life and whom she wants to be like. The paradox is that many women grow up knowing that they do not want to be like the adults who were available as their models, yet they have no one else to emulate. As adults, women are burdened with the task of erasing their dysfunctional ways of behaving and developing positive patterns that will make life more rewarding.

Four of our young women clients, Lynn, Mandy, Marie, and Pearl, were discussing some common concerns. Lynn, who had come for therapy because she could not get along with coworkers, said,

We've been talking about how we grow up patterning our lives after the models who have influenced us. I realize now that my models are not to follow. Not wanting to be like them, I don't have any guidelines, and this is why I feel so adrift. I couldn't admire my mother; she was always so beaten down, complaining, and ineffective, and I was deathly afraid of my father. He was an angry, frightening man who was usually drunk and abusive. I never enjoyed school and had few friends. I remember as a little girl going alone to the ice pond and skating by myself; there was no one I wanted to be with. I grew up to be a loner and I've never learned how to get along with people. I feel adrift, washed around without being able to reach out and make contact with anyone. I'd like to change, but I don't know how.

"My models were not to follow, either," Mandy said, "but for me it was different." Mandy had come for therapy because she did not like herself. Fettered by her inner timidity, she sensed that the big things in life were eluding her while she was fretting about the small ones. "My parents were so concerned with me that they wouldn't let me make any mistakes. They fussed over every detail of my life. Even when I was in college they tried to insulate me by always jockeying me into needing them. I've grown up to be as anxious and troubled as they are. I still start and stop everything I do a dozen times. I know I'm stuck in a dead-end job because I don't take risks. So, although my models are not to follow, I've done so without wanting to. It's hard for me to change, too."

"I've had a different modeling problem," interjected Maria, who had described herself in early therapy sessions as angry at life and not knowing how to change.

The models that I admired and would have liked to follow were all men. I was always adventuresome, eager to embrace life in big chunks; I felt frustrated when I was held back from taking chances. I remember how I wanted to travel; it had been my dream to visit Morocco and wander around the country, mingling freely with the natives. I could have done it if I'd been a man, but it was unsafe for a woman to do that on her own. I let people talk me out of that dream. Even in thinking of a career, most of the things I wanted to do, like being a commercial airline pilot, were unheard of for women. I've been miserable knowing I couldn't follow the models I admired and hating the choices open to me.

"I've come to realize that my models were so perfect that they weren't to follow. either," said Pearl, whom

247

no one would have suspected of trying to be perfect. She was twenty-seven, with no life goals, little education, and a dissatisfaction with everything she tried.

Maybe if I hadn't felt so inadequate in relation to my parents and my older sister I wouldn't have rejected their way of life. I can remember as a little girl feeling ugly, tongue-tied, and awkward around my mother, whom everyone admired for her beauty and gracious hospitality. I never knew what to say when we had guests; I was sure she was ashamed of me. I also felt dumb because my report cards were never as good as those of my sister. Since it seemed impossible to be as good as a model mother and a smart sister, I gave up. Instead of trying to equal them, I stopped trying to achieve at all. That's why I'm so miserable today. I still feel inadequate and don't believe I can ever make up for the years I've wasted.

To these women can be added a long list of others whom we see in our practice, women whose models are not to follow. They have found that lacking good models accounts in great part for their feeling of being awash in a sea of indirection. Not having had an affinity with their models left in them a void, not knowing how to be as individuals and how to act in relation to others.

The models who influence a girl as she grows into womanhood include peers, siblings, teachers, and other adults whose impact shows up in the design of her adult behavior. Some are public models, only a part of whose lives are open to view. Movie stars, recording artists, and other heroines whom young women emulate are incomplete models. Their public image reveals only the part of them that their press agents promote. Other models for growing-up girls are their peers, who provide for most young people a stereotype of sameness rather than individuality. Many young women insist that they are expressing their individuality; instead they are carbon copies of their contemporaries. Older siblings are also models to be either admired or rejected. As a matter of fact, all women in all their roles show how girls can grow up to be. But for most women, the paradox of modeling can be traced to their interactions with their parents, which has consigned them to a limbo between never being finished and being finished the way they do not want to be. For that reason, we will look in this chapter at the way parents may be models not to follow.

The primary way that children learn is by imitating the behavior of their parents. (Small children are not even aware that other adults are different from their mothers and fathers.) They copy their parents, often without even realizing it. This was brought home when we were doing play therapy with children. In the playroom we had toy telephones. If, in their play, children used the telephones, they unconsciously modeled adult conversations. We could hear exactly how their mothers and fathers expressed themselves when we heard what the children said. They had learned their parents' speech patterns and imitated them perfectly. Unless something intervenes, children will be inclined to sound even more like their parents when they grow up.

"I seem to be like my mother."

For some women, the paradox of models is that, although they see the dysfunctionality in their mothers and fathers' lives and know that they do not want to live as their parents have, they still tend to become like them. It is difficult to shape new chips from old blocks.

That is what Lannie said when she sat weeping in therapy. "I feel so terrible. My mother was a bitter, nagging woman, and I'm afraid I'm becoming just like her. She blamed everyone else when she was disappointed, and I know I do the same thing. No one likes being with her anymore because she is so critical and unpleasant. I don't want to be that way. Yet no matter how hard I try to be more positive, I always backslide into those old negative patterns."

Lannie had been struggling in therapy for a long time to outwit the perversity of internalized parental patterns. In fact, neither of her parents had been posi-

tive models. Her father balanced her mother's critical-
ness by being passive. Lannie scorned him for that. She
could not remember a teacher she had admired nor an
adult friend who had influenced her enough to make
her believe that it was rewarding to approach the world
positively and accept setbacks with good humor.

For women who would like to be different from the
models who shaped the raw material of their formative
years it takes a great deal of work, thought, and support to resolve this paradox. It involves weeding out
well-established habits of dubious worth and replacing
them bit by bit with more functional ones. First, habits
that need changing must be identified. Next, gains that
come from maintaining those habits must be understood. Finally, new models must be found to use as
guides.

Ordinarily, a woman's most important model is her
mother, whether she sees her positively or negatively.
No matter how much a woman does or does not want
to grow up to be like her mother the gentle coaxing of
her mother's familiar ways influences her in the same
direction.

We do not want those of our readers who are mothers to feel guilty if they see themselves in some of the
examples we present. Most of the lovely qualities that
women have are attributed by them to the example of
their mothers. We have worked with many women who
have received the priceless treasure of their mothers'
love and are sufficiently inspired by their mothers' examples to want to identify with them. We are happy
for them and expect that they will pass these gifts on to
their daughters. However, women who have had poor
examples and whose lives reflect this find themselves
being poor models for their children. If you see parts
of yourself reflected in this chapter, you, too, are a victim of poor modeling, and probably your mother was
as well.

We have much empathy for mothers who have been
a disappointment to daughters in their uncertain path of
development. Although those daughters who have been
hurt by the relationship may not agree, we know that it
has not been easy for their mothers, either. They, too,

did not have good models from whom to gain the assurance and serenity needed to be the parents of daughters who would want to take the measure of their mothers' molds and fill them. Many mothers who are inadequate models also suffer from the paradox of guilt. Although they had no skill, resources, or power to prevent the repetition of unsuccessful patterns in their children, logic cannot quell a mother's sense of responsibility for what happens to her daughter. The paradox of modeling is then repeated in succeeding generations. Our hope is that by focusing on the destructiveness of the paradox women will learn ways to break the downward spiral wherever it is recognized; future generations of women will then have at least one fewer paradox with which to cope.

As young girls grow up, they tend to see their mothers in one of two ways: as the kind of person they can identify with and would be pleased to follow, or as a woman they dislike and never want to resemble. If a girl likes her mother the way she is, she is likely to identify with her and learn to do things and relate to people as her mother does. She grows up feeling comfortable with herself as a woman. She feels confident in her mother's love for her and her love for her mother. But whatever a daughter's feelings about her mother, she is apt to adopt more of her mother's characteristics than she realizes.

Some daughters see so many flaws in their mothers that they do not want to be like them at all. Yet, ironically, they pick up the very characteristics they dislike. This is how it was for Susan. She described her mother as chronically emotionally crippled. Married to a domineering man who needed to control his wife and children, Susan's mother was not allowed to assume an adult role. Decisions about herself, the children, and all family affairs were made without benefit of her opinions or in spite of them. Nursemaids took care of the children, disciplined them, and discouraged them from looking to their mother for anything. Important decisions were made by Susan's father. If her mother was unhappy with the way things went, her complaints were not taken seriously. Susan's mother became increasingly depressed and physically ill when she became aware that she could affect only the trivialities of her life.

Susan saw her mother as literally lacking in any redeeming qualities. She knew she did not want to suffer from the same "sour-personality disease." The tragedy was that in not having any other mother model to follow, Susan had inadvertently become very much like the woman she disliked. When this possibility was suggested to her in therapy, she vigorously denied it. Yet, what else could explain that she had accepted her father's domination just as her mother had? She felt powerless in most areas of her life, and her behavior was characterized by complaints about everything she was unhappy with. She bumped along in ruts rather than searching for ways to correct situations she did not like.

Susan did not see that her married life was very different from what her mother's had been and that different behavior on her part might bring rewarding results. She had a loving husband who urged her to come for therapy because no matter what he did she was critical and complaining. In therapy Susan was shown that she typically reacted as her mother had, even when the situation was quite different. Her daily catharsis of complaining had her mother's stamp on it. Feeling self-righteous, Susan did not recognize how out of place her reactions were. She did not know how to change, since she had never known a mother who was different and she had no other models to follow.

When her therapist was able to show Susan how she was the victim of a paradox, her resistance weakened. She could look more objectively at herself, safe in the assurance that she was not to blame for her shortcomings. She could, in time, shed the life sentence by which she was condemned to mirror her mother's model, and could carve out an identity from her own raw material.

"Even a good model can be bad."

At other times, seeing her mother as a perfect model can produce a paradox of modeling for a woman. A young girl who sees her mother as a perfectly finished woman, full-blown in her perfection, unrealistically assumes that she, too, should be faultless. She cannot expose her feelings or inadequacy or her mistakes to a mother who seems to be without fault. Striving to copy her model, she sets goals for herself that elude accomplishment. As she is faced with her own limitations, she either gives up or tries too hard. In either event she feels that she falls short of her mother's example and is inadequate.

That is the irony of the paradox of modeling. Although a "perfect" mother could expect to inspire her daughter by her example, her excellence may, in fact, frighten her daughter away from trying. How many daughters have felt more adequate when their mothers were not around? How many daughters stood back, assuming failure in advance, waiting for their mothers to show them the way to do things?

Pat was a young woman who had wanted to be like her mother, but considered that she had failed. She saw her mother as the nicest person in her life. Pat remembered her mother as loving and happy, with a good sense of humor and an ability to be serene even in trying times. Pat hoped to grow up and be just like her, to have her children love her as Pat had loved her mother.

Pat put her mother on a pedestal. From her own vantage point she failed to see that her mother was human, had faults, and made mistakes. It was not until Pat was an adult in therapy that she realized that her mother kept a careful lid on her own can of worms. Pat had always believed that she had to be perfect to be worthy of a mother of such illusory perfection. When she looked back as an adult, she saw belatedly that her mother had not demanded perfection of her; the pressures came from her own internalized standards.

In trying to make her mother proud of her, Pat had set unreasonable challenges for herself and usually gave up when she found them unattainable. She expected that her mother would disapprove if she showed weakness or fear, so she kept her feelings and her mistakes to herself. She floundered without direction and grew up sabotaging the development of aspirations unique to herself; every wall seemed too tall for her to climb.

The important message for mothers is that although it is desirable to be achievement-oriented models for their daughters, it is also appropriate to reveal one's humanness to children. Small children see loving mothers as perfect even if the mothers themselves do not. Youngsters are hesitant to reveal their imperfections to paragons of virtue. To be human and real is better than to be perfect and illusory; it makes for much better models for children. Daughters need to see their models making mistakes in order to learn how to handle their own imperfections. Daughters then will feel secure knowing that they, too, can be human and will feel free to expose their own ragged edges and holes as they learn from their mothers' examples.

We are acutely aware of this. It was after our children were adults that we learned how differently they, as children, had perceived us from the way we saw ourselves. One said, "I always saw you as so dynamic and thought I had to be that way." (This is a totally different perception from that of the one of us in question.) Another said, "You were always the center of attention and so well liked." (Again, a very different view from that of the author, who saw herself as shy.) We look back now and wonder about the many opportunities we may have missed, while trying hard to be good mothers, to let our children see us as approachable, because we failed to show them that we were fallible.

Women who have not seen flaws in their parents probably have not learned how to handle conflict. If they never saw their parents quarrel amicably, they had no example from which to learn skills to resolve differences with their peers, with authority figures, or with their spouses. If they are kept in the dark about family tragedies, finances, and other plans, they will grow up having to learn everything the hard way. This is inadequate, paradoxical modeling. It is a model not to follow, because it provides no modeling at all for many of life's ordinary and extraordinary encounters.

Sometimes to grow up to be like one's mother may not prepare a woman to live in a world that does not stop for people to get on. To be a carbon copy of one's mother dilutes the uniqueness and flexibility necessary for a fully expanded sense of oneself. There are many situations today in which a traditional model of past generations will not provide the variety of alternatives needed to meet the complexities of today's living. For instance, a woman raised in a small town in a financially secure home who never saw her mother struggle without money may find it very difficult to live in a city apartment, to be transferred across country, and to cope with inadequate finances, creditors, family illness, and the loneliness of living in a strange city. The support on which her mother could count is not a part of the daughter's life in which each day will bring challenges of its own.

Sometimes mothers know that they do not want their children to follow their modeling, yet the influence of their actions is subtly effective and their daughters grow up to follow in their footsteps. This happened to Nancy, who wanted an easier life for her children than hers had been. She came to therapy distressed that her daughter, Ruth, would not listen to her. Ruth seemed determined to make the mistakes that Nancy had hoped to protect her from.

Ruth loved her mother very much and had always looked up to her. Anything her mother did had seemed okay. Since her mother had not held herself up as perfect, Ruth had no problems in trying to be like her. She described her mother as fun-loving, carefree, creative, and not run of the mill. Nancy had been divorced after Ruth's youngest sister was born. She worked very hard to support herself and her daughters at a beans-and-bread level. Ruth saw her mother make many choices that were somewhat unconventional, but they looked fine to her daughter because it was her

255

"mom who did them, and whatever mom did was okay." Lacking other adults to associate with, Nancy shared her feelings with her daughters and they became almost like a group of peers. By the time Ruth was an adolescent, she already saw herself as an adult, her mother's equal.

Realizing that her mother frequently had sexual relationships, at seventeen Ruth accepted this as appropriate behavior for herself and became involved with a young man. It was this that distressed her mother. She had hoped that Ruth's life would be different from her own difficult one. It was her dream that all her daughters would see college as a door to a better life; she was afraid a sexual involvement would lead to marriage and the end of school for Ruth.

When Ruth and Nancy came to therapy, it was evident that Ruth felt very comfortable living with a young man outside "the holy bonds of matrimony." Unconventionality did not distress her; she had known it all her life. Nancy finally came to understand that since she herself had modeled an unconventional way of life and had proven to her children that it was satisfactory for her, she could expect that her daughters might follow her example. Ruth, having accepted a peer and supportive role with her mother, did not feel the need to please anyone in what she saw as adult choices.

Children imitate the socially acceptable behaviors of adults. Mary, who instilled a love of learning in her children by reading to them daily, recalled the happy summer afternoon hours of her childhood when she sat on a blanket under a tree while her mother read to her. This was a model Mary was happy to follow. But there are many ways in which even loving mothers provide paradoxical models for their daughters. Nora's daughter sat with her in therapy and called herself stupid. Nora disagreed, saying, "Why would you say a thing like that?" When asked by the therapist if she thought that she had taught her daughter this self-criticism by her own behavior, Nora was dumbfounded. She had not realized that she regularly put herself down and was chagrined to see that her daughter had indeed learned the habit from her. She had not thought of herself as modeling for her children when she did this. She could see that she needed to work on another paradox, that of self-esteem, in order to be the kind of model her daughter could profitably follow.

Louise knew that she had a hard time refusing even inappropriate requests and often felt imposed upon because friends and coworkers took advantage of her weaknesses. No matter how often she scolded her daughter Lou Ann for being an easy mark with her school friends, the child did not seem to learn to stand up for her rights!

Mavis had learned as a child to do each task perfectly, regardless of how long it took. Her mother's favorite expression was, "Anything worth doing is worth doing right." Mavis lived by this rule and was meticulous about her housework, cooking, and laundry. She could not explain her impatience when Betty, her ten-year-old daughter, cried if there were mistakes in her homework!

"Be like my mother? Never!"

Many of the women we see as clients have consciously rejected their mothers as models. Marlene reported hating her mother. She felt that she had been punished all her life by a harsh and unfeeling mother. When Marlene was a little girl, she had to work much harder at home than her classmates did and was beaten if her work did not meet her parents' standards. She always felt poorer than other children because her parents did not buy her simple things that would have helped her to feel more like her classmates. She could not understand why her mother prevented her from taking part in school plays, joining the school band, or going out for athletics. Marlene wanted to do these things very much because she was an only child and lonely for other children's companionship.

Marlene's mother had a Vesuvius-like temper, which erupted without warning. Having scrapped all pretense of restraint, she freely scolded, yelled, and blamed. Her target of choice was usually Marlene, who learned to protect herself from verbal abuse by shutting out what she heard and from physical abuse by running away and hiding from her violent mother.

During all of her childhood Marlene had no understanding of the pressures under which her mother lived. She was not told in ways she could understand about the problems of poverty, illness, and insecurity that triggered her mother's punishing outbursts. She knew only that her mother seemed a terrible woman whom no daughter would choose as a model. When she came for therapy as an adult, Marlene was still suffering from the effects of her hurtful experiences.

"Even as a child," Marlene said. "I knew I would be different from my mother when I grew up. Today if anyone even suggests that I'm like my mother, that's all I need to hear. I'll go to any effort to change. I learned from my own painful experience how important it is for a daughter to have a validating and tolerant mother," For Marlene, the paradox of modeling was that, having had such a threatening model, she repressed her feelings and for many years lived on a plateau of alienation. A barrier had been built between herself and her mother that she might never want to remove.

"Martyrs are a tough act to follow."

When Carmen was twenty-one, her mother died of a neglected illness. Everyone knew that if she had been able to afford medical care she might have lived: instead, she had kept her illness to herself. Her death culminated a lifetime of putting everyone else first. She had scrubbed other people's floors to buy school clothes for the children. She had gone hungry so they could eat. When she was asked what she got out of life, she had said, "The love of my children." When they were grown up, she seemed ready to die, and did, a super-martyr, unsung except within the narrow circle of those who knew her well.

As she grew up, Carmen saw her mother as a very positive model, hard-working, soft-spoken, uncomplaining, and generous to the point of sacrifice. Carmen

258

and her seven brothers and sisters felt this was the way a mother shoud be. Carmen hoped to be just like her mother.

When Carmen married and had children of her own, she, too, sacrificed herself for them. They had music and dancing lessons, which the family could ill-afford. They did not have to help at home if it interfered with school projects or fun. Not having as extreme financial hardships as her mother had suffered, Carmen would have felt guilty if she did not give generously of herself to her children. She always found time to attend a ballgame, bake cookies for Brownies, or car-pool for a special event, even if she was left with no time for herself. Finally, her children were grown and needed her no more. Unlike her own mother, Carmen did not die at this point in her life; she did become severely depressed, however, and that brought her to therapy.

Only then, with the help of her therapist, could Carmen examine the sacred doctrine of martyrdom, which she had thought was such a good model. At first she resisted, but later she saw that perhaps she had hurt herself without helping her children by investing so much of herself in them. Perhaps they, too, felt guilty and resentful about some of her help. They might have been less alienated, yet more independent, if she had not sacrificed so much for them.

Carmen was a highly intelligent, creative woman. Her depression lifted as she looked at her potential and realized that a few brief years of study could equip her to find her own place in any number of areas. Although the paradox of modeling had grounded her for many years, she knew that the last half of her life could be tailored to fit her yet-to-flower potential. She was hopeful that she would be able to model for her daughters a way that they, too, could break new ground.

Not all martyrs are so benign that their daughters want to follow them. When Rhea came for therapy as a young woman, she told about her childhood resentments. Rhea's mother divorced her husband when Rhea was a baby and worked industriously to support her two children. Rhea had appreciated the financial

259

struggle her mother faced, working as a secretary and raising her children without support from their father. She unselfishly did the things she thought would benefit them. As a young girl, however, Rhea came to resent the strings her mother attached to the good things she did. She would buy Rhea a small gift and then leave a note saying, "I got this for you; now you can do the ironing for me." Or she would allow the children to have a birthday party and insist that they plan everything to her satisfaction.

Operating from her position as a martyr, Rhea's mother had induced a great deal of guilt in her daughter. Rhea had even felt guilty enjoying camp because she knew how hard her mother had worked to make it possible. Unable to do the things she thought were expected of her to equal her mother's sacrifice, Rhea reacted with resentment. Because she saw her mother as overpowering and did not feel safe confronting her directly, she acted out, as many children do, by underachieving scholastically. To the horror of her mother, Rhea dropped out of school in the tenth grade. Rhea never questioned that she loved her mother, but she also knew that she felt angry toward her and did not want to follow her martyr's example. She both loved and resented her mother, and these feelings often clashed, preventing the two women from sharing good times.

Rhea was able to resist her mother's modeling to an extent; she grew up to be very different from her mother. As a girl she had known and admired other women who seemed to get more out of life than her mother did, and she consciously tried to model herself after an aunt with whom she spent a lot of time. It was only when she was married and had a family of her own that Rhea felt the urge to come to therapy to resolve her ambivalent feelings about her mother. The unfortunate thing was that so many years had been wasted and so much potential undeveloped during her years of resistance. Once she dealt with all of the old distress and no longer felt guilty about her mother's martyrdom, Rhea came to an important realization: She no longer had to blame her mother. Sometimes it takes a long time to understand this. Even when a mother's behavior hurts her daughter badly, she is acting out of her own distress and is, for the most part, motivated by love.

Of course, this does not deny that the hurts are real and have to be dealt with. Nonetheless, it is not functional to dump on another person old feelings about past hurts. This only encourages that person to be defensive, or even self-righteous, and escalates alienation. By the time Rhea and her mother came together for therapy, they had each spent time with us individually and had a clear understanding of what had gone on to create the barriers between them. Rhea, who was now a mother herself, understood her mother better and her resentment had dissipated. Her mother could let go of her self-righteousness when she saw how such feelings were distancing her from a daughter she loved. Talking together in therapy, each was able to express to the other positive feelings and to ask for what she would like from the other in the future. They were able to solve their modeling paradox, because, like most mothers and daughters we have worked with, they wanted only the best for each other.

This applies even to those martyr mothers whose lasting gift to their daughters is guilt. Seriously eroded in her sense of self-esteem, Mona was a twenty-nine-year-old college professor when she came for therapy. Stuck in the mire of self-blame, she did not seem to be growing and taking risks as her colleagues were. She was coasting along without promotions while everyone else seemed to be going someplace. Even though her work was satisfactory to others, she saw herself as treacherously close to the academic guillotine.

Mona's mother, Alice, had supported both Mona and her own invalid mother. She had never said so openly, but her sighs and attitude of resignation had made it clear that she would welcome relief from her burdens.

Alice was a perfectionist and had very rigid ideas about how things should be done. Rather than let her growing daughter learn by doing chores in a child's way, Alice did the cleaning, cooking, shopping, and laundry after coming home from a full day at the office. It seemed plain to Mona that her help was not wanted because she could not do anything well enough. She never had the thrill of challenging her abilities, struggling until she succeeded, nor did she have a chance to learn from her mistakes. Mona could even get out of her single chore, doing the dishes, if she had anything else to do. "Go on and play; I'll do the dishes. I don't want you to miss any fun," was the message she remembered hearing from her self-sacrificing mother.

As an adult, Mona realized that she was firmly tied to her mother by cords of guilt. She understood how hard her mother's life had been and how little she had been allowed to do to lighten her mother's load. Now, Alice was calling in the IOU's. She felt that she had the right to criticize, direct, and control Mona's life. The guilt that this aroused in Mona was matched by her anger at her mother's blatant coercion. The paradox of modeling had served to separate them and caused Mona to say frequently, "I never want to be like my mother."

"Fathers are important, too."

The first man in a woman's life is her father. Much of her later life and her relationships with men are influenced by the way she and her father interacted when she was a child. If she was afraid of her father, she is likely as an adult to be afraid of all men. She is likely to see other men as the authority figure her father was. If she and her father had a mutual respect for each other, she is likely to develop robust affiliations with other men free of early fears and safe from the disease of static dependence.

Fathers can be excellent models for women, offsetting the press of society to fit a rigid mold. How a father relates to his wife, children, and to others has an effect on whether or not his daughters will establish direct, open, and honest relationships. Daughters who have basked in the nourishing climate of a positive reciprocal bond with their father grow up feeling comfortable with men, liking them, being able to negotiate differences with them and to enter lasting, honest relationships with men. They are not threatened by authority figures and get along well with most people.

Some fathers, though, are overbearing. Some are weak. Some are rejecting. Some are angry and frightening to their daughters. The daughters of these fathers are more likely to suffer from the paradoxes in this book, and they may develop psychological problems when they cannot resolve the paradoxical messages.

Renee's father was an abusive, autocratic, loud man before whom the whole family wore a protective mask of obedience. Renee remembered feeling the need to stay close to him and, at the same time, being frightened by his loudness and cruelty. Because he doled out the goodies, Renee did not dare to alienate him; yet her days were filled thinking up acceptable schemes to isolate herself from the unpleasantness of her home.

Renee said, "My one abiding memory was of being yelled at and punished. I was never told what I had done to provoke his outrage or how I might have prevented it. I could usually outrun a spanking, but I was really terrorized and felt helpless when he abused my mother."

It took a long time in therapy for Renee to see that even as an adult she reacted to other loud, controlling men as she had to the model she grew up with. It was as if they became her father and she made a nightmarish regression to the helplessness of her childhood. "Finally," she said, "I know now that I can interact with men in peer relationships. When I see us as equals and don't buckle under to their aggressiveness, I can stand up to them, I can have an impact on them, which influences how they treat me. By remaining helpless in the past, I may even have elicited control and punishment from men. Since I have improved my self-esteem and become assertive, men treat me with more respect."

With the confidence that comes from successful experiences, Renee went on to develop more communication skills. These made it easier for her to move from blaming all men for what her father had done to her to having the power to effect change herself. The modeling paradox had told Renee that all men were like the frightening model that had been imprinted in her mind. Its resolution freed her to trust.

Vera's father was a model who left her feeling a great need to replace him in her life. She remembered him as happy-go-lucky, loving, and attentive. She recalled joyous childhood days, sitting on her father's lap, playing with him, and enjoying all the rewards of being his little girl. In the innocence of her years, she did not know that he was irresponsible and improvident. Her mother divorced him when Vera was six years old, and she never got over the fact that he disappeared from her life. It became obvious to her in therapy that she had grown up mourning her loss and longing for someone to take her father's place.

None of the men whom Vera met were as perfect as the father she remembered. Her life had been characterized by a series of disappointing relationships and several in-and-out marriages. She did not realize that her memory was embroidered by fantasy. Because she had grown up without her father in the home and had idealized him, she thought every man should be at least twice life-size. She expected a man to give her everything she desired, with no compromise or negotiation on her part. She visualized developing with every new man the kind of relationship she had enjoyed with her father as a child. Thwarted by reality, disappointed by the narrow humanness of her mates, she saddled them with accountability for her pain. In therapy she learned to focus on the loss of her father as the source of her distress. When she was able to do this, she no longer needed to put her baggage of blame on men's backs when they did not fit her impossible requirements. She could look forward to building relationships with real people who had real faults and imperfections, rather than on an idealized model.

Growing up in a home with a weak father can create psychological problems for women that become paradoxes of modeling. When a daughter sees her mother in a critical light, and does not want to be like her, it may be because of a father who is unwilling or unable to accept responsibility yet has made his wife look like the bad guy while he is, in fact, the poor model. His failure puts an extra burden on his wife. Those wives who have kept their families afloat by unselfishly assuming the initiative often do not feel good about themselves. They find little support for stepping in and filling a vacuum left by an ineffective husband.

As Nora said in therapy, "I was called castrating and emasculating when I did what I had to do to keep our family's head above water. My husband could never hold a job, and I had to take charge. Yet even our children blamed me for usurping his prerogatives. No one gave me credit for assuming responsibilities which had to be met. In trying to correct a problem I was told I was the problem. Even the kids saw him as a nice, gentle, harmless guy, and they felt sorry for him because I was impatient with him."

Counseling such women, we encourage them to see that they are not guilty. We ask them to look at whether they are accepting other people's neglected responsibilities because it is necessary or if it is possible that they are doing so because they are anxiously attempting to keep everybody happy. If so, they may be reinforcing their husbands' irresponsible inactivity, which is the real source of the problem. Instead of facing this issue, they perpetuate a vicious cycle that insures that no one will be happy. Women sucked into this whirlpool need to get to the point of personal comfort where they can concern themselves with other matters while allowing their husbands to succeed or fail, letting them suffer the consequences if they do not accept their obligations.

Alcoholic father are poor models. If a girl sees her drunken father as mean and abusive, she often reacts by insulating herself from him and identifying with her mother, treating her with pity and understanding. If, however, her father seems to be a nice guy when sober, a daughter is inclined to feel forgiving, maternal, and sympathetic toward him. In order to excuse his alcoholism, she frequently blames her mother for his drinking problem.

Nita did this. She grew up in a home with an alcoholic father who was pleasant and social, drank regularly, and acted as if his contribution of congeniality made up to his family for his other shortcomings. Her mother accepted that if there was going to be food on the table and if the mortgage payments were to be met, she would have to provide the money. She reached into her slender purse of skills and went to work at a menial job to bail out the family. Nita had warm feelings toward her father and a fearful attitude toward her mother, whom she saw as always tired and short-tempered. Although she loved them both, she felt protective of her father; he seemed unable to be anything but what he was. He died when she was in her early teens, and she felt an unspeakable sadness. She had no one to tell that she had not seen him as the failure; it was her mother whom she believed had failed by being so critical of him.

Women who grow up in homes with fathers like Nita's have conflicting feelings about themselves in relation to men. They tend to make either/or choices. Looking for a model of masculine strength, they are unprepared to relate to strong men. Often they choose weak men like their fathers. If their fathers seemed like failures, they hope in some way to make their husbands into the men their fathers should have been.

If, like Nita, they see their fathers as acceptable, they may marry weak men, unaware that they will live over their mothers' grief. An additional handicap for daughters from families with strong mothers and weak fathers is that, as a result of not liking the way their mothers handled their roles, they have not learned to value other women and tend instead to distrust them.

A little girl relating to an angry, critical, and punishing father may be traumatized for life. Threats not actually carried out may be even more frightening to a child than the punishment itself; she never knows when the ax will fall.

Maria's father was verbally abusive and hostile to

her. He dispensed whippings at the slightest provocation. She carried a memory of this model into her marriage and feared her husband Chuck as much as she had feared her father. Chuck was a hard-working and ambitious person who did not intend to frighten his wife. Nonetheless, Maria responded to his wishes as though they were commands. She was so afraid of displeasing him that she became passive and seldom took the initiative in anything. He became annoyed by her timidity. The cycle began: The more timid she was, the more annoyed Chuck became and the more she feared that he would became angry and lose his temper.

Maria did not realize that by fearing Chuck she was keeping the cycle going. When she came for therapy she was the prototype of many women we see. She said things like, "My husband won't let me," "I don't have any choice," "He will blow up if I spend money," and "He will never change." Maria believed the things she said, but they were really excuses she used for not taking charge of her life. The frightening model of her father had convinced her that it was safer to retire to a sanctuary of compliance than to risk life in the arena.

"I learned about sex from my parents."

Modeling also accounts for women's attitudes about sex. Ideally, a young woman will develop a positive attitude toward her sexuality at home by observing and adopting her parents' healthy attitudes about sexual intimacy. This does not always happen. Edith grew up hearing her parents fight about sex. She felt sure that anything that caused so much quarreling could not be associated with love. The message Edith got from her mother was the classic, "Men are no good, and you would do well to avoid them." From her father she got the unspoken message that a woman should not talk about sex with men. Although the subject of sex was not openly discussed, the oblique references were crystal clear: All men wanted from women was their own sexual gratification. It was plain that Edith could best please her parents by stifling her own sexuality.

Edith married the first man to whom she felt sexually attracted, largely, she realized many years later, because she felt a need to legitimize her yearning for him. She had ambivalent feelings when she married. If she pleased herself by enjoying sex, she would displease her mother. If she followed her mother's advice and rejected sex, both she and her husband would feel cheated. In therapy, Edith learned that her parents' modeling was at the bottom of her ambivalence about sex. Edith and her husband would have to create a sexual intimacy and assurance before they could enjoy their sexuality as her parents had never seemed to do.

The absence of good parental models would not be so critical if women could find direction elsewhere. For women who do not want to follow traditional roles, there are few models available. There are many female teachers to admire in elementary school, but few female professors in college and even fewer in graduate school. A banker or business executive who is a woman recognizes that there are few women in high-level business and government positions to serve as examples for aspiring young women. This is a great deprivation for women. Men have traditionally had mentors who showed them the ropes, befriended them, and helped them along the way up. Consciously or unconsciously, male protégés pattern themselves on the successful behavior demonstrated for them, and they are encouraged in their aspirations. If a woman chooses a man as a model, she risks being accused of losing her femininity. If she follows stereotyped female models, she is accused of unfairly using her sexuality to compete with men. The poignancy of this paradox is clear to anyone who has traveled an uncharted path.

Women who are trying to resolve the paradox of modeling know their task is like trying to build a house without a blueprint. In resolving the paradox they need time, effort, and emotional support to erase deficits and establish the credits of new models to follow. We encourage women to look to other women for inspiration and example, to identify in other women the qualities they would like in themselves, and to aim consciously to develop them. A woman who is a good model for others is like a pebble thrown in the water; her influence spreads in gentle ripples, nourishing the spirit of those she touches, stimulating the rising confidence of those who follow.

CHAPTER XII

Sexuality

"That is the way men like women, but I don't dare be that way."

Women see men reacting positively to sexy, alluring, glamorous, and seductive women. This model of sexuality is held out as an ideal for which women should strive. The same men, however, give the message that they expect their women to be modest, demure, and virtuous. The paradox is the double message: A woman should be both a whore and a madonna. This expectation has caused women to feel distressed and confused about their own sexuality.

What is the image of the ideal woman that men would have us strive to achieve? The ideal woman is everywhere, adorning almost every media message. She is a combination of youth, beauty, and other physical attributes that excite desire. She is the stimulus for dirty jokes, insolent stares, and brazen propositions, as well as sidelong once-overs and nocturnal fantasies. She is the temptress, seductress, whore made socially acceptable in the name of business. The practice of objectifying and commercializing female sexuality is degrading for women; this degradation is felt in an undefined uneasiness, uncertainty, embarrassment, and even shame that women feel about their sexuality.

At the same time that women are bombarded with this image of female they are told more quietly how to be feminine. They are to be madonnas, pure, sweet, and gently smiling, revered and good, but not quite real lest they fall off their pedestals. Madonnas are special women of whom much more is expected than of a whore, and the expectations are quite different. The whore is for excitement and enjoyment, for having fun, for experiencing fantasy and freedom. The madonna is for gentle pleasure and comfort, for settling down, and for building a home. She is to be supportive, happy, nurturing, compliant, and submissive—the perfect mother of a man's children.

The expression of a madonna's sexuality, too, centers around a man. In public she is to be modest, demure, and attractive, so that her partner is enhanced by being with her and other men envy his good fortune. In private she is to become whatever best suits her partner's fancy: a passive, undemanding (and thus unthreatening) recipient; an aggressive, initiating Jezebel; an earthy, warm mother figure; a stimulating, innovating turn-on; or perhaps, at one time or another, all of these.

Gender identity is biologically determined and something one is powerless to control. Female sexuality is part of women every moment of their lives and is present in every cell of their bodies. Ideally, a woman's sexuality should be so much an integrated part of her that there would be no need to single out sexuality as a topic for discussion. Unfortunately, this is not the case. Instead, it has been the foundation upon which sex-role stereotyping and female socialization have been based. Indeed, women's sexual behavior, the means through which they express their sexuality, has itself become a painful paradox that has created confusion and generated feelings of self-doubt and low self-esteem in women.

In recent years much has been written about human sexuality; much more needs to be learned about female sexuality. It should be understood, however, that we are not attempting here to deal definitively with the subject of sex. The focus of this chapter is on the paradox of sexuality to which women have been exposed and their attempts to resolve the conflicts created by double messages.

Sex-role stereotyping and the paradox of sexuality have a powerful impact on all women, whether they have chosen heterosexual, homosexual, or asexual lifestyles. The paradoxes with which women are shackled are not affected by choice of sexual partner. The partners could be changed; the conditions of the double-bind would for the most part remain the same. Sexuality and sexual behavior are only part of life, whereas sex-role stereotyping can govern life. It begins in the cradle: the effects may last to the grave.

Most of the heartbreak associated with female sexuality originates from a narrow focus on women as sex objects, rather than as people who are also women. The fact that female sexuality is expressed in affiliative, nurturing, affective, emotional, and problem-solving capacities in all areas of a woman's life—not just in sexual encounters—has been largely ignored. Female sexuality has been tightly circumscribed by centering it around women's function as sexual partners.

Being thought of primarily in terms of their sexual behavior and potential as sexual partners has made women feel objectified: that is, they feel like things, rather than persons. They see themselves as sex objects because they are treated that way. Objects are to be used, most frequently for practical purposes, but sometimes just for amusement or as a source of pleasure and beauty.

Women have been given the double message that as sex objects they must be forever provocative, voluptuous, and nymphlike, even while they maintain their purity, naiveté, and youthfulness. Women are expected to be both whores and madonnas, yet they are told that there are two kinds of women, *either* whores or madonnas. No matter which choice a women makes, she is putting herself in a subservient role, since her sexual behavior is prescribed by men. In making this choice, women allow men to make the self-serving decision about how female sexuality can be expressed.

There is no denying that in prescribing women's sexual roles, men have created Superman imperatives and destructive inhibitions for themselves. All the same, women have been even more encumbered than men because they have been in dependent roles where direct confrontation must be avoided. They have been encouraged to seek either roundabout, manipulative solutions, or passive, helpless adjustments to the paradox of sexuality.

From the contradictory message that says, "I can degrade you and simultaneously love and cherish you," comes most of the yes-no quandaries women experience about their sexuality, If women accept male descriptions of themselves as whores, they must either learn not to feel, lest they, too, experience the humiliation reserved for this peculiar profession, or they must accept themselves as sex objects, designed to please men. A third option is to become madonnas, ignoring the siren song of the media and remaining aloof from their own passions, perched on the pedestal of purity.

The greatest distress of this paradox is probably felt by women who fit neither the stereotype of femaleness nor that of femininity. What about women who are too tall or too short, too thin or too fat, too bright or too dull, too uneducated or too educated, or too whatever more or too whatever less than it takes to attract and please a man? Not having the accoutrements of either mold, they must strive to compensate in some way to avoid feeling devalued and inadequate. Women who are not able to make up for their supposed shortcomings see themselves as full of insufficiencies, as not measuring up to the ideal of what a real woman should be. They regard themselves as rejects in the male-female game.

The criteria for a "real woman" change regularly. Currently a really real woman is super-everything: super-beautiful, super-sexy, super-talented, super-intelligent, super-educated, and super-successful in her combined roles of sexual partner, mother, homemaker, and career woman. For all but a few women, aspiring to this is folly; failure seems guaranteed. Such unrealistic criteria encourage a woman to look for a man to rescue her from failure, rather than for a partner to enhance her life and share intimacy and responsibility.

For some women, this analysis of the paradox of women's sexuality may seem to be a harsh generalization that does not fit them. Some women grow up in a wholesome environment that fosters a healthy appreciation of their sexuality and their capacity to express it in an appropriate, self-determined manner. Their sexual identity is not limited to brazenly female or benignly feminine pigeonholes. It is an important part of their birthright. Observing other women, however, they can see how the malevolence of the paradox of sexuality has both captivated and violated them.

The incidence of rape, incest, and child pornography, in which females are usually the victims, is rising. Pornographic literature and prostitution are commonplace commodities. Billboards and movies feature women in chains. Bars titillate their patrons with hostile "entertainment" featuring females with thrust-out breasts being sprayed by male customers with streams of water from toy water pistols. In therapy, clients report having been sexually abused as children, often by male relatives, including their fathers and stepfathers. They talk of their resentment and revulsion when they are forced by their partners to participate in sexual experiences they do not want. These practices are perpetuated in the name of sexual pleasure and lovemaking. The sickness women feel at being used in these ways comes from their intuitive knowledge that these atrocities are no more than thinly disguised manifestations of the anger, rage, and violence with which the powerful victimize the weak.

It seems quite likely that the paradox of sexuality originated in men's attempts to alleviate their fear that women would punish them in the most vulnerable area of their masculinity—their sexual capacity. By creating two kinds of women, men hoped to act out their own hostility as well as their fantasies with every man's whore and to establish safety and affiliative bonds with their own personal madonnas. Unfortunately, men's fears and anger toward wanton women has carried over into their personal relationships with the women they love. The contempt that men feel for whores is sensed by their madonnas, who are ashamed and humiliated by their own sexuality.

Despite the sexual revolution and the efforts of the

women's movement to give women comfortable control of their bodies and their sexuality, women still feel pressured to become either the willing dupes or the innocent victims of the paradox of sexuality. The feelings generated by this conflict range from mild annoyance to disillusionment, disappointment, anger, and rage; from surprise to disbelief, shame, humiliation, and degradation.

"My parents expected me to . . . ."

Girls acquire their attitudes about their own sexuality from their early family experiences. In some homes, the sexual aspect of oneself is seen as wholesome and natural. Discussions of sex are usually encouraged, and guidelines for sexual behavior are established. Problems then revolve around how and when the passionate side of oneself will be expressed.

In other homes, sexuality is viewed with caution, or even fear and suspicion, as if it were Eve's apple, not to be acknowledged lest it be eaten of. When the subject is avoided entirely, children do not interpret such avoidance to mean that sex is unimportant, nor even that it has a proper place, but that it is so important that it must be denied completely. Problems of sexuality then revolve around how girls feel about themselves as sexual beings as well as how they behave sexually in response to their feelings. Hand-me-down parental values are plugged in as rules for playing the male-female game.

The decision about how they will act sexually is one of the issues young women are concerned and anxious about. They do have many other concerns, however, such as leaving the safety of home, their parents' happiness, handling responsibility and freedom, maintaining individuality, making personal choices without sacrificing their values, and being accepted by their peers. Sexual behavior is not the central focus for most young women. Some parents fail to understand this and react as if every decision of their daughters' lives involves sex.

Gerry's father accused her of having sex with boys

when she came home late several nights in a row. He had forgotten that she had an after-school job and worked until closing time in a drugstore to earn Christmas money. Kathy remembered the time she was fifteen and had for months been in love with a boy who had not so much as spoken to her. Finally he asked her to go to a movie. After several dates with him she told her mother how much he seemed to like her and said dreamily, "Maybe we'll get married." Her mother sharply replied, "Are you trying to tell me you're pregnant already?" Both of these parents had assumed, and voiced their assumption with clublike bluntness, that sex would be the Pied Piper's tune of their daughters' downfall.

Sometimes these assumptions are correct for, as a result of parental attitudes, resentful daughters learn early that they can use sex as a weapon with which to win power games against their parents. In Cookie's home, every evidence of her sexuality was viewed with alarm. She did not remember having masturbated when she was a baby, but she realized as an adult that when her mother walked up to her crib, smelled her hands, and slapped her, it must have been associated with that.

As Cookie grew older, her mother and father constantly expressed their fear that she would succumb to the pleadings of boys with little honor and big ideas. In her preteen years, she was not interested in sex. As a teenager, she saw her parents as punishing and rejecting. She realized that the way she could hurt them most was to be sexually active. She began having sex with many men, including her father's friends.

In therapy Cookie learned that by using her sexuality to punish other people she had cheated herself out of the positive fulfillment that might have accompanied sexual experience. By exploring her anger and learning nondestructive ways to discharge it, she shifted emphasis to her sexuality as a source of pleasure. She claimed her right to choose sexual companions for positive reasons rather than as missiles aimed at her parents. Cookie had dared to be the way men seemed to like women; now it was time to be a woman she liked.

Carolyn's older sister, Beverly, was a fiercely competitive student whose bedroom walls were covered with evidence of her academic success. Perhaps in a well-meaning effort to keep Carolyn from feeling inadequate about her average grades, her mother and father showered her with compliments about how pretty she was. She was taught from her earliest years that her talents rested in her "natural" beauty. She was subtly encouraged to act in enticingly sensuous ways, but cautioned to be innocent and virginal. The message was strong: her value was in her sexuality, and it was a marketable commodity if she remembered that only when a girl married was she to have sex, and then only with her husband.

Carolyn remembered that in grade school, even though her best friend was smarter, she did not have naturally curly hair, soft brown eyes, and a happy laugh as Carolyn did. If she could not be smart, Carolyn decided that she would be beautiful and have many successful, handsome, and eager men fall in love with her. "Beverly got books for Christmas and money to put in the bank for college," Carolyn told her therapist years later. "I got dresses with ruffles and ribbons for my hair and, when I was sixteen, a little diamond on a chain. All I had to do was ask, and they gave me whatever I wanted as long as it was to make me look prettier. They seemed pleased that I had more boyfriends than any of the other girls. I got the idea very early that they thought the only thing I could do with my life was to catch a man. A man would be my chance for success."

As an adult, Carolyn found this success elusive, for she did not live up to her own image of the ideal woman. As beautiful as she was, her mirror reflected flaws. For one thing, the sexuality that Carolyn had so frugally saved did not burst forth once she was married. At first she feared that she had sold out to the wrong man, but after her third love affair sputtered out the notion that there was something wrong with her demanded recognition.

As Carolyn got older, she felt at a disadvantage when she compared herself with younger women. Each morning was an ordeal as she became increasingly caught up in what she called her beauty work. Exercising and dieting when the sand began to settle in her hourglass figure; meditating to reduce the frown lines of her stress; plucking, manicuring, curling, and moisturizing all took many hours of every day.

And then she was thirty-seven. Carolyn was a beautiful woman, although she did not think so. She felt increasingly depressed as middle age beckoned. Her resolution to the paradox of sexuality had failed. She had never become the sex object she had been encouraged to be. Instead, she was a self-centered woman, obsessed with her looks and angry that she could not stay young forever.

Most women have learned so well that they are supposed to look like flawless masterpieces that it is unusual to find a woman who feels happy about her body. Even those women who feel confident about their beauty focus on how to improve it and remove the imperfections that are obvious only to them. It is sad to hear a woman say, "I never wear shorts because the inside of my knees are fat no matter what I do to get rid of the bulges," or "I don't dare wear sandals because my middle toe is longer than my big toe, and it looks so gross!"

Other women have tried to resolve the pain of being compared with a female ideal by ignoring their physical appearance. Husbands may complain about overweight wives who wear frumpy clothes and outdated hair styles. When this happens, some men retaliate by losing interest in sex or by rekindling their desires with someone new. Rebecca mentioned, "My husband constantly nags me about being overweight. He won't accept that I've got a lot more important things to think about than how I look. He tells me that my appearance justifies his stepping out on me because who could stand having sex with me."

On the other hand, a man may be secretly or openly relieved when his wife's youthful attractiveness begins to wane, for then he does not have to worry about competition from other men or maintaining his own looks and vigor. Edna knew it had been that way for her. "As my husband developed a paunch and lost his hair, he encouraged me to overeat and always managed to keep us broke so there was never any money to spend on me."

The same secret relief may also be true for women. Aggie confessed that she was happy to see her husband gain weight, because other women would not see him as handsome. Jackie insisted to her husband that she loved his bald head, but knew that what she really felt was relief that he was no longer the superjock he used to be. Judy purposely picked a man fifteen years her senior. She thought her youthfulness would be insurance; she would not have to compete with women to hold an older man as she might have to if she married a man her own age.

Women do not have to feel guilty for wanting to be healthy and beautiful. Nevertheless, health care should not be in the service of someone else, but for oneself. Caring about their bodies must be an outgrowth of women's concern for being integrated, fully-functioning persons, and not a misguided attempt to reach a resolution of the paradox of sexuality.

"I really don't trust women."

For many women the paradox of sexuality is expressed in jealousy and competitiveness with other women. In trying to be what they think men want them to be, they compare themselves with the women men associate with and desire. Other women become the enemy; and men become the coveted and jealously guarded prize.

Lea came to therapy burning with the green-eyed monster of jealousy. It threatened to destroy her relationship with her boyfriend Dick. He was the manager of a large department store, an ambitious, successful young businessman who constantly told Lea that he loved her and saw her as physically and intellectually desirable and stimulating. He nullified these reassurances by telling Lea that he only hired attractive female clerks. He further damaged his credibility with frequent judgments about how her girlfriends measured up, and he kept his roving eyes busy when he and Lea were together.

Dick saw his behavior as his male prerogative; Lea saw it as intolerable. It was for her an extension of the humiliating competition she had faced as a girl when her mother had charmed her boyfriends so convincingly that they ended up coming to visit her mother instead of Lea. Her parents were divorced when she was fourteen, and she became an also-ran in the let's-fight-over-him game with her father's girlfriends.

It was jealousy that prompted her in therapy to sit on the edge of her chair and spit out her hurt. "Men can't be trusted. All they care about is sex. They're not interested in a woman for anything else. And women! They don't care whose guy they're after as long as they get a man." The issue underlying Lea's jealousy was that no matter how hard she tried to please a man, she thought she would never be pretty enough, good enough, or sexy enough to keep him.

It is a tragedy that women have been taught to compete with each other for men. Discussing this in group therapy, one woman said she suffered pangs of jealousy when she went to movies with her partner and watched the beautiful, larger-than-life sirens of the screen. She saw them through a mixture of heartache and envy, compared herself unfavorably with them, and thought that her partner did, too.

Another woman mentioned that she hated to go anywhere with her husband because women openly flirted with him as if she were ready to be put on the shelf. A third woman said that she had been to a party the previous week and felt miserable because a gorgeous woman had been there and many of the men paid attention to her. "I'm sure every one of those men yearned to be with her," she said.

Eva created her own paradox of sexuality and needed to come for only four therapy sessions to resolve it. She was afraid that her husband was pairing up with other women because she was so fat and unattractive. Although she had no evidence that her husband was searching for a replacement, she thought that with a wife who looked like she did he could be expected to seek out another woman. In fact, Eva was strikingly beautiful and only slightly on the plump side. Her therapist insisted that Eva focus on her positive qualities instead of predictions prompted by jealousy. In trying to identify what she valued in herself, Eva bumped into her lack of self-appreciation. Her jealousy was a projection of her own feelings of insecurity and inadequacy. Her husband was imperfect in some ways, but he was not interested in making conquests.

Eva was able to resolve the paradox of sexuality she had created when she understood that other women were not the problem, nor was her husband. The problem was that she was trying to compete with a stereotyped version of what she thought a man would want her to be. When she could value herself, she was free. When Eva terminated her brief therapy, her confidence in herself and her own sexuality fully expanded, she said, "My entire life has been changed."

Some women, even though they are certain that their partners are eternally looking for extracurricular women and that there are always eager females willing to respond to men's sexual advances, feel no hesitation about their own faithfulness, saying, "Of course, I know I would never become involved with anyone else."

Hildie, though, was different. She believed that the surest way to keep her love life secure was to keep her boyfriend insecure. She played a seductress role with other men whenever she had a chance. "I never actually have sex with any of these guys, though," she said. "I just make sure I always have someone in the background, hovering around and waiting to really appreciate me. It keeps whomever I am with on his toes. I'd rather be the one to be fought over than to be doing the fighting!"

In refusing to see men as the prize, Hildie had made herself the prize. She did not realize that in her own way she, too, was trapped in the double-bind of sexuality, or that she had tried to resolve the conflict by playing a game that was punishing to her as well as to her sexual partner.

Cora played the temptress role because it gave her license to express sexual fantasies she enjoyed, but which she thought a "normal" woman would never have. By pretending to herself that whatever she did sexually was to please her partner, she could participate without guilt and without assuming responsibility for her own desires. Cora was aware at a deeper level that she was pretending. Even though she yearned for a long-term relationship, her fear that she was sexually abnormal kept her moving from one partner to another lest, in getting close to a man, she might inadvertently reveal her "perversions."

For Hildie and Cora and for countless women who play the temptress role, the emotional costs were high, the risks of failure and rejection great, and the long-term rewards illusory.

"I try not to think about sex at all."

Most young women do not express their sexuality by playing a seductress role. They integrate their parents' discomfort about sex and suffer pain, embarrassment, confusion, and guilt, which spread listlessly over their adult lives. Prevailing attitudes in our society about sex range from rigidity to permissiveness. They serve both to reinforce and negate the spoken and unspoken messages of parents, peers, and teachers. Feeling immobilized by these contradictory attitudes toward sex, the conflict of sexuality becomes. "I can't be a whore or a madonna. I don't dare to act either way."

A woman who has made this decision may enter a committed relationship thinking that it is proper for her to be artless and uninformed about her own sexuality. She often expects her partner to teach her what she needs to know so that they can slip easily into loveland. Such thinking is based upon the double standard that maintains that women should be beginners and men should be sexually experienced at the outset of any relationship. The man becomes the dominant one, the teacher, and the women becomes the subordinate one, the learner. This sets the stage for the extension of dominance-subordinance into all areas of interpersonal interaction in the relationship.

When Connie married Marty she was uninformed about sex. They had petted some before marriage, and, although she was surprised at her responsiveness, she had held tightly onto the reins of her passion. Connie was proud of the fact that she had come to her marriage looking forward to sex. Expecting that her husband would know everything about making love, she believed his expertise would awaken her dormant sexual capacity. Unfortunately, after eight years with Marty, Connie felt frustrated by dreams long deferred. Her sexual capacity was still untapped. Marty was disgusted with her awkwardness and inhibitions. Connie felt more and more rejected, dissatisfied, and disappointed because, having saved herself for him, she had expected to be rewarded with pleasure.

Under the barrage of negative messages about herself from Marty, Connie's self-esteem ebbed. She decided that she did not want to go on feeling miserable the rest of her life. If she could prove to herself just once that she was "okay sexually" she would recapture the assurance of her youth. She actively sought out and found another man. He felt comfortable in his instructor role, and she was delighted and pleased with the confirmation of her sexuality that this single experience gave her.

When she came for therapy, Connie blamed Marty for not being a good teacher. Like many other women, she had only done what society expected of her. She had kept herself chaste, thinking that sex would automatically become a beautiful experience once she married. She felt embittered and cheated; even though she had fit the purity criterion of the double standard, the happiness she had promised herself had eluded her.

Women who have attempted to resolve the paradox of sexuality by becoming a madonna think that they must play a respondent role in sex. Lannie felt unhappy because she wanted sex more often than her husband initiated it, and this did not fit her image of how she thought she should feel. Although it was fairly easy to arouse him, she felt cheapened when she took

282

the initiative and frustrated when she waited for him to act. She interpreted his lack of interest in sex as a rejection of her. Also, although her husband assured her that he liked having an initiating partner, he obviously seemed to enjoy sex much more when he was the instigator.

Lannie recalled a comment he had made that a woman who really enjoyed sex was insatiable and could not be satisfied by one man for very long. She suspected that he harbored an unacknowledged fear that once a woman's sexual potential was aroused, her sexuality would become uncontrollable and she would be "driven from man to man" in an effort to quench her appetite. "What nonsense, what a primitive suspicion," Lannie exclaimed. "I don't dare challenge him, though. He'd feel I was attacking his rationality as well as his performance. I guess I just have to keep quiet."

Men must take responsibility for perpetuating the misperception that a woman is more feminine and desirable when she is sexually receptive than when she is sexually assertive. This attitude has given men control of sex and has encouraged women to play the madonna role. It has drawn a sharper line between *female* and *feminine*, and has created distress and confusion for women who do not want always to play a receptive role.

Jennifer and Frank came for therapy together. Both were victims of the paradox of sexuality. He believed that he had a right to have sex whenever he wanted to. She believed that this was true and that she should be able to comply.

From the time she was eight until she was ten, Jennifer had been molested sexually by a "kindly" neighbor. Unable to avoid him, she kept quiet while her terror increased. As is true for many women when such a thing happens, Jennifer felt ashamed of herself and believed that being a girl made her vulnerable to abuse.

In marriage she tried to avoid sex even though she felt extremely guilty, thinking she was letting Frank down. He was a warm and affectionate person who loved Jennifer dearly. Since he knew she loved him, too, he was bewildered and hurt by her withdrawal. At the same time, he felt angry.

Frank seized upon any exchange of affection between them as a cue for intercourse. Knowing this, Jennifer began to avoid physical contact with him. She stopped greeting him with a kiss when he came home in the evening, stiffened up when he hugged her or they brushed against each other, and clung to her side of the bed. In his anger, he pressed harder; she shrank back even further into herself. Their alienation reached the point that they rarely talked, yet both of them realized that their commitment to each other was still strong and deep despite their problems. They began therapy.

Few women have partners who are willing to share responsibility for sexual difficulties. Many men take the "you have a problem" route. They are quick to send their wives for therapy when there are sexual problems. Other men adamantly refuse to admit that there are any problems at all. It serves them well that a woman who will not discuss sex is no embarrassment to a partner who feels threatened about his sexual adequacy. The paradox of sexuality protects such a man. If she tries to be a madonna, she can feel guilty about not being a temptress. And the reverse is also true: If she plays the role of a whore, the problem can be explained readily by her failure to be a madonna. Either way, she is responsible.

"He's supposed to be in charge when it comes to sex."

Most women give men credit for sexual relationships when they are good and are willing to protect men by assuming responsibility when relationships are bad. Perhaps women perpetuate this unequal responsibility for the pleasure and pain of sexual behavior because they have been assigned the role of protector of men's egos and masculinity. In this role, women have been given, inadvertently, power over men. In making sexual performance the fundamental proof of their manhood, men are pressured with psychological factors that can be potentially much more damaging to their erectile capacity than are physical or environmental factors. They fear that an angry, hostile woman, unless restrained by the paradox of sexuality, can devastate a man with a disdainful sniff, a cutting remark, or a cold shoulder. The whore and the madonna paradox seems to be a manifestation of the fear and anger men feel toward women because of their own sexual vulnerability and their yearning for safety and intimacy.

Perhaps as a result of men's attempt to equalize the balance of sexual power, most women have been conditioned to doubt almost everything about their sexual behavior. If a woman does not want sex as often as her partner does, she feels withered with inadequacy; if she wants sex more often than he does, she may feel ashamed of her "wantonness." If she does not want to join him in novel sexual experiences, she feels prudish; if she is interested in experimenting and he is not, she thinks that she is expecting too much of him. A woman may believe that if she is not whatever her partner wants sexually he will think he has a right to look for substitutes. When a man makes inappropriate sexual advances, a woman assumes that she has somehow elicited them. According to some views, a woman is responsible when she is raped, even though rape is known to be an expression of violent rage, not of sexual feelings.

Some women are in therapy a long time before they feel comfortable talking about sex. They have learned to inhibit their sexuality to the extent that they even see acquiring information about sex as unacceptable. For them the feeling persists that "nice girls don't do it, unless they are married, and they *never* talk about it." They believe it is less appropriate to be concerned about sexual problems than about problems in any other area of their lives. Taken to the extreme, it is as if they were saying to themselves, "If I think about sex, it is as bad as if I am lusting after a man." This attitude leads to the denial of sexual impulses and inhibits curiosity so that sexuality is effectively suppressed. This convolution of fact protects women from feeling guilty.

As therapists, we can easily empathize with the bewilderment many women feel when they realize that they must rethink years of conditioning. They spend many hours in therapy learning to be comfortable with their sexual assertiveness. At the same time they must struggle to change patterns of thinking about their sexuality and they have to develop new ways of behaving sexually. These changes may arouse feelings of anxiety about relating differently to sexual partners, perhaps partners with whom they have had years of negative experiences.

It is a challenge for women to assume responsibility for their own sexual pleasure. It is understandable that they may feel shy, timid, and embarrassed when they try out behaviors that express their newfound appreciation of their capacity for pleasure. They feel vulnerable, because new behaviors are uncomfortable. Their confidence is fragile because they are not yet sure of what their rights are and what their partners' responses will be. They may catastrophize that men will be repulsed or angry, or will see their changing as a demand or a signal that they yearn for other men.

The one sexual responsibility that men still seem to claim for themselves is that of bringing women to orgasm. The notion that sex is not important to women except for procreation, that it is a man's right and a woman's duty, has largely been dispelled. This idea was replaced with the misconception that women enjoyed sex primarily for the warmth and closeness associated with it. Female orgasm was not considered important; the temptress existed solely for a man's pleasure, while the madonna was passive, receptive, and undemanding as long as tender consideration accompanied a man's gratification. Then another notion became popular, perpetuated largely by men, that sex was more pleasurable for men when women had orgasms. The demand that women have orgasms simultaneously with men's became the mark of sexual achievement through which both partners earned their credentials as successful lovers.

The next step, the rediscovery of women's capacity for multiple orgasms, underlies today's prevailing sexual attitudes. This revelation has become, for women who are multiorgasmic, confirmation of their innate sexual potential. For women who are not multiorgasmic, it has uncovered nagging doubts that they will ever be adequate. For men, continuing to believe as they do that they should be the sexual aggressor, the demand to produce multiple orgasms in their partner exerts even greater pressure to perform and fear that they cannot. Nevertheless, men continue to see a woman's orgasmic "response" as a man's achievement, while maintaining that if she is nonorgasmic there is something wrong with her.

A woman needs to learn that she is in charge of her own body. The use of a woman's orgasm to enhance a man's sense of masculinity is an abrogation of her rights and a violation of her person. A woman is neither a man's property nor his plaything. Such thinking is a remnant of the time when a woman was seen as chattel, and it needlessly feeds the distress and confusion a woman feels about her sexuality.

Much of the emphasis in therapy in the past has been on helping women adjust to their partners' sexual expectations. As therapists, we prefer helping people with sexual problems by working with both partners. It comes as a surprise to many couples that the ideal sexual relationship is one in which each partner takes responsibility for his or her own sexuality. Upon reaching this understanding, both of them can become involved in a joint effort of discovery and change, individually and as a team.

Sometimes a woman's partner sits in the safety zone and refuses to become involved in therapy. When this happens, she often finds that she can change effectively alone. Her understanding and sexual growth is precious to her whether or not her partner is willing to be part of it. In addition, as she changes, her partner will change in response to her.

What is to be done about the pervasive negative effects of the paradox of sexuality? What is the resolution women can hope to achieve? We see our task as therapists as that of helping women acquire positive feelings about their sexuality, from which they can develop a capacity for sexual enjoyment. Then they can choose either to exercise this capacity or not to do so, depending upon their own best interests and their concern for others.

Sexuality is only one aspect of being a woman. She is first of all a person. As she resolves the paradoxes of equality, self-esteem, affiliation, dependency, emotionality, perception, conflict, and guilt, she will learn to value herself as a person who is proud to be a woman; worthy of receiving love, success, and respect; sure of who she is and what she wants; and assertive in expressing her complete personhood. Once a woman truly cares for, appreciates, and likes herself—once she loves herself—she will be prepared to express her capacity for affiliation, effectiveness, and sexuality.

CHAPTER XIII

Psychosomatics

"Getting sick isn't so bad; there's a lot of strength in being weak."

For one who has no other way to exercise power, sickness can be a useful tool. The paradox for many women is that when they are sick they receive the love, attention, and cooperation that they do not get at any other time. Sometimes sickness results in gaining a control over others that is unattainable when one is well. Although this paradox is rarely verbalized, it has been experienced widely, often without one's realizing it.

If you have ever experienced butterflies in your stomach you can understand psychosomatic illness. Butterflies are a minor physiological reaction to fear of stress, while psychosomatic illness is a more serious bodily reaction to more serious traumatic situations.

Psychosomatic illness is a complex subject, and we

cannot in the space of this chapter provide our readers with a complete understanding of the phenomenon, nor of the power people have to control their bodily health. Many books have been written about these subjects. We are concerned here only with the paradox of psychosomatics as it operates in women's lives. In the terms of the paradox a woman receives love, attention, and cooperation from others when she is ill and experiences feelings of power in her illness that she would not have if she were well.

The paradox of psychosomatics works in various ways and serves various purposes for the women who suffer it.

● It results from inhibiting spontaneous emotions and behaviors that do not fit the stereotype of amiable and confirming femininity.

● It rescues women with no other viable alternative from the frustration of unresolved conflicts.

● It is a respectable escape for women when the pain of illness seems less excruciating than the pain they have to confront when well.

● It takes the pressure off overwhelmed women who have found no other way to lighten their burdens.

● It gives otherwise unarmed women weapons with which to control and punish.

In discussing how we would proceed with this chapter, we were aware of the strong indignation we feel when we think of the paradox of psychosomatics. We are indignant that we live in a culture in which the secondary gains that people get from being ill often make illness seem preferable to good health. We are indignant that people have had to suffer illness in order to find an unconscious escape from harsher realities. We are indignant that people who have had no recourse except being ill have lost years of vitality and healthful living in a dysfunctional effort at coping. We are indignant that other unresolved paradoxes in women's lives are responsible for their succumbing to this one. We are especially indignant because psychosomatic illnesses are seen as more feminine than masculine.

Although men also experience psychosomatic illnesses, they do not experience the paradox as women do. Our culture reinforces health in men while it accepts illness as a normal state for women. Research has shown that doctors take men's symptoms more seriously than women's and attempt more actively to identify and cure men's illnesses. Women's symptoms are often seen as neurotic manifestations peculiar to women, and are treated with tranquilizers or other palliatives, often including a patronizing pat on the head. We are indignant about that, too.

It is important to understand that people who suffer psychosomatically do not consciously choose to do so. The secondary gains that sometimes come from illness are not originally anticipated. It is, however, a nice feeling to be taken care of and loved when sick, and this does discourage some people from getting well. Nevertheless, most people resist being labeled psychosomatically ill.

Typical of the many clients we have seen who resisted was Betty, who came reluctantly for therapy because her medical doctor had referred her to us. He was not the first doctor who had suggested psychotherapy for her.

At first Betty was indignant at her physician and distrustful of the value of psychotherapy. Her first words revealed her strong feelings: "I don't know why I'm here. I'm really sick, and I don't know how talking about it will make my pains go away or give me back my strength. I'm disgusted with my doctor; I think he just doesn't understand what is wrong with me in spite of all the tests and X-rays he's taken. I'm sure there is something he has missed." She added that part of her reluctance to come was because she would be ashamed to have anyone know that she was seeing a psychologist. They might think she was crazy, not sick at all. She found it painful enough to be sick without being accused of imagining her ills.

Betty had suffered from a variety of ailments and had spent much of the previous two years in bed or in doctors' waiting rooms. She thought that if her illnesses were psychosomatic, it meant they were all in her head, which she understood to imply they were imaginary, something her body told her was not true. If they were all in her head, she felt it meant she should be able to control them if she tried hard enough. Not being able to do this would suggest an unacceptable weakness on her part.

Betty was relieved when her therapist explained that psychosomatic illnesses are real physical illnesses, but that they combine emotional and physiological factors to produce symptoms. She had as much chance to prevent a psychosomatic illness by putting her mind to it as to prevent appendicitis. Psychosomatic illness, which is a physical reaction to a traumatic situation, reflects emotional distress that has not been handled in a functional way, either in the present or some earlier time. Her physical symptoms could be improved through therapy if she could identify and deal with emotional distresses that added their mischief to her illness.

Although developing psychosomatic illnesses is not a functional way to elicit reinforcement, it is a phenomenon that exists in many women's lives. There is an absurdity in the idea of gaining from suffering, yet there are complex factors in women's experience that can explain why illness sometimes serves women better than good health.

The rewards of illness accompany its debilitation. Illness sentences women to passive appreciation of the largess of others and cuts them off from the esteem-enhancing rewards that healthy persons earn for themselves. In this chapter we look at several common ways that the paradox of psychosomatics operates in women's lives.

"It's all right for a 'lady' to be sick."

The paradox of psychosomatics is tailored to fit the stereotype of femininity. For nonassertive women who are amiable and conforming, illnesses are often the result of the inhibition of spontaneous expressions that would not be seen as ladylike. Most "ladies" have pushed down within themselves a well of feelings that

291

seem unsafe to tap, but which later push their way to the surface with a gush of malevolence. Recent research has established that the health of married women who feel ambivalent about adjusting to their roles is much poorer than it was when they were single. Weary women who feel beaten down and helpless have found that they could give up the struggle and retire in pain to darkened rooms without being seen as less womanly.

Rosalie had wracking headaches when she was referred by her medical doctor for psychotherapy. She reported that they often come when her high school students seemed out of control in the midst of lively and controversial discussions. Sometimes headaches came when she wanted to be alone and fellow teachers dropped in on her unannounced. At other times a headache was triggered when she felt taken advantage of. She listened with disbelief when her therapist said that she was probably angry, that there might be things she needed to say, but would not let herself express. "Do you mean," she said, "that angry thoughts are trying to push out of the top of my head because I won't let them out of my mouth?" Rosalie could not have said it better!

Anger was not an acceptable feeling for Rosalie, since she thought it very unattractive in a lady. She had been raised to be amiable and compliant. When she was a child, her parents praised her and friends sought her out because of her pleasant disposition. To be around anyone who was angry set her escape reflexes in motion. By the time she was an adult, Rosalie could not recognize her own anger and believed she did not experience it. She was hooked into the paradox of psychosomatics and did not know that her headaches served to replace her anger and to elicit solicitude from others. It was more acceptable to her for ladies to have headaches than to be angry.

Discussions in therapy helped Rosalie isolate other areas in her life in which she denied her spontaneity and paid for her cordiality with a crashing headache. She saw that this happened when important issues were hotly discussed among her friends. For instance, she sympathized strongly with the farmworker movement and the problems of other minorities. It bothered her to hear unjust criticisms of powerless people. Yet she sat silently, and her head punished her for her cowardice about speaking out.

Rosalie's favorite hobby was oil painting in her garden. She enjoyed being alone among the flowers she loved and luxuriated in this special time of pleasure. On occasion, a neighbor man in whom she had no interest would drop by as soon as she went outside and engage her in conversation. She wondered why she got a headache every time. She learned in therapy that rather than let him know that she did not want to visit with him, she had been polite while her angry feelings clashed like cymbals inside her head.

Rosalie experienced the paradox of psychosomatics as a result of her well-integrated instruction in ladyship. By inhibiting her honest feelings so she would not appear unladylike, she violated her right to express her opinions and choose how she would spend her time. She was so accustomed to being amiable that when she was imposed upon the imperatives of her childhood reappeared, telling her that she must be sweet and kind regardless of how she felt. Having no place else to go, the feelings she could not destroy by her friendly smile signaled their rebellion.

Rosalie's experience is shared by many married women who attempt to conform to roles about which they feel ambivalent. We have dealt in previous chapters with the expectations made of women in marriage, expectations that are either unrealistic or for which women are unprepared. Recent research has established that married women experience poorer emotional health than they did when they were single and that married women as a group seem to suffer more than single women. It is reasonable to suggest that psychosomatic problems play a role in this. The body of a married woman may in this way object to seemingly endless days of boredom or back-breaking burdens. Since women are readily excused for illness, getting sick becomes preferable to complaining and is not as threatening as change might be.

That is the way it was for Patricia, a client who was sick and sick of being married. She told us, "I don't know what's wrong with me. When I watch television commercials I think I must have tired blood. But I think I'm too young for that." It seemed to Patricia that all the zip had gone out of life. She felt constantly dragged down with one respiratory infection after another. "The funny thing is, I was never sick before I was married. I even had perfect attendance in high school." Discussion revealed that Patricia was not as happy in her married role as she had expected to be. It seemed that staleness had crept up and overtaken her, and she was numbed by the dullness of her days.

Angela, another client, was suffering from the backlash of trying to prove her ambitious mother wrong. She was experiencing depression, which has been called "the illness that has no name." She felt as bad as if she were physically ill. As she described it, "I know that I'm closing the curtains on life. I can't sleep at night, but in the daytime I can hardly keep my eyes open. I sit all day and watch soap operas, drinking too much, and ignoring the kids. Each night I tell myself, 'Thank God, one more day is gone.' "

Angela's mother, who had resented giving up her own career when she married, had repeatedly warned her daughter, "The worst thing that can happen to a woman is to be stuck at home as a wife and mother." She steered Angela through career preparation routines designed to insure that she would take the world by storm. Annoyed by her mother's pushiness, Angela resisted her ambitions for her. She married at nineteen and plunged into housewifery, a role that fit her only until the heat of her rebellion cooled. Depression, her helpless response to a disagreeable life, settled over Angela like a black cloud once she sensed the mounting evidence that her mother had been right. Housewifery was a flop, and Angela bottomed out in the paradox of psychosomatics. Her depression had lowered her resistance and she suffered from frequent respiratory infections.

News stories occasionally report cases in which after the death of one partner, the other dies suddenly. The second death is ascribed to a broken heart—once the loved one was gone, there was no further reason for living.

The paradox of psychosomatics usually works in a less dramatic way when women who have been badgered until their resistance breaks give up and retreat into sickness. Their sickness is accepted; their previous pleas have gone unheard.

It was this way for Ruby, a legal secretary who felt helpless to defend herself at work. Sickness was certainly not something she intended, but it proved to be a "ladylike" way out for her. When she came for therapy she was painfully thin and so nervous her hands trembled as much as her voice did. She recounted a history with a boss who saved himself from ulcers by aiming his violent outbursts of temper at her, regardless of who had pushed his anger button. She said,

> I've been intimidated for years by his screaming and cursing, but every time I wanted to quit I realized how scarce jobs are so I tried to take the lumps silently. I was actually afraid to face up to him and quit, even though my insides curled up every time he bellowed. I finally got so nervous, I lost weight and I could hardly type a letter. One day I just gave up; the dam broke, and the tears rushed down my cheeks. Surprised, my boss asked me what was wrong. I blurted out my feelings, ashamed and helpless. The irony of it is that once he wore me down to the level of a sniveling child, he became very nice and considerate. The trouble is, I don't know how long it will take me to get my nerves settled and my weight back. I just wish he could have been more understanding without my getting sick.

"I have no other alternative."

Some women see no alternatives to the situations in which they find themselves. For a capable woman, trying to fit into dependent and submissive roles may cause such frustration that she sees no acceptable way to behave. Being sexy or charming does not suit her, but getting sick rescues her from the frustration of holding down her abilities so she will not outshine a man. In addition, dependent women who are hostile and angry, yet are unnerved by their low self-esteem, do not dare to take chances. In becoming sick they have conflicts resolved in their favor or, better yet, avoid conflict entirely by removing themselves to the sickbed, an effective throne from which to elicit cooperation.

Rebecca demonstrated how a capable woman can become so frustrated that she will develop a full-blown illness to prevent a more threatening explosion. In her case, one paradox led to another. Her efforts to live out the myth that the man should be head of the family pressed her inexorably into the paradox of psychosomatics. It was not until she came to therapy that she realized that the painful arthritis that might someday cripple her completely could be connected with the frustration of her considerable talents.

Rebecca's first words in therapy suggested what the root of her problems might be. She said immediately, "My husband is a very good businessman." Experience has shown us that such a statement may be a denial of the real source of distress. It can mask suppressed rage, as it did in Rebecca's case—rage that she was a capable woman whose talents were being stifled as she tried to conform to a dependent role.

Rebecca and her husband Tony had worked together for twelve years in their advertising business. They were very different. Tony approached things with caution and deliberated a long time before making decisions. Rebecca's style was spontaneous, outgoing, and confident. Unfortunately, their business was not financially successful and Rebecca was frustrated and unhappy in it, although she hated to admit it.

Rebecca had enjoyed considerable business success before she married Tony. She had eight years experience in advertising and was well respected for her creativity and her ability to carry through. When Tony, who worked for a rival agency, proposed marriage, she fastened her hopes to his dream and together they started their own agency.

By the time Rebecca learned how differently she and Tony worked and how frustrated she felt working with him, their business was deeply in debt and she saw no alternative but to stay and press herself harder to work their way out. During the years she stretched her capacities and bore two children, whose care she combined with her job.

When Rebecca felt uneasy about her negative reactions to the way Tony did things, rather than challenge him she pitched in harder to smooth over the rough spots. As she described it,

> I knocked myself out to develop creative ideas, but they were often wasted because there was no one to follow through on them. The accounts I developed dried up because I didn't want to take the leadership role and act like I was taking over. I suppose I could have charmed Tony with pleasing ways or flattered him in an effort to make him do things the way I thought best. But those ways don't agree with me. Instead, the rage of frustration grew in me until I thought I'd burst. I was afraid of what would happen if I did let my feelings out, so I swallowed them and learned to be faithfully inattentive to any rumblings of rebellion I felt.

Sickness became a way out for Rebecca. The anger that she held in found a home in her joints and stiffened them with arthritis. Had she resolved the earlier paradoxes, she might have learned more effective ways than getting sick to cope with frustration, anger, and conflict, ways that would have better suited an assertive, forthright, and goal-oriented woman like herself.

Rebecca was able to do this in therapy. Starting with the paradox of equality, she saw how she had been socialized to play a role of submissiveness that did not fit her at all. Reinforced by the importance of affiliative relationships and feeling that she needed to depend upon someone, she looked up to Tony and denied her perceptions when she felt she was right and he was wrong. She avoided conflict and took responsibility for the harmony of their relationship, a relationship based on a fantasy she felt safer not to examine.

Rebecca described it as a humbling experience to see for herself that "a bright, capable woman like me could use sickness to run away from problems, but I believe that is what happened. I couldn't accept my feelings about our business, but I could accept my illness. Since it seemed inevitable, I didn't blame myself for it. Tony was always considerate and understanding when I was in pain and would do anything to help me. I would have hated myself if I'd ever blown up at him since he was so nice. I couldn't tell him I was crippled by feelings I couldn't express. I didn't know it myself!"

"Illness is a respectable out."

Illness gives some women a respectable escape from difficulties that may seem more agonizing to experience than sickness itself. Illness has glued together many relationships that could not stand the test of good health. A fragile woman can expect not to be criticized. For timid women, not confident in their relationships, being sick is like insurance against being abandoned. Disappointed women who have not been able to admit their hurt have swallowed their pain. For these women, the pain of illness is less excruciating than the pain of their disillusionment; their bodies cooperate perversely by giving them demanding symptoms to think about. Among these women are mothers who have lost their reason for living when their children are grown and their nest is empty. What more respectable way is there to get attention when a woman is no longer needed than by being sick?

A girl can learn very early in life, yet never realize, that illness can provide her respectable refuge from difficult dilemmas. In Ruth's case sickness was accompanied by the rewards of more attention. It was as if she had said to herself, "I only get attention when I am sick."

Ruth came to therapy when she was twenty-two to

try to formulate some vocational goals for herself. She was strongly convinced that her poor health would limit her ability to succeed in any demanding job. She was looking for one that a person who may not be able to work every day might expect to succeed at.

Ruth's father had died when she was five. She never forgot the feeling she had at that time. She was sure that his loss was more devastating to her than to anyone else, since she had spent more time sitting on his lap or walking through the woods with him than anyone else had. He had known how to make his little girl feel important.

In the period immediately following his death, no one paid much attention to Ruth. She felt pushed aside in favor of business details and out-of-town family. Bewildered, she did not know what to think. Life without her daddy did not seem very promising. She had her first respiratory attack a few nights after the funeral. Frightened by Ruth's alarming symptoms, her mother gave Ruth her undivided attention.

From then on, Ruth got sick whenever a situation suggested that she was unloved or neglected, which happened frequently in her much-changed world. Her daddy was gone forever, and her mommy now had to go to work. She frequently had difficulty breathing when her mother disciplined her. When her mother began dating again, Ruth felt frightened that her fragmented world would disintegrate further. Often an attack would come just before her mother was to leave for an evening of fun. Ruth felt very loved when her mother would cancel her own plans to stay home with Ruth.

Although she outgrew her respiratory problems, Ruth had other illnesses as she grew older. Her health became a primary concern in making family plans. They even moved west to help her allergies. Ruth never became very robust in spite of her mother's diligent attention to her daughter's persistent symptoms.

In the spring of her senior year in college, when Ruth had compelling evidence that she would flunk several courses, she developed unexplained stomach pains and had to drop out of school. Since she was welcomed home with sympathy and love, it was easy to focus on the happiness of her homecoming. Unnoticed was the fact that her illness had provided her with an easy out.

Ruth's psychosomatic pattern had started in early childhood, and by the time she was an adult it was a well-ingrained habit. At no time had Ruth realized that she might be unconsciously using illness to get attention and to feel loved. For Ruth the paradox of psychosomatics had cheated her out of the joys of childhood that a healthy girl would have enjoyed. Illness was a morbid pipeline to the rewards of love and feeling important. As a child of five, she had not known any other alternative. As an adult, she could take better paths to win the reinforcement she wanted. She could attract attention because of her positive qualities, not because she was pathetic or helpless.

Like many people suffering from psychosomatic problems, Ruth resisted change. Challenged by members of her young women's therapy group and supported by their encouragement, she worked through her initial feelings of embarrassment and became indignant when she realized that she had been cheated by a paradox that had given her small gains for big losses. Once she had experienced indignation, she was able to focus more on good health than on sickness. When she was willing to risk success, she applied herself to a job and proved to herself that old patterns can change. The ghosts of her old paradox had been challenged and laid to rest.

Rosemary found that illness gave her a respectable escape from disappointment and also protected her from criticism. She had two major complaints when we first saw her: "My health is so poor that I frequently can't leave home for weeks at a time," and "I'm thoroughly and completely disgusted with my husband, who never tries to get ahead." Rosemary was caught in the runaround of projecting onto her husband her feelings of disappointment in herself. Her girlhood ambition had been to be a dancer. Trained in ballet and an outstandingly talented performer in her hometown,

300

she arrived in New York ready to see her name in lights. She found that there she was just another aspiring dancer. Frustrated at the elusiveness of the Big Time, she got sick, pocketed her untested potential, and returned home to marry the man who had promised he would always wait for her. Rosemary's disappointment was so intense that she buried it under the mantle of respectable symptoms. When asked by well-meaning friends about her thwarted plans, she explained that she was too sick to put the necessary effort into a career. In private, she unleashed the fury of her disappointment onto her husband, disguising her pain by focusing on his real and imagined failures. She wanted him, through his accomplishments, to bring her the star status she had not earned for herself.

Rosemary kept busy caring for her health and enjoying the solicitude of a husband who never questioned that sickness had tragically subverted her great career.

Velma, a young housewife, seemed to be having more illnesses every year. She had married John when he was a young engineer as unsure of himself as she was of herself. Able and hardworking, he shed fears with each promotion. He gained confidence from his enviable successes, but Velma felt threatened as his career carried them into sophisticated circles where she was expected to entertain. What preparation had her childhood on a dairy farm given her to plan and carry out elaborate parties and to make conversation with strangers? Certain the John was disenchanted with her lack of sophistication, Velma feared he would abandon her in favor of a woman who would be a better social asset. She noticed that, although he was disappointed, he would leave a party early if she got sick. In time she seemed to be sick a lot, and this provided a respectable excuse to keep them home and a good reason to avoid entertaining. Although John missed his friends, he accepted that Velma could not help her poor health. Of course he would not leave her. The paradox worked for her!

Marsha became almost an invalid as her children

301

were growing up and no longer needed her to be closely affiliated with them. When they were little she basked in the warm pleasure of doing things for and with them. The children were admired for their appearance and excellence in school, and being their mother enlivened Marsha's days and nourished her spirit. Their accomplishments became her rewards, and she felt like a most successful mother. To her dismay, as they grew older they became resentful of the controls she exerted in their lives. They sidestepped as she pushed them forward.

Marsha inadvertently found that she could be reassured of her children's caring when she was ill. Sickness became a way of life for her. Unfortunately, it was a precarious way to hold her family close to her, since it depended upon their goodwill, which was by that time on the decline. As her complaints increased the paradox backfired. Her children became alienated and avoided her, unaware that her sickness was a pathetic expression of her need to stay connected to them.

When her children are all grown and the nest is empty, a woman who has stayed healthy throughout her children's lives often finds herself falling apart. Yvonne, a woman of fifty, put it this way, "When my children were sick, I was always healthy; I *had* to be. My husband worked long hours, and I often had to be mother and father to them, and always held up. Now that they are grown and gone, I have nothing to keep me busy, I'm falling apart. I've been to the doctor ten times in the past six months, and take several medications. I wake up in the night, sweating and shaking, convinced that I must have cancer. I remember longingly the years when each child-filled day exhausted me so much that I didn't know what insomnia was." Yvonne was a pitiful example of the many mothers in our culture who, after devoting the middle third of their lives to raising their children, find they have no design to fill the yawning years ahead.

There are other situations in which being sick has

provided women with a respectable escape from harsher realities. When Sara's father died she felt so weak she was unable to help select a coffin. A friend went in her place. Everyone agreed that Sara should not be pressured at such a time. Norma developed such severe stomach cramps on the way to the airport that she begged off flying, which she had always feared. Her friend understood her embarrassment and comforted her. Zelda did not like big parties, and her in-laws were planning one for Christmas Eve. She had a migraine and could not go. Her husband stayed home with her because he did not want her to be alone on the holiday. Virginia hated housework and cooking. When she got bronchitis, she stayed out of the kitchen and her roommate did all the cooking. She still seemed too weak to cook even after several weeks. All this time her roommate uncomplainingly kept on with the kitchen detail. In each of these instances such solicitude and love was shown the woman who was sick that it is likely that the sickness would strike again in similar circumstances.

"It takes the pressure off."

The paradox of psychosomatics also serves to take the pressure off women, although in doing so it extracts at least a pound of flesh. A woman who is overwhelmed by responsibility may break down, only to find that others cooperate better when they see her as deserving of help because she is sick. Women who live in frightening circumstances may feel safe only when they are seen as too weak to be abused. Dependent women who are sick can expect to be taken care of. Sickness provides justification for staying in a rut of passivity rather than confronting the indignities of a dominant-submissive relationship.

When responsibilities seem overwhelming and the pressure is unbearable, one effective way to get out from under the burden is to develop an illness. This not only lightens the load, but assures the sufferer that others will come forth to offer cooperation. Nelda, a widow, found to her surprise that this was the way the

303

paradox worked for her. "Can you imagine the irony of it?" she asked. "All those years I begged for cooperation and never got it, but once I was flat on my back, no one could do enough to help."

Nelda had heavy responsibilities. She had supported her three children by working as a nurse's aide. She gardened, sewed, and did whatever else she could to stretch a dollar. She would come home at night, tired to the point of exhaustion, to find that the chores the children were assigned were still undone. Wearily, she pitched in. She was resigned to the fact that it was easier to do the work than to argue.

When we first saw Nelda, the strain had caught up with her. She was recovering from a heart attack. She needed vocational guidance, since she would have to plan a less strenuous life for her future. She frankly admitted, "Although my heart attack seemed like the end of the world for me at the time, it drew the whole family together. The children are all eager now to see what each of them can do to help. My mother used to quote an expression, 'God writes straight with crooked lines.' I guess my illness is an example of what she meant."

For a frightened woman, sickness can take the pressure off in relationships where she does not feel safe. Lorraine is an extreme case who was brought for therapy by her husband Don because he "hated to see her suffer so."

Don insisted that he loved Lorraine very much and would do anything in his power to help her get well. In fact, he had been marvelously kind and patient during her many illnesses. He outlined a history of their life together. During their fifteen years of marriage, Lorraine had several serious abdominal operations as well as what had been described as a nervous breakdown. She seemed timid and retiring and had spent most of her life indoors, usually confined to bed. They no longer went out socially and never entertained. Their friends had gradually dwindled. Don did not object to the expense of her many illnesses because, obviously, she could not help being sick. He searched for remedies, hoping she

304

could become once more the happy, healthy bride he had married.

Don was a self-made man. He owned several businesses, which he ran with an iron hand. Controlled on the surface, he blew his stack if things did not go his way. His employees had learned to acquiesce to avoid his temper, so violent that he had been known to break furniture in his rage. Although neither of them realized it, Lorraine had found a sure-fire way to avoid his punishing outbursts. She got sick.

Therapy gave Lorraine a chance to examine the malevolence in her life with Don and to understand the dynamics of their alliance. It became clear that she was appropriately frightened of Don's temper and that the only time she really felt safe with him was when she was sick. When she was well, he treated her with the same harshness he used with others; when she was sick, he was all solicitude. He padlocked his temper then and reacted with loving concern.

Lorraine's fears had begun on their honeymoon when a blown-out tire catapulted Don into a rage. She had never seen him act that way during their courtship and was overwhelmed by the experience. She drew herself closer to her side of the car as the first of her many stomachaches began to gnaw in her middle.

Lorraine had always dated men who treated her with gentleness and kindness. Don had done this until they were married. Unprepared as she was for this outburst on their honeymoon, she stifled her fears; they settled in her stomach where they began their mischief. After the honeymoon was over, Lorraine found that Don frequently took out his anger on her. Her ears were no longer too delicate for profanity; he did not mind her seeing the dark side of his personality. If a business deal did not go well, Don was complaining and critical when he got home. If a screw dropped while he was repairing something, he cursed loud enough for the neighbors to hear. If their dog knocked over its water or tripped him, Don kicked or abused the animal. Lorraine was never certain that she might not be the next victim of his anger.

The paradox of psychosomatics came to Lorraine's

rescue by providing safety when she was sick enough to elicit pity. She could live with her pain better than she could live with constant fear. Being sick enabled her to avoid Don's worst qualities and experience the gentler parts of his personality, which were otherwise suppressed. In taming a tyrant with her sickness, Lorraine made it safe to stay dependent upon Don. Illness justified her passivity and guaranteed his benign dominance.

"I can control and punish."

Giving women the power to control and punish is another way that the paradox of psychosomatics affects women's lives. Women who have not resolved the conflicts generated by other paradoxes do not have effective skills with which to communicate and negotiate with others. Unfortunately, they have found that it is possible for weak people to control strong ones; sick women can keep generations of family members in line by a well-turned phrase or a guilt-inducing sigh. Having produced the guilt, they can easily punish those who resist.

In order to resolve the paradox of psychosomatics in their lives, women need to look at the gains they may be reaping from illness, some of which involve controlling and punishing other people. Women who lack communicative skills and do not feel good about themselves find themselves at a loss, unable to ask directly for what they want and too unsure of themselves to stick with negotiations to hammer out compromises. They have learned, as subordinate groups have throughout history, to use manipulative ways to slide through life. It may be that the only way they know to achieve a sense of control in their lives is to use their weakness as a strength, disarming the opposition with the tyranny of helplessness.

Control of others by sickness ranges from such claims as "I need to sit in the front seat of the car so I won't get carsick" to "If you don't finish law school and take over my practice, the work will kill me."

The woman who never felt much direct power in her

family finds that a few well-timed heart palpitations can bring everyone else's plans to a halt; a phone call in the middle of the night will bring anxious relatives and friends to a sufferer's bedside; the thought of a loved one languishing alone keeps family members from leaving a sick one behind to take well-earned vacations; growing and grown children allow their dreams to collapse so their sick parent will not be unsettled by their independence. It is simply a matter of the weak controlling the strong, paradoxical because of its absurdity, dysfunctional because goals met by indirection bring out or cater to the worst in people.

Why do we let a person who is sick control us? Because we would feel guilty if we stood up to them. Guilt induction is the powerful, effective tool used to control others through illness. It can lay low the hardy but unsuspecting soul, and can punish those who refuse to succumb. This is the way a group of our clients described how people used guilt induction to control or punish them:

Pam said, "My mother-in-law! She expects me to call her daily, although, curiously, she doesn't expect her son to. I feel like a worm if I neglect to call her one day, and the next day she reminds me that a telephone call can do wonders to brighten up a sick person's life. It lets her know she is *loved*! I feel both guilty and punished and end up apologizing. Yet I don't believe it is right that I feel so obligated."

Regina said, "My parents control me through guilt. For years I've wanted to take a cruise for my vacation. Yet every year I save up my vacation time and spend it at their home. They say they are too feeble to visit me and 'Who knows whether we will be around next year.' I can imagine how I'd be punished if I told them I'd like to take my chances on that and do something just for myself for once."

Nora berated herself, "I don't have the patience to endure quietly when my mother calls me long distance and unwinds all her bitterness on me. She zeros in on me as if my leaving home were the cause of her illness. I feel guilty living so far away, so I think I should be patient when she attacks me. She controls me to the extent that I can hardly enjoy my life. And since I refuse to move back home she puts the guilties on me!"

Mary Jo's business partner controlled her. "He has a heart condition that he plays to the hilt. He doesn't grasp his chest and collapse into a chair, but he might as well. He makes it plain that I don't dare add to his stress. He has become so anxious that he needs to control everything. I'm afraid to insist that he allow me some decisions about what we do and the way we do it. I wouldn't want to be responsible for what might happen if I challenged him."

"How about this for being controlled by the weak?" asked Cheryl. "I can't even leave my children in the day-care nursery to go shopping. The first time I did, the baby cried herself sick. I haven't had the heart to do it again."

To these women can be added countless others who have been punished by sick people who found the paradoxical power to control in a way that only the most secure can resist.

The resolution of the paradox of psychosomatics is not easy. First, as with all paradoxes, women who suffer from it should not blame themselves, but see that they are once more the victims of their feelings of powerlessness. When other paradoxes are resolved, women will have the power they need to act directly in their own best interests and to elicit positive responses from others. They will see that indirection as a model for behavior is not worthy of them. They will see several reasons why it is a mistake to depend on sickness. At times the gains of attention and caring may not come; sick people are frequently ignored. What is even worse, people who are sick run the risk of appearing unattractive, disliked, and distrusted. Having developed a passive or a complaining personality, they are not likely to be listened to when they most desire it. Resolutions of conflicts are generally avoided and the person who is sick has little chance of making an impact when decisions are made. People who are sick miss out on what they really want to experience by not being able to participate fully in life.

Plainly, the paradox of psychosomatics is too high a price to pay for the privilege of securing love, cooperation, safety, and high self-esteem, all of which are part of a woman's birthright and can be gained in more functional, direct ways. The resolution of this paradox leads to revitalization and reintegration of a woman's healthy self and to reality-based relationships.

CHAPTER XIV

Fear

"I want to want to, and I won't."

Women have not been encouraged to see themselves as courageous, nor to take risks in order to grow. They have been expected to suffer in silence when life is unpleasant. Their fears increase, and they become immobilized. They may develop a pattern of expressing desires upon which they never act. The paradox is that women tell themselves they are undecided when, in fact, their fear guarantees that they will not do anything. Such women exemplify the adage, "Not to choose is to choose not to."

Fear is one emotion that underlies all of the paradoxes discussed in this book. In this chapter we focus on each paradox to show how a woman's fear can rule her decisions as surely as external forces do.

The paradox of fear is the conflict generated by women's knowledge that they are desperately unhappy and their fear of pursuing changes in their lives, the outcomes of which are unknown. Women who let fear control them are immobilized in the dead space between gaining the prize of personal growth and competence and surrendering to their own resistance. This is not surprising, for women have been told repeatedly that they are weak and should expect protection in their dependent roles. They have not been credited with being courageous. A woman may need encouragement to venture from safe backwaters to the fearsome mainstream of life. Encouragement, however, is seldom enough; sometimes fear dictates that she will settle for the distress of the paradox she is trapped in rather than risk following an unknown route to freedom.

Women who are caught in the immobilizing paradox of fear often verbalize the first half of the paradox. "I want to want to." Their wish to act is acknowledged, but action halts there; the decision, "and I won't," overrules their wish. These are the women who come to therapy only once or twice, and those who come demanding quick relief in the middle of their crises. In their initial therapy sessions they are confronted at some level with the paradoxes of their lives. The second half of the paradox of fear, "and I won't," is much tougher to swallow than the first half. Overwhelmed with fear, their wish for a resolution of their conflicts fades into the impotence of choosing not to do anything.

"How can I be both equal and inferior?"

Annie came for one or two therapy sessions on three different occasions. The first time her therapist saw her, Annie's husband Jack had demanded a divorce. Their relationship had been as stormy as the blustery winter day they met. At that time, Annie was in love with Roger, whom she wanted to marry. Roger had just broken their engagement because he decided he was not interested in marrying anyone, even though he said he cared for Annie a great deal. He thought it was unfair to continue seeing her, knowing that she wanted to marry him.

Feeling rejected, Annie quickly attached herself to Jack, rationalizing away her resentment when he was late for dates, made crude comments about other women, and erupted in anger. Annie had always been treated with respect and appreciation until she met Jack, and she responded to his behavior as if it were a challenge instead of a warning that he was not the kind of person in whom she should invest her devotion. Given time to recover from her bankrupt love affair with Roger, Annie probably would not have married Jack. Unfortunately, she became pregnant on the one occasion he cajoled her into having sex, and they hurried off to the justice of the peace within three months of their first date.

Jack was not any more considerate after marriage than he had been before. Annie found herself bombarded with the paradoxical messages of equality. He believed Annie should work until the baby was born, since they were "equal partners in a giant venture." Annie agreed that she should work, but not that they were equal partners. While her earnings went into a joint account, Jack seemed to think that he was entitled to spend the money he earned without consulting her. He said that since he was the head of the family and knew about finances, he would make the decisions. It chafed when Jack's decisions involved such things as a new camper for him and going to the laundromat for her, hunting trips with his buddies for him and sitting home with the television set for her.

Once the baby was born, Jack began spending more evenings away from home, saying, "Well, it just doesn't make sense for both of us to sit at home with a kid." Unable to accept this position, Annie fought back with temper tantrums or sullen silence. Jack reacted to this by staying away from home even more. Annie began to realize that she was caught in the conflicts inherent in trying to be equal with a man who wanted to maintain a dominant-subordinate relationship.

When she first came for therapy, Annie had two children and only minimal job skills. Jack had threatened divorce because she was, as he put it, "one long complaint after another." Everything would be fine, he said, if she would take care of herself and leave him alone. Since she would not do this, he wanted out. The fear of losing Jack at that time in her life was overwhelming to Annie. Examining solutions to their conflicts, however, was equally frightening, and Annie cancelled her second appointment.

311

Five months later Annie returned for therapy, strong with temporary resolve to stick with therapy until she found answers for her latest crisis.

"Last week," Annie began, "the school called and said I had to come in for a conference. Their teachers say that Jackie has been talking back and getting into fights and Teddy sits and daydreams without doing any work. When I told Jack he said, 'What do you expect? Jackie hears you bitching all day, and Teddy gets away from it just like I do, except I leave home physically and he just does it mentally.' Once again, Jack's pointed the finger at me."

Annie kept her next appointment. Her concern for her boys' distress put enough starch in her backbone to work out some short-term plans to help them correct their behavior at school. She realized, though, that she was procrastinating when it came time to resolve her own problems. "I have to stop doing this," she said. "I can't go on this way with Jack, feeling beaten down and fighting back with anger all the time. That gives him justification for what he does, and that's not the real issue. The real problem is that I resent being treated like an inferior. If I could stop feeling so bad, then I could decide what to do. I'll be back next week and start focusing on myself. Once I feel better about myself, I'll be able to do something about the situation with Jack."

Perhaps unconsciously Jack knew that Annie would not tolerate his behavior and would leave him if she felt equal to him. In any case, she cancelled her next appointment, saying that he refused to let her spend the money. Jack's intervention reaffirmed the inequality in their unhappy alliance and allowed Annie once again to avoid facing her fears.

Several months later Annie made another appointment. She had discovered that Jack was involved with another woman. When she had confronted him with what she knew, he said that the affair had nothing to do with their marriage. He no longer wanted a divorce; he just wanted Annie to get off his back and leave him alone.

I think he did this deliberately to hurt me. He wants to rattle my cage so he can feel better than I do. I just finished my first semester of college and got terrific grades. Remember, you and I had talked about my doing that, so I'd have something to feel good about as well as learn some job skills. That's one thing I wasn't afraid to do for myself. Jack seemed to resent it, because he sure made it difficult. He refused to stay home with the kids, and I had to hire babysitters. Then he complained because I was spending the money. Every time I had to study for an exam, he started an argument. He must have wanted me to fail.

Annie was no doubt correct in assuming that Jack did not want her to go to school. He seemed to give her just enough punishment to keep her defeated and helpless, and just enough hope to keep her tied to him. In any case, she felt less fearful after two sessions and was strong enough to demand that Jack come with her for therapy. But her strength soon ebbed. Annie cancelled her next appointment, explaining that Jack insisted they be referred to a male therapist who would be able to understand his position.

Annie remained rooted in the charade of male-female roles. Procrastination interspersed with just enough therapy to help her through each crisis was the way Annie's fear fixed her in her place.

"I've done so well—why do I feel so bad?"

Christine's story demonstrates the paradox of fear in another way. Her husband Andy was ambitious, well-educated, and capable, whereas she described herself as a quiet, gentle follower. She tried for several years to please Andy by entertaining his business friends and associates, going to conventions and conferences, and being available for cocktail parties and dinners. She forced herself to be outgoing, social, and a decorative asset in his drive toward success. Christine tried to fit the image Andy wanted. Because the fit felt wrong, she was plagued with feelings of low self-esteem. She

313

became increasingly nervous with strangers and, according to him, did not sparkle and put others at ease.

Christine was caught in the paradox of self-esteem. Despite having done well filling the role her husband assigned, she still felt bad. His critical messages futher eroded her sense of worth. She suffered in silence, afraid to disappoint Andy by telling him that she would like to trade the glamour of her public image for a comfortable homemaker role.

At the time Christine came for her one and only therapy session, she was already frozen in fear. She came only because her husband insisted, saying, "If you could see how nice people are and how impressed they could be with you, you wouldn't be so depressed. You'd be the cheerful, happy wife I know you can be."

At the end of her session, after discussing that she would really like to tell him, "There's nothing wrong with how I really am; it's only in trying so hard to please you that I do my best and still find I'm not good enough," Christine said, "I haven't decided if I'll come back or not." Her therapist sensed that in not making the decision to return for therapy, Christine had in fact decided not to. Wanting to be herself was much different from resolving to become herself.

"Without you I'm nothing; with you I lose my sense of identity."

Denise had been taught that she would be a real woman, warm, loving, and fulfilled, when she was affiliated with a man. Her father taught her that winning another person's approval was the most important skill a woman could have. He frequently told her to be just like her please-everyone mother. Her mother was a willing model, and Denise learned to be compliant, amiable, forgiving, generous, and thoughtful. She was a "perfect" daughter, loving toward her parents, popular with her teachers and her classmates, and an obedient worker.

The summer she graduated from high school, Denise became engaged to a man she barely knew. The rewards of belonging to him made up for his dullness.

Although her parents approved of the engagement, they wanted her to stay at home and attend the local junior college. Denise felt some frustration with them and a tremor of independence, but being afraid to risk their displeasure she complied with her mother and father's wishes.

College gave Denise a taste of life she had never dared to envision. She met a young man who told her that she had much to learn and he would like to be her teacher, because he saw "smoldering fires burning beneath a compliant facade."

Denise came for therapy full of turmoil. "I'm not so naive that I believe his line," she said, "but I know that in a way he's right. All my life I've gone along with everyone else's wishes because I was afraid of not having anyone. I needed them. Now I realize I don't even know myself; I haven't any idea of who I really am. Yet I'm committed to school here and to marriage. I'm just nineteen, and I can predict just about everything that will happen to me for the rest of my life. I need to find out what I want, instead of just going along with what everyone else wants for me."

Unfortunately, Denise's fear of displeasing her parents and her fiancé, of cutting her affiliative bonds with them, was stronger than her wish to test the uncertainties of creating her own destiny. Therapy would have involved disengagement from others' objectives for her and cultivating her own. For Denise, *disengagement* translated into *disintegration*. Her fear dictated that she would choose not to act.

Sometimes women do not continue with therapy because their affiliative need seems so strong that they cannot risk the disapproval of their therapist. They think that if they told their complete story, their therapist would be shocked and rejecting. Therapy is most helpful when clients are able to fully disclose and share their thoughts and feelings, both positive and negative. Knowing this, their fear of being judged tugs too powerfully, and they do not return.

Not having been in therapy before, other women may interpret a therapist's statements or questions in terms of their fears. They are afraid that in order to overcome the paradox of affiliation, they will have to end their present relationships. Others interpret messages to mean that they must stay in relationships whether they want to or not. These fears are groundless, but there may be no way for a new client to know this, especially in the beginning. It takes time to establish trust.

"I have to destroy myself in order to survive."

Karen was thirty-two when she came to us for therapy. She had two children, ten and seven, and was in the middle of a divorce. She had never worked during her marriage; her husband Jerry had not wanted her to. "I'm so disgusted with myself because I quit school years ago thinking I'd never need a job, so why stay in a grind I didn't enjoy." Karen had filed for divorce and had planned to move to another state where she had an aunt with whom she and the children could live. Karen would work at whatever job she could get while she went to secretarial school.

Jerry was not interested in untying their matrimonial knot, and he pulled out all stops, even using the children to intimidate Karen into staying with him. Karen had little money for a lawyer, whereas Jerry had control of their savings, a good income, and the potential to markedly increase his salary in the future. He sued for custody of both children.

Karen's attorney advised her not to move away and to settle for joint custody. "I'm being blackmailed," she said. "Last night Jerry came over and said I had two choices: I could either remain married to him or lose the kids. He kept telling me that he earned a lot of money and I didn't even have a job, and no judge in the world would let me keep them under those conditions."

Caught in the paradox of dependency, Karen could see no alternative that would not sentence her to a lifetime of loneliness. She could continue the custody case and risk losing both her children; she could do as her lawyer suggested and try to keep both of them at least part of the time; she could ask for custody of one child and let Jerry have the other one; or she could stay married and watch the light of her independence flicker out. Karen felt whipped; it seemed that she must give in and stay bound to Jerry to keep her children. The pattern of letting Jerry rule her life had the appeal of the familiar. He had told her what to do and how to do everything, in part because she had been so dependent upon him. She knew that staying with Jerry meant that his anger at her wanting to leave would destroy the small essence of herself, the last remnants of her identity, that she had tried to maintain by seeking a divorce. She also knew that she could not settle for joint custody because, if she lived in the same city as Jerry, she would be a sitting duck for his barrage of punishments.

Not only was Karen herself immobilized with fears, she immobilized her therapist as well by refusing to return for therapy, saying, "There's nothing you can do. Why should I burden you with my unsolvable dilemmas?" Karen rejected the answer: "Because at the very least, you deserve someone to talk to, someone to give you support while you go through this appalling experience, and someone with whom you can share your anger, fear, and grief. No matter what you decide, the one thing you can be sure of is that you are going to be with yourself, so you need to feel as good about yourself and the choice you make as you possibly can."

"I can be emotional, but I mustn't upset anyone."

Elena was sent to therapy by a public agency. Her first husband had left her for another woman, leaving her with two daughters to support. Apparently, at that time Elena resolved never to let another man hurt her, Instead, she set in motion conflicts revolving around the paradox of emotionality, for she decided to use her attractiveness and charm to keep herself and her children safe and secure. The first thing she did was look for a promising husband who would accept her for her "feminine" emotions and would never jiggle the lid on her well-buried anger.

317

When she was twenty-five, Elena married again. Her new husband was twenty years her senior. He had a comfortable home and a small business. She treated him with kindness and courtesy. They had a marriage of convenience in the beginning. When she was thirty, the comforts of convenience turned into the obligations of bondage. Her husband became seriously ill. Elena nursed him for five years, including the last year when he was bedridden and unable even to feed himself. Everything they had, including their home, was sold to pay his medical bills.

When Elena's husband died, she went to work in a department store. Within a few months she was severely incapacitated with migraine headaches and was no longer able to work. In desperation, she turned to public agencies for assistance. The physician who examined her when she applied for a government-funded training program told her that her physical condition was caused by emotional distress. Elena's acceptance into the program was made contingent upon her receiving therapy.

The first appointment was scheduled, but Elena did not appear. Upon inquiry, Elena said she had no intention of coming for therapy. The agency scheduled a second appointment; Elena came and spent most of the time denying any feelings about anything that had ever happened to her and refused to return for therapy. Her agency scheduled another appointment. Elena came three hours late, apologized and left.

The decision was made not to schedule any other appointments for Elena. Therapy is a mutual effort of client and therapist. Elena had a right not to come, and she knew the consequences of her decision. We suspect that she had long been afraid of her smoldering anger, and her fear was that therapy would ignite fires she might not be able to quench.

Sometimes women do not continue with therapy because they believe that they are at a point where doors have slammed permanently shut and they cannot turn back to change the structure of their lives. It is true that the foundation choices women make tend to demand that building blocks be positioned in a somewhat determined pattern. Women who come for therapy only once or twice are often unable to see any hope for remodeling their present environment.

When Edith came to therapy, it was obvious that she was agitated about the marriage she was about to enter. In her therapy session, she listed many valid questions about going through with the marriage. Having listed her doubts, she dismissed them. She stated that her dress was bought, the invitations were printed, and under no circumstances could she back out now.

This is another example of a situation where a therapist has little influence on a client's decision. At best, her therapist could only help Edith to examine alternatives and make her own choice. She already had made her decision and was unwilling to explore other alternatives.

"I don't see it the way you do, so I must be wrong," and "I have to resolve differences without facing the issues."

Dorie suffered from the paradoxes of perception and conflict. The thought of initiating any resolution of conflict frightened her. She wanted to trust her perceptions, but the paradox of perception kept her from acting on them. Her husband Pat believed that women were best suited for supportive roles and men should be the strong ones, the managers and protectors of the family. Occasionally, he asked Dorie to help out in his business. He would have liked her to do more for him, but she resented his looking over her shoulder, because she was a faster learner and in many ways more capable than he was. She felt especially angry when Pat asked his brother, whom Dorie saw as having little to contribute, to be a partner in the business.

It made no difference what I said to Pat before he took his brother in. I suggested that he give him a job without the partnership, but for some reason Pat wouldn't go for that. Then I suggested that a year's trial would be good; I just couldn't see that it would work out, and any legal hassles would be avoided. I guess Pat thought he was going to turn a green kid into a superbusinessman. I don't really know what he thought; he never discussed it with me.

He still doesn't tell me anything. He says that I don't know about business. He makes me wonder at times if he might be right. He wants me to shut up and listen to him gripe and complain while his brother tears down everything Pat builds up. The worst problem is that Pat expects me to listen in silence, agree with him and then go and do whatever he wants. If I don't, he blows up.

The thing that really makes me mad is that Pat should listen to me and never does, and I'm not able to get that across to him. I wish there were something I could do, but I know there isn't. No matter what I say, it just creates more conflict.

Dorie's feelings of immobility, helplessness, and anger kept her from acting on her perceptions and insisting that Pat confront the issues of their conflict. His arrogance kept her feeling powerless and afraid. She failed to return to therapy, choosing instead to remain ineffective in the middle of the struggle.

"I'm responsible for everything and powerless to effect change."

Angie came for therapy caught in the paradox of guilt. She was married to an alcoholic whose dependence upon her galled her at the same time that it fed her need to be wanted. Harry had lost his driver's license, and Angie drove him to his night watchman's job every night and picked him up in the morning, even though she was often late getting to her own job because of it. They had no children, and her job allowed them to just keep up with the bills. By working, Angie protected Harry from having to worry about the family income.

In her first and only therapy session, Angie alluded to feeling responsible for his weaknesses. In truth, it was her honest efforts to compensate for his inadequacies that allowed him to be irresponsible. Angie also said that Harry did seem to need her and she liked being needed, although she felt guilty, suspecting that she was getting psychological gains by supporting his dysfunctional behavior. Angie was able to see that her own growth and freedom from guilt depended upon her allowing Harry to suffer the consequences of his own behavior. At that point, her fear of dealing with the pain of growth overwhelmed her, and she said, "Well, there are worse things than Harry's drinking." Angie quit therapy.

Sometimes women are as uncomfortable with their successes as they are with their failures. Julie had struggled desperately to resolve the paradoxical notion that she was responsible even though she had no power. She was coordinator of a large, federally funded health program. Her boss was a politically ambitious man who saw the program as a steppingstone for his career. Her board of directors, on the other hand, was interested in Julie's successful translation of the philosophy of the program into action. Often the interests of the board conflicted with those of Julie's boss. At these times, he portrayed her as the villain, letting her be the scapegoat for failures. When there were successes, he accepted the accolades. Julie struggled doggedly for over a year, accepting responsibility for resolving unsolvable problems and creating harmony between people who were unreconcilable.

At the end of that time, her boss resigned to run for public office and Julie was offered his job. She came for therapy twice bcause, she said,

I keep looking around for my old self, the one who felt so lucky to have a job, who was so scared of getting fired if I made a mistake. My successful self feels so new and strange, it's as though I don't even know myself at all. I don't know what I think and feel. Before I focused everything on other people and felt guilty and responsible for anything that went wrong, whether I had anything to do with it or not. I had nothing left over to give to myself. Now I find myself in a new role and I wonder who I

321

am. It was really tough to be responsible *for* other people, and it's much easier now just to be responsible *to* people in certain areas or for certain things. I'm just responsible for myself now, yet I don't know anything about myself! I'm scared, but I know that I'm someone I can learn about!

For Julie, it was very important that support be available to her, lest her fear of success force her back into old patterns. With a little encouragement she found it easy to become an expert about herself and to give up trying to be an expert for everybody on everything else. She sought therapy because she recognized that her fear could force her to return to an old and paradoxical pattern. She refused to let this happen to her.

"I lose, especially when I win."

Yolanda knew that her conflicts were self-generated remnants of a poverty-stricken childhood. She came for therapy once, describing how she was unable to control her spending patterns. As a child she had longed for the clothes and homes she saw other children enjoy. She compared her own hand-me-down clothes, practical shoes, and plain little bedroom that she shared with two sisters to what she saw on television and in magazines. She remembered poring over the mail-order catalog, picking out all the things she would buy when she grew up and married a rich man.

When Yolanda initiated therapy, she was twenty-five, still hoping to affiliate with oil wells or diamond mines. She had many dates and kept herself in the limelight at parties and on vacation weekends, hoping her own personal millionaire would be attracted by her good looks, wit, and charm.

"There's part of me that won't wait, though," she said. "I keep trying to make up to myself for all the things I never had. I'm a shopperholic. I spend all my spare time browsing through stores, picking up little things for myself, and I feel better. I have charge accounts all over town, and I always spend to the limit of my credit. I know that I should budget, but I don't."

Yolanda, too, was a one-time client. She called and cancelled her next appointment, saying she could not afford therapy. Actually, she could hardly afford not to come, for her fear of never getting enough in life dominated her adulthood. Yolanda was caught in the paradox of mythical thinking. Unable to confront herself, she hoped that a wealthy and generous benefactor would come along and save her from her extravagant spending patterns at the same time that he made her feel secure.

Becky, too, was caught in a myth. She had built her life on a fairy tale in which she was Sleeping Beauty waiting for someone to rescue her. It did not matter who wakened her; a boyfriend, her mother, father, teachers, or even a magical therapist would do. She saw as her role being passively receptive. She was beautiful in an exotic, cool way, and thought that all she had to do was remain visible and available and something marvelous would happen to her.

Becky came for therapy because it seemed she had been waiting a long time for her magical awakening. In the meantime, everything seemed unimportant and she felt vaguely angry. She was not aware in the beginning of therapy that she was hoping to be rescued. Her therapist asked her, during the second hour, if she ever saw herself as waiting for something. Becky looked very thoughtful and then said, "Well, I guess I'm waiting for you to make something good happen right now. As a matter of fact, I felt kind of angry with you because I'm just sitting here sounding dull and feeling bored and you're not doing anything about it." There was another long pause, and then she asked. "Do you suppose *I'm* the part of my life that's boring? Maybe I could make things happen for myself."

When women discontinue therapy after only one or two sessions, there is little a therapist can do. For Becky, being able to answer her therapist's question honestly allowed her to examine a pattern that was sabotaging her realistic hopes for a satisfying life. By using her therapist as a mirror to reflect the fallacy of her mythical thinking, she could resolve the paradox of

323

fear. She could change, "I want you to do it because I can't," to "I want to do it myself and I will."

"My models are not to follow."

Alice saw both of her parents as appropriate models for her to emulate. Her mother had devoted herself to making it possible for her husband to succeed as a surgeon. As part of this devotion, Alice was taught to be a loving, compliant daughter who would make her father's time at home pleasant. Her mother died just before Alice's fifteenth birthday. Trained to please "the doctor," as he was called at home, Alice tried to fill her mother's role.

Unfortunately, "the doctor" was a perfectionist. Like many people who demand a great deal of themselves, he expected perfection from anyone he was associated with. Trying to emulate him and because she wanted to please him just as her mother had taught her to, Alice learned to avoid his disapproval by being careful not to make mistakes. The safest way for her to do this was to rely on her father as the final authority on everything. This allowed Alice to maintain the illusion of being as perfect as "the doctor" seemed to be.

Alice began therapy when she was twenty-eight, within a few months of her father's death. Her life seemed empty without the two people upon whom her efforts had always centered. She was full of fear about the future and felt a rising resentment about her past. Her mother's role, that had seemed so right for Alice at fifteen, had become rooted in unthinking compliance. Following that example had stifled Alice's growth toward adulthood.

"The doctor," too, had proved disappointing as a model, for his perfectionism had been motivated by selfishness. Alice was beginning to realize, as she looked at the pattern of her life, that he had neglected his family almost completely in favor of his work. He had taught Alice to keep busy and look on the bright side so he would not have to think about her loneliness. He had discouraged her from trusting other people, thus keeping her isolated and dependent upon him. He had insisted that her job was in the home, thus keeping his own life comfortable. He had preached that thrift was a virtue, thus keeping for himself the financial rewards of his career. He had allowed Alice to sacrifice her future for his convenience. Now that "the doctor" was gone, Alice had no one to tell her what to do. She feared that she would make mistakes, do something stupid, get sick, or die of loneliness. Most of all, she feared that learning to be herself instead of trying to be a reflection of her parents was an overwhelming task.

Alice's fear won out. She fell back on "the doctor's" attitude about money to explain why she could not continue therapy. Her father had made careful arrangements for the management of his estate after his death. When he died Alice instructed his legal and accounting firms to continue handling her affairs just as her father would have done. "The accountant hasn't set up my budget for this year, so I'm trying not to overspend," she said. "The doctor hated wasting money." Alice believed that the money she had inherited from her father still belonged to him. She felt guilty spending it in ways she knew he would not approve.

Many women think, like Alice, that the family money belongs to the person who earned it. They believe that a wife should be thrifty and has a right to spend money only with her husband's approval.

Other women see themselves as unable to afford therapy because family budget priorities put their needs last. They know that if they had a broken leg, they would have it taken care of. Indeed, if another family member had a psychological problem, they would see that help was forthcoming. When it comes to themselves, however, it is difficult for women to accept that their emotional well-being may be more important than other family needs that are routinely met.

This was brought home to one of us when the question of therapy came up in an all-female group. At least ten places were suggested where women could go for therapy that was free or at reduced rates. When the question came up in an all-male group, several men stated that money was not their primary concern. They would go only to the best therapist, and they expected to pay for expertise.

> "That is the way men like women, but I don't dare be that way."

The paradox of fear is vividly expressed in conflicts involving sexuality. Bea came for therapy because her boyfriend was interested in sexual experimentation and Bea was not. Many of the novelties he suggested were unexciting and even repulsive to her. "I wish I wanted to do whatever he asks, but I can't. I'm so afraid that he'll find someone else who is more uninhibited," Bea said. "Maybe I'm a prude. He's not satisfied with me at all. Can you do something so I'll be more accepting of him? Are there books I could read that would help?"

After reading, Bea was still uninterested in his suggestions. It did not occur to Bea, as it does not to countless other women caught in such a press about their sexual performance, that his demands were unreasonable. He had a right to ask for what he wanted; Bea had a right to say no to his requests. Furthermore, Bea had a right to ask for certain sexual behaviors from him, including that he stop making demands she was unwilling or unable to meet. She could also have pointed out that if he continued to make such demands, she would continue to feel sexually inadequate with him. She then would be even more uninterested in sex and in their relationship. Perhaps she would be the one to decide to leave him for someone less experimental.

Ellen's fear of her own sexuality fixed her between the stove and the table, right at the refrigerator. To save herself from the risks of becoming involved in alliances that would threaten the possibility of sex, she protected herself at an unconscious level by eating and gaining weight. Then, to console herself because she felt unattractive and rejected, she ate and added more unwanted pounds. Food became a substitute for all the things she wanted, including her sexual identity. Her eating patterns became the focus of her world, and her weight became a heavy blanket of protection, isolating her and keeping her safe. It also kept her wishes, hopes, and dreams well hidden from both herself and the world.

"Getting sick isn't so bad; there's a lot of strength in being weak."

Daisy looked as sick as she was when she came to therapy. She was probably a small woman even when she was well, but apparently she had lost a great deal of weight, for her pantsuit hung on her in baggy folds. Her voice was weak, and her motions feeble and shaky. Her physician had referred her for psychotherapy; he could find no organic reason for her physical symptoms.

Daisy's husband Howard was a quiet man who rarely interacted with Daisy and their teenage son and daughter. Family life was predictable: In the winter they went to the children's football and basketball games and had guests over for Thanksgiving and Christmas. Saturdays they puttered around the house; once in a while they went shopping, although Howard refused to buy clothes for himself and was not interested in what Daisy wore. Whenever she asked him how she looked, Howard gave a perfunctory nod. In the summer, they went on an occasional picnic with the children, and sometimes to the zoo or the amusement park.

The surface of Daisy's life seemed placid enough, but undercurrents of anger rippled to the surface as she went on with her story. Their son was interested in auto mechanics, she thought, perhaps even engineering. "But do you think Howard even bothers to show him how to fill the gas tank on the car? Oh, no! He takes off for the service station all by himself, without a word. And Nan, too, notices her father's silence. The other day she was crying in her bedroom because he didn't speak to her or give her a smile when she offered him some cookies she had made. It's downright cruel to treat a sensitive girl that way."

Daisy felt that Howard was being cruel to her, too, when he withdrew in silence. "I've been noticing that if I bring up anything I'm mad about, his ulcers act up.

He sighs and takes his medicine. Several times lately he's tossed and turned all night. I worry about him more than I do about myself."

Daisy and Howard were involved in a very destructive contest. Whenever Daisy felt strong enough to point out how angry she felt toward him, Howard's stomach signaled his next move. The only time he seemed strong, considerate, or talkative was when she became ill. Daisy genuinely hated being sick, but feared being well; when well, she was unable to stifle her wish for closeness with her husband and her anger that he rejected her. The only way she knew how to keep him well was to be sicker than he was. This was the single method she knew to gain control and some rewards in a relationship with a man she found dull and distant.

What Daisy wanted was for Howard to be strong enough so that she could be well and still be able to depend upon him. Perhaps the illness she was experiencing did have a name: heartsickness. Whatever the name, her longing for intimacy is familiar to many women.

Almost all women who come for therapy experience fear. Fear of change, or of not being able to change; fear of success, or of failure; fear of becoming dependent on the therapist, or of being rejected; fear of having to act on one's rights, or of not being allowed to act on them; fear of responsibility, or of irresponsibility; fear of being too emotional, or of not having any feelings at all; fear of having to confront one's self, or of not liking what one sees.

The paradox of fear for women is that the conflicts generated by unresolved paradoxes leave one immobilized. Most women, however, find relief and new hope to resolve paradoxes when they follow their natural, healthy impulses to self-exploration and growth, and search resolutely for an authentic identity.

RESOLUTION OF PARADOXES

CHAPTER XV

Resolution of Paradoxes

As you read the first fourteen chapters of this book, it is likely that you saw your own life reflected in the stories of the women we have written about. Which paradoxical conflicts are you enmeshed in and what can you you do to resolve them?

This chapter will help you to answer these questions. We will present the characteristics of the thirteen paradoxes in a series of questions about how you see yourself and how others see you. If you answer yes to many of the questions about a particular paradox, this indicates that this paradox is operating destructively in your life. Following the question, we will offer concrete suggestions and useful tools to help you change dysfunctional habits and self-defeating attitudes that have locked you into paradoxes.

We do not mean to suggest that breaking these constraints will be easy. Unfortunately, there is no quick magic, no simple prescription for change. Complex and difficult dilemmas do not have easy solutions and paradoxical double-binds are among the most subtle and pervasive influences in women's distress. Our work with women in psychotherapy is devoted to the arduous, sometimes lengthy task of supporting women as they move out of controlling situations into self-determined effectiveness.

There are, however, things you can do on your own. We have confidence that with courage and strength you can improve your life. The suggestions we have outlined here are starting points for change. With perseverance and practice, you can identify the paradoxes that have entrapped you, choose alternatives that will make your life more rewarding, and act to implement them. If the task seems overwhelming, do not hesitate to call upon the skills and help of a psychotherapist to ease the way and speed up the process.

EQUALITY

Do you see yourself as:

- less important than men?
- filling subordinate roles that are assigned to you because you are a woman?
- struggling with the notion that caring for others is a woman's most important task, and you don't like it?
- discriminated against by a double standard for men and women?
- sacrificing your goals in favor of a man's?
- choosing a traditionally "feminine" career because you are a woman?
- dominated, but afraid to fight back?
- pitying women who are not wives and mothers?
- crediting men with being more capable than women?
- believing that men's opinions are to be trusted more than women's?
- agreeing that boys are more entitled to education than girls?

Do others see you as:

- treating women with less consideration than men?
- accepting subordinate roles in relationship to men?

- passive and deferential with authority figures?
- not having developed many facets of your personality?
- limited in your knowledge?
- narrow in your interests?
- afraid to challenge people who are dominating you?

How can you resolve conflicts caused by being told that you are both equal and unequal at the same time? First of all, you can recognize that although sex-role stereotyping is pervasive and has influenced you, you can dilute its effects and resist its erosions in the future, thereby changing the course of your life. Consider that the average life-span of a woman is seventy-six years. Decide how much of your life you have already lived and how many years you can expect to have ahead of you. Some of you will be pleasantly surprised to find that you have not yet lived a third of your expected years. Others may have another quarter of a century in which to grow, change, and enjoy life. What you do with the rest of your life is up to you.

If you see yourself as less important than men, you need to tell yourself that it is stereotyped thinking that has assigned women to an inferior status. Such thinking has no basis in fact. Learn to make judgments for yourself based upon individual differences, not sex differences. In other words, in thinking of a career for yourself, think in terms of, "Does this occupation fit my specific abilities?" rather than, "Is this a good career for a woman?"

Challenge decisions that put you in subservient positions simply because you are a woman. In a division of labor at home, decide who does what on the basis of interest and ability, not sex. It is fine for girls to mow lawns and for boys to cook. In relationships, suggest to your partner that you both examine your roles to see that one of you is not dominant while the other is subordinate.

If you are uncomfortable with the notion that caring for others is a woman's most important task, recognize that women have been strongly socialized to like a caregiving role and this accounts for their acceptance of it. You have a right to choose your role based upon your wants and aspirations. Whatever your choice, you can enjoy your role and still not be limited by it. Realize that child-rearing takes only the middle third of a woman's life. Plan for your pre-family and post-family years so you will not be dependent upon anyone else.

Read widely. Keep an open mind about women's issues and see to it that you do not make judgments based on ignorance or sterotypes that have been used historically to keep women down.

Look at what is involved in the changes you want to make to break out of a position of inferiority. It is true that as you challenge sterotypes other persons will be threatened, especially those who have gained by dominating you. Accept that your changing will be difficult for them, but do not let them deter you. If you have been submissive, passive, and dependent, you will find as you become spontaneous, effective, and self-directed that you are more vital and interesting. The very persons who were once threatened by your growth will come to appreciate, respect, and enjoy you more.

It can happen to you! If you take a positive attitude, accept yourself as the equal of men, and expect positive reactions from others, you are likely to succeed. Breaking out of this paradox will make it easier to resolve all the later ones.

SELF-ESTEEM

Do you see yourself as:

- feeling worthless?
- inadequate in many areas?
- generally anxious and uncomfortable?
- unable to take risks and fearful of failure?
- sensitive to criticism and worried about what others think of you?
- apologizing for yourself and putting yourself down?
- unable to aspire to high goals and not accomplishing much?
- putting yourself last?

- feeling that nobody could really like you?
- easily influenced by others?
- uncomfortable when you receive compliments?
- not worth spending money on?

Do others see you as:

- not liking yourself?
- tiresomely self-critical?
- in need of constant reassurance?
- avoiding close relationships by pushing others away?
- protecting yourself by not taking risks?
- having a "yes, but" response for every nice thing someone tells you?
- misunderstanding what others say?

The downward spiral of self-esteem can be reversed in two ways: through positive, rewarding achievements and through mutually enhancing relationships with people you respect and admire. The key to increasing your self-esteem is to make opportunities to gain these reinforcements.

First of all, make a list of the negative feelings you have about yourself. These are the feelings you can learn to live without. Opposite each of the negative feelings, list the positive emotions with which you want to replace them. The rewards for not changing are to remain mired down in fear of failure, feelings of inadequacy, and anxiety and concern about your supposed shortcomings. The rewards for changing are the replacement of these self-defeating miseries with feeling good about yourself and achieving competence.

Take another sheet of paper and write down all of your strengths. Include positive attributes, such as your self-awareness, your intelligence, education, skills, and job training; avocations you are interested in; and your accomplishments. In a second column, list your weaknesses, like your fear of new situations or your tendency to let yourself sit at home because it seems safer than getting involved in something new. See your strengths as a foundation upon which you can build a positive self-image, assets you can make use of so your weaknesses will no longer be overwhelmingly defeating to you. Your weaknesses are important only when they stand in your way. In being aware of them, you can take action to alleviate their harmful effects. For example, if you are afraid to speak up in large crowds and you are offered a job that would involve a great deal of public speaking, then your fear could become a stumbling block to achieving a goal. At that point you will have to decide whether your fear will control you and limit your choices or whether you will overcome it.

Once you have assessed your strengths, rank them in order of importance to you. These are your personal resources; the tools you can use to begin changing how you feel about yourself. Now let your imagination take off and list all of the things you might like to do or wanted to do as a youngster, from being a chemist to losing fifteen pounds, and from getting a private pilot's license to learning to bake cream puffs. Aim high; dreams do not cost anything, and they can become reality as readily as your catastrophes can. Be sure that your secret ambitions are at the top of this list, and do not let scoffers and pessimists influence you.

If accomplishing these goals costs money, plan how you can get it, rather than letting financial worries deter you. Tell yourself, "I'm worth spending money on." A college degree, for instance, does cost a great deal, but breaking down your objective into successive steps toward the goal may mean that each semester's expenses are manageable. Four or five years from now you will have finished what you once only hoped for; if you had not dared to dream, the time would have passed without your having achieved your goal.

Once you have listed your objectives, separate them into long-term and short-term goals. Then decide which ones are the most important and which are the least important to you. If your number one long-term goal is to become more comfortable in social situations, plan how you will accomplish this. Do not begin by throwing a dinner party for fifteen guests, half of them people you hardly know. Instead, smile and say "hello" to your neighbors when you happen to meet, ask a good friend out to lunch, and speak first to your fellow employees, rather then waiting for them to make friendly overtures. They may feel as timid as you do.

Break down each goal into small steps that you can climb one at a time, and keep your eye on your success at each step, instead of evaluating whether or not you have reached the top. Reward yourself along the way with self-validating messages; tell yourself what a good job you are doing and how proud you are of yourself. This will help you to feel good and will chase away your suspicions of worthlessness.

If you fail now and then, do not punish yourself with put-downs and backslides into, "I knew I couldn't make it." Go back and review your list of negative feelings; they are what you have to lose by picking yourself up and encouraging yourself to try again. Develop support systems, such as a study group if you are in school or a best friend you can call and say, "I need some encouragement." Tell others about your plans and goals and ask for the support and rewards you need.

Use the achievement of short-term goals, like finishing a gardening project or a letter to an old friend, as rewards along the way. Seek out positive people and avoid critical ones; you are too hard on yourself already and you do not need anyone else to drag you down. Do not apologize for yourself, to yourself or anyone else, with statements like, "How could I be so stupid," or "I'm always making a fool of myself." Do not blame yourself. Expect people to like you; they will when you project a self-accepting attitude.

Take an assertiveness training class so you can learn to say what you are thinking and develop skills to respond openly and honestly in interactions with others. Tell people when you feel bad or scared; saying the words aloud dissipates the feelings, whereas keeping them inside increases their clout. Also, focus on other people from time to time by asking them how they are feeling about things that are important to them and showing an interest in their lives. In short, do for them the same things that you enjoy having done for you.

Learn to give compliments; they are readily available, priceless gifts. More important, practice accepting compliments with a smile, a direct look, and "Thank you."

AFFILIATION

Do you see yourself as:

- centering your life around relationships?
- needing to feel you belong to someone in order to feel at ease?
- important because of your affiliation with someone else?
- incomplete without someone to belong to?
- worthless if you lose the person you belong to?
- feeling it is more important to love than to achieve?
- basking in the reflected glory of someone else's accomplishments?
- willing to do anything for the person you love?
- someone who goes along, but is not sought out for herself?

Do others see you as:

- not having an identity of your own?
- incomplete without your "better half"?
- an extension of your partner?
- bereft if you have no partner or role with which to identify?
- needlessly self-sacrificing for those you love?
- anxious about losing your loved one?
- incapable of earning your own rewards?

What can you do to change the feeling that you are nothing unless you are connected to somebody, but in being connected you lose your sense of identity? First, accept the fact that affiliative relationships are good and do bring rewards; it is only when you invest too heavily in another person that you lose your identity.

Examine your attitude toward your relationships. Do you find your life revolving around someone else? Do you feel important because you are somebody's mother, wife, daughter, or friend? Do you get pleasure from, or brag about, their achievements rather then your own? If so, learn to look to yourself and identify your own good qualities. You have internal resources that you can develop to build a support system based upon your dormant abilities. The items on the list of your strengths that you made to improve your self-esteem are the basis for an identity of your own. Do not let people introduce you as Sam's wife, mother, daughter, or friend. Insist that you be acknowledged as yourself; you will be when you put your assets up front.

Look also at why you have chosen to be committed to the people to whom you are connected. Are you attracted to them because each of you brings out the best in the other, or have you latched onto other lonely souls to fill up a hole in yourself? A good way to judge the quality of a relationship is to determine whether you admire in the other person those qualities that the individual values in her- or himself. Good affiliative relationships are built on such mutuality and do not deplete or rob the identity of either person.

Having many acquaintances provides variety in your friendships while keeping you from having all your eggs in one emotional basket. No matter how good a relationship is, do not limit yourself to it. Widen the circle of your friends and acquaintances; people of different ages, different economic levels, different nationalities, and with interests new to you can add excitement to your days. When you share parts of your life with them you will not be bereft if the special one moves out of it.

Look to other involvements besides friends for satisfactions. Maybe you have put aside your own goals and ambitions in order to consolidate a relationship. In doing so you robbed yourself of identity-producing resources! Develop your talents; explore new hobbies. Some women go back to school (community colleges offer a variety of courses ranging from personal interest classes to career development). Or get an advanced degree. Look back at the fantasies of your childhood and see if you might now pursue what you were once interested in. Many midlife careers originate with such introspection.

Maybe a job would be the answer to help you find your own identity. The rewards for women who work are more than financial. Involvement in the wider world helps you to be more interesting and vital. Knowing you are respected, depended upon, and valued for what you do helps you to feel like somebody in your own right.

You can avoid much of the hearbreak that comes with too strong affiliative ties by learning to accept dissimilarities in people. Remember that women are encouraged to look at affiliative relationships to give their lives meaning, whereas men are rewarded for being goal-oriented. If you are in a male-female relationship and you feel cut off because the man in your life does not understand your need for togetherness, discuss this different orientation of women and men with him. You can both change some; he can put more into the relationship and you can become more accepting of his involvement with goal achievement.

By becoming less vulnerable in relationships you will be able to judge the actions of your loved ones by their yardsticks, rather than your own. Do not demand that others do as you do. Maybe your way of showing love is to shower someone with affection, to plan happy surprises, and never to forget a birthday. But theirs may be different. Learn to look at their way of showing love as just as genuine as your own. Accept it as a mark of their uniqueness.

DEPENDENCY

Do you see yourself as:

- unable to reverse previous choices that have put you in a dependent position?
- needing someone for financial or emotional security?
- inadequate, with your best qualities destroyed or fading?
- afraid to risk taking chances that might mean losing your security?

338

- helpless and unable to take charge of your life?
- trapped, stifled, and destroyed by giving your power to the person you depend upon?
- lulled into passivity by being taken care of?
- comfortable not having to make decisions?
- unprepared to provide a future for yourself?
- hesitant to take steps toward self-determination?
- giving up because you see no way out?

Do others see you as:

- weak and childlike?
- waiting for someone else to act so you can follow?
- leaning too hard in your helplessness?
- taking advantage of them?
- passively putting up with that you do not like?
- easy to outgrow and to be set aside when someone better comes along?

If you have answered yes to most of these questions, your life still may not be as bad as it looks. If you are sensing the destructiveness of the paradox of dependency, there are alternatives. You can identify some for yourself and move out of relying upon someone else to a point that you can want, but do not need, to be committed to someone.

Begin by assessing your present situation. Ask yourself the following questions: What is keeping me dependent upon someone else? Is it emotional, financial, or physical need? Does my dependency involve the needs of someone else, perhaps someone who would do just as well if left to her or his own devices? How long must this dependency last? Until the children are in school? Until I get my education? Until the house is paid for? Dependency does not need to be a life sentence; you can qualify for parole any time you are ready to get out.

Look at the alternatives you have. If you cannot find any, seek some professional help. A psychotherapist is trained to help you identify choices that were hiding in you all the time. Be audacious in your search! Think of wildly unrealistic solutions. You will be surprised how often they contain the kernel of workable plans. It just *seems* impossible to get a job or a degree, to become an author, or to sell your paintings. Many women who once thought they could not went on to reach such goals once they challenged themselves to get started.

If you are psychologically dependent, look at how you and your partner are reinforcing this. Give up little-girl ways; they are beneath the dignity of a woman. Search for other people in whom to invest some of your attention; you and your partner will both feel less burdened. Examine the rewards you are getting from being dependent, then compare their small comforts to the destructiveness you are experiencing. See what being dependent is doing to your disposition; if you do not like the results, this will be additional motivation to change. Check out, too, whether someone is gaining at the expense of your being dependent.

Identify the emotions that dependency generates in you. Feel those feelings of helplessness, inadequacy, frustration, and powerlessness. Then move on. You will find that these feelings will go away when you start to move. In the case of powerlessness, recognize that to feel powerless is to be powerless. This will change when you hitch your own strengths and power to your plans.

If you have been afraid to take risks lest the fragile security of your relationships be lost, do what other women have done. They considered the messages they told themselves to keep inactive, messages like, "My husband won't let me," "He will divorce me if I challenge him," "I'm not smart enough," "I'll probably fall flat on my face," and 'The children need me." They are all false messages that scare you into staying in a dependent role. The experience of other women is that when they stop leaning, they are better liked, respected, and admired.

In moving out of dependency and into self-directed effectiveness, you can identify the rights you may have given up to keep the peace. You have a right to put yourself first in some things and to explain to others that your being a martyr will not help either you or them. You have a right to set goals for yourself and to ask for cooperation in reaching them. You have a right to develop your autonomy and the confidence that comes from experiencing your competence. You have a right to insist that relationships be interdependent, so that everyone involved can enjoy both the rewards of independent activity and the security that comes with commitment. Do so.

EMOTIONALITY

Do you see yourself as:

- unable to express negative emotions?
- fearful of making others uncomfortable?
- always having to be cheerful?
- suppressing anger, disappointments, and frustrations?
- blowing up over little things?
- assuming responsibility for the feelings of others?
- trying to keep everyone happy?
- deserving of criticism for being emotional?
- feeling guilty because you have negative feelings?
- being a burden on others because you are emotional?

Do others see you as:

- easily hurt because you are too emotional?
- too nice, easygoing, and tolerant of others?
- bending over backwards to please?
- manipulative because you cry instead of saying what you feel?
- unpredictably hotheaded?
- too sensitive to be told the truth?

Being emotional is a rewarding, valued, and healthy part of you. Your emotions become your adversary, however, when you follow the dictates of the emotionality paradox and try to express your feelings without upsetting anyone. How can you unravel the complex threads of this double-bind? There are several steps in this difficult process. First, it is time to give up the notion that being emotional is a characteristic reserved for women, something you must apologize for or keep

341

in check unless your feelings are used to make others feel good.

Second, you will have to let go of the idea that only positive emotions are acceptable, that negative emotions must not be acknowledged even to yourself and must not be disclosed because they will make others feel uncomfortable. Refer back to the list of your negative feelings that you wrote when examining the paradox of self-esteem. These emotions release their gnawing grip when you discharge them. Expressing your negative feelings has a twofold advantage: It gets rid of the pressure of suppressed feelings and helps you to feel better about yourself, and it unravels the tangles of the paradox of emotionality.

Step three involves reexamining the assumption that other persons will be angry, rejecting, or punishing if you are not always happy and other-oriented. You have undoubtedly learned from painful experience that people react negatively when you disclose the full range of your feelings. In an assertiveness training class you will learn invaluable skills for expressing both negative and positive emotions in a nonthreatening manner so that others hear and respond in mutually productive ways.

Remember that it is patronizing to assume that someone else is too weak or too sensitive to be told what you are feeling. If others see you as too sensitive or too emotional they will shy away from being honest with you. Let them know you are not too fragile to hear the truth. Their feedback will help you to clarify misunderstandings and to change your own behavior should you want to do so.

Disclosing your negative feelings can be distressing for you as well as the one with whom you would like to communicate. Begin slowly; you do not have to move from suppressing your feelings to being completely open and honest with everyone. You would not want to do this. Instead, start at the beginning and ask yourself, when you feel uncomfortable, nervous, or anxious, what you are feeling. Do not ask yourself, "Why am I upset?" Instead, seek answers to these questions: "What am I feeling?" "What is happening to elicit

342

these feelings?" "What can I do about it?" "How can I change what is going on?" "Why" questions frequently have no answers, and even if there are answers, they will not necessarily help you to feel better. "What" and "how" questions almost always have productive answers readily available when you look for them. If not, then you can move on; there is no reason to feel miserable about something over which you have no control.

Once you know what you are feeling, you can decide what you will do to discharge your feelings. Sharing them with the person directly involved may not be possible or desirable. You can choose to discharge them by writing them down, pounding a pillow, or talking aloud as if the other person were present. After you have released the pressure of stored-up resentment in these private ways, you will be able to express your anger constructively and will have no need to feel ashamed or guilty about how you handle your negative emotions.

Learn to be comfortable about saying no. You are not responsible for others' feelings, anymore than they are responsible for yours. Refusing a request is a simple right you can act on, just as you would encourage those you love to do. Crying because you feel sad or happy, being nice because you feel nice, and doing considerate things for people are also your rights and you can act on them, too. Your emotionality is an important part of you, just as your intellectual and physical components are. It is a resource you can use to live your life in self-rewarding and other-enhancing ways.

PERCEPTION

Do you see yourself as:

- able to rely on your own viewpoint only until challenged?
- uncertain about how to act?
- unable to trust yourself and looking to men as authorities?
- constantly needing confirmation about what you are thinking and feeling?
- not having worthwhile opinions?
- afraid to be different from others?

- unwilling to speak up for fear of looking silly?
- concerned about being wrong and making mistakes?
- adjusting your perceptions to fit those of others?
- ready to assume you are wrong without questioning others' viewpoints?
- valuing men's opinions more than women's?

Do others see you as:

- being uncertain about your own opinions?
- looking to men as authority figures?
- afraid to speak up and act on your rights?
- quiet and cautious about expressing yourself?
- not wanting to get involved?
- backing down readily when challenged?
- afraid to be wrong?
- unsure of yourself?

The paradox of perception immobilizes women with self-doubt. Moving out of uncertainty and indecision involves trusting your own perceptions. This is a learning process. The first step in this process is to examine again your list of strengths and positive attributes. These are your resources, the things you do and know well, the things you feel confident about. Realistic self-appraisal can tell you those areas about which you can feel proud while you continue to expand your knowledge and those for which you need and want additional skills or education. Identify what you do not know and learn what you need to know to be comfortably informed in areas that are important to you. Let your curiosity loose. Learn about new things. Dig deeper and expand your knowledge in those areas in which you already have a foundation.

The second step is to give yourself permission to make mistakes. Remind yourself that mistakes are opportunities to learn, grow and change, not shameful personality flaws. Remember, being wrong about something does not make you wrong about everything, nor does it mean you are a failure or a bad person. It only means you misperceived. Speak up even though you are not fully informed or absolutely sure of what you are discussing. This gives others a chance to add your input to their own, rather than feeling annoyed with you because you are unwilling to contribute or sorry for you because you seem afraid. Listen when you do get involved; this, too, is an opportunity to learn. You can always say, "I'm glad to hear that," or "I didn't realize that was the case," if you get information that conflicts with what you thought.

Look closely and critically at the stereotyped belief that men are more intelligent, more rational, and more knowledgeable than women. None of these qualities is sex-linked. By making men the authority figures, you deny yourself the opportunity to become an expert on yourself, keep yourself immobilized in self-doubt, and place an unfair burden on men, for although they may welcome their authoritarian roles, they suffer from always having to be right and having to offer constant reassurance to you.

Take back the power you have given others to inhibit you with a questioning look, a curt dismissal, or an uninformed challenge. Act on your right to express your thoughts and feelings. No one gives you this right; it is yours to exercise. Change your quiet and cautious image by speaking up. Others will respect you for taking risks and will welcome your involvement.

While you go through this difficult process of becoming confident about what you know, become involved with positive, supportive people. Validate yourself when you do step forward. Focus on the positive responses you get and enjoy your successes. Put your wishes into action. For instance, instead of thinking, "I don't agree with what he's saying," speak up. Say, "My understanding is that . . ." or "In my opinion . . ." This is the way you test your perceptions. The worst that can happen is that you will find out you are wrong. Then you can correct your misperception. This replaces self-doubt with self-confidence and resolves the paradox of emotionality.

345

CONFLICT

Do you see yourself as:

- playing a peacemaker role and trapped in the middle of others' difficulties?
- feeling responsible for creating happiness and harmony?
- looking for indirect ways to make peace because anger is "unfeminine"?
- fearful of direct confrontation and unable to challenge others even when you would like to?
- believing that it is best not to speak up when someone is angry?
- telling yourself that nothing is worth a fight?
- backing down and feeling like a loser?
- giving up in defeat and hopelessness?
- getting out of situations to avoid risking a fight?
- fighting over inconsequential issues in order to avoid big problems?

Do others see you as:

- a pushover when any dissension threatens?
- in charge of maintaining the peace?
- a diplomatic mediator who will accept responsibility without confronting anyone?
- someone who will go along because it is easier than facing unpleasant issues?
- manipulative and guilt-inducing because you avoid direct ways of settling disagreements?
- afraid of healthy confrontation?
- making heroic efforts that are doomed to failure?

Resolving differences without facing the issues is an impossible task in which you eventually become the loser. Moving out of this paradox is frightening because your fear of conflict is firmly entrenched and, in many ways, may be based on a realistic appraisal of another person's aggressiveness. If the task seems overwhelming or too tough to handle alone, get professional help.

Learn how to communicate assertively. Once you have learned assertive skills, you will be more likely to get positive reactions from others and you will be better prepared to handle their negative responses.

Find out whether or not you are scaring yourself out of taking action by telling yourself that if you do act, something terrible will happen. Answer the questions, "What is the worst thing that can happen if I bring up this issue?" and "What is the best thing that can happen?" Ask yourself, too, "What are the consequences if I do not deal directly with this?" Keep your objective in mind when you get involved in open confrontation. This helps to keep you from getting sidetracked in bickering.

Take small steps. Begin by facing the issues in disagreements over small problems, like whose turn it is to feed the dog and what movie you will go to with a friend. After your confidence and skills improve, you can tackle the explosive problems that you have long avoided or tried to solve without direct confrontation. This involves preparation; doing your homework is an essential part of the process. Analyze the basic issue involved to help you organize what you want to say. Make sure you discuss *only* this issue. Practice aloud how you will initiate the discussion. Anticipate what responses the other person may give; this will help you to avoid being distracted if they bring in unrelated problems. Remember, you have a right to expect others to become involved in conflict resolution. If they refuse to do so, then you can decide what independent action you want to take.

Keep an open mind so you can hear nondefensively what the other person has to say. If you find out that you are wrong, say so. Apologies are healing for all concerned if the apologizer is genuinely sorry. You do not have to apologize for yourself or for acting on your right to express your thoughts and feelings, but you can say, "I'm sorry this happened." Be flexible about the outcome you are seeking—everybody wins when a compromise is made, whereas insisting on having things your way may be self-defeating.

Refuse to be intimidated by someone who uses anger

or the threat of anger as a weapon to keep you in line. Certain issues are worth a fight, and creating harmony at the expense of your own churning stomach is not a happy alternative to sticking up for yourself. Force yourself to break your pattern of withdrawing from the heat of the battle by firmly and calmly insisting upon your rights. Self-respect and improved relationships are powerful reinforcements available to those who take difficult risks.

Challenge others when they say, "Now don't get upset." Tell them that you have a right to feel angry and the responsible approach is to confront the difficulty, not to bury it. Do not complain helplessly to others about your difficulties; take steps to resolve them. It is not possible to go through life without discord and conflict. Honest and direct confrontation is positive and essential in relationships that are spontaneous, flourishing, and nurturing for the people involved.

GUILT

Do you see yourself as:

- generally acting more responsibly than others do?
- powerless to change the things you think are wrong or are uncomfortable with?
- lacking when you cannot change things?
- guilty about situations you have no power to control?
- responsible for others' failures?
- anxious and frustrated?
- trying hard to make up for someone else's shortcomings?
- always worrying?
- cooperative, while others thwart your good intentions?
- unable to stay out of other people's business?

Do others see you as:

- loving, but misguided?
- overanxious?
- too worried about their business?

348

MYTHS

Do you see yourself as:

- disappointed that life has not worked out as it was supposed to?
- disillusioned in relationships?
- cheated out of your dreams?
- not wanting your heart's desire once you get it?
- still thinking that life should be easy?
- looking for someone to rescue you?
- looking for happy endings?
- still hoping for magic solutions to difficult problems?
- unprepared to face the realities of life?
- asking, "Why me?" when things go wrong?
- expecting the impossible?

Do others see you as:

- like a little girl and emotionally immature?
- living in a dream world?
- expecting always to be rescued?
- disappointed in others and blaming them for your troubles?
- expecting too much of them?
- complaining?
- ungrateful?
- unreasonable?
- impossible to please?

If you grew up believing in myths and your dreams have backfired, life may seem like a cruel hoax. Nothing turned out as it was supposed to. There was no pot of gold at the end of the rainbow, and when you got your heart's desire it was not what you wanted. Where do you go from here?

You can start by recognizing that you have been cheated by a fantasy. Face the anger you feel because you were told that all you would have to do was to sit passively and grow up and you would be rescued to live happily ever after. You have good reason to feel disillusioned. Do not tell yourself that it is wrong to feel as you do. To deny that you were ill-prepared for the realities of life is to perpetuate a myth. Do recognize that you are not alone; most women in our culture were cheated in the same way.

Take a good hard look at your dreams. Were you, like many other women, led to expect a fairy-tale romance? A life of ease? No-fault children? Dimes that would stretch into dollars? Did you also hope that relationships would be trouble free? That poverty would not pinch? That there would be magic solutions and happy endings if you just waited long enough? Take some time and shed some tears, if necessary, over the loss of your dreams. There are no magic solutions, and happy endings come only for those who work for them.

Now, put those dreams aside and assess what you have. That is reality. Do not imagine that if you could just replace your faded Prince Charming with a new one that the dreams would be reborn and you would have another chance. It was the illusion that was at fault, not the prince you married. He may be as disillusioned as you are.

Starting at the point where you are now, decide what you can do with the rest of your life. Instead of blaming anyone for your plight, ask yourself, "How can I change what I do not like?" Look for strengths you have not tapped and talents you have not developed, and use them. Do not expect life to be easy. It is enough for it to be rewarding.

MODELS

Do you see yourself as:

- resembling people you do not like?
- feeling adrift?
- acting in ways that you are not proud of and feeling that you cannot stop?
- not knowing how to change when you do not like what you are?
- trying to live up to others' expectations?
- wondering what is wrong with you?
- making the same mistakes your parents did?

- not measuring up to your ideal?
- feeling unliked and not knowing why?
- giving a bad example to your children?
- pretending to be someone you are not?

Do others see you as:

- resembling your parents, whom you criticize?
- a carbon copy of another generation?
- being unaware of your objectionable qualities?
- unwilling to change?
- rigid and unbending?
- vacillating and unsure of yourself?
- clinging to a group identity instead of developing your individuality?

If you have been caught in the paradox of modeling you are struggling through perilous waters without a navigational chart. Is there any way you can improve your course now? If you do not like the way you see yourself, you can search for new models and develop new ways to behave.

Awareness is the starting point of growth. Knowing and understanding that you did not have good models can make it easier to accept yourself and your imperfections. You are probably not as lacking as you think. Search for your good points. Validate yourself for them. You will move closer toward becoming the way you would like to be if you appreciate and build on what you like about yourself than if you blame yourself for your imperfections. Tell yourself that you have a right to feel good about yourself.

Seek out positive people to associate with; their attitudes are likely to be contagious. Think of people you know and like and make a list of them. Then add the names of public figures whom you admire. What do you like about each person on your list? Note their good qualities next to their names. Maybe you admire a friend's patience or ability to listen, or the poise of a public figure. Analyze what seems to go into their behavior. Is there any reason you cannot set yourself a goal of developing one new trait a year patterned upon something that you admire in a model on your list?

Modeling is such a subtle process that characteristic ways of behaving are picked up on a subconscious level. In attempting to erase dysfunctional habits or patterns, do not blame yourself for them. They come from the adults you knew as children. If your father shouted, shouting will seem natural to you, unless through some turn of events you come to see the distress it evokes in others. If pouting was the custom in your childhood home, that, too, becomes a habit for the next generation. At least until someone or something effectively intervenes.

As you become aware of the modeling process and look back on the models whom you may not have admired, there is another possibility for growth. As an adult you can sometimes look through the distress that bad models caused you and move on to understanding that your models also suffered from poor modeling. Perhaps you can move to understanding and forgiving them.

Remember that just as you had models, you also are a model for others. Think of what kind of models you would have liked and aim to be that kind of inspiration for those who follow you.

SEXUALITY

Do you see yourself as:

- living up to your partner's sexual expectations instead of your own?
- feeling responsible for your partner's pleasure and afraid of failing to please?
- feeling uneasy about your sexuality?
- uncertain of how to act sexually?
- valued only because of your ability to please sexually?
- unable to say no to sexual demands?
- needing to pay for things with sex?
- using sex to get what you want?
- different sexually from what you think you should be?
- living up to images that do not fit you?

354

Do others see you as:

- uncomfortable about your sexuality?
- either prudish or wanton sexually?
- using sex to manipulate them?
- centering your efforts around your sexual attractiveness?
- rejecting of your own sexuality?
- susceptible to a man't attention?
- chasing after men?
- avoiding sexual contact?
- valuing yourself in terms of your sexual conquests?

The instruction to be both a whore and modonna is impossible to follow, since by definition these are mutually exclusive roles. To resolve this paradox, you must decide for yourself how you will express your sexuality, rather than using it in a stereotyped way that fits someone else's expectations and desires.

Step one in resolving the paradox of sexuality involves banishing the notion that men have the right to tell you how you should act and how you should think about yourself sexually. These important questions are for you to decide. It is true that your partner has a right to make requests of you, and you have a right to make requests, too. Both of you may grant or deny these requests. You are not, however, responsible for seeing that your partner is sexually satisfied. Be assertive and learn to say no comfortably if that is what you want to say.

Each person is in charge of both giving and receiving pleasure in lovemaking. Sex is not a service one person provides for another on demand. It is a positive communication of intimacy that two can share.

If you feel uncomfortable about your sexuality and uncertain of how to act sexually, become informed. Read current books, find the answers to questions you have about your reproductive system, and learn about your body. Explore your feelings about your sexuality with a psychotherapist and in a women's group. This can help to banish your doubts and inhibitions and instill confidence in yourself. Also, expose any old sexual hurts that you have buried; they may be stifling your sexual self. Discharge your grief over sexual experiences that have traumatized your development or caused you to shut down sexual expressiveness. Overcoming these distresses helps you to be more accepting of your own sexuality and less critical of the behavior of others.

If you are fearful of sexual contact, remember that you have a right to establish the conditions of your relationships. A partner may be fun to play tennis with, but not to have dinner with; fun to dance with, but not to go camping with; fun to be affectionate with, but not to have sex with. Do not make the mistake of evaluating a man you have just met from the perspective of whether or not you would want to have sex with him or marry him. You can cut yourself off from interesting and happy times with this attitude and almost guarantee that love affairs will end in hurt or disappointment because they are based on superficialities instead of genuine caring, knowledge of each other, and mutual trust and respect. In brief, when it comes to overcoming fears of sex, move slowly.

Stop comparing yourself to and trying to pattern yourself after mythically perfect women from either side of the whore-madonna imperative. You are a special woman. Your sexuality is only one part of you. It is one component of your uniqueness, rather than a representation of your totality.

Go back to the list of your strengths and positive attributes. Did you include any reference to your sexuality? If not, add it now. If you did, was it your most important or valued attribute? Probably not. In any case, all of these qualities add up to who you are. Develop all of the characteristics you value about yourself. When you see yourself as a total person, you will project yourself in this way and others will respond to you as a person who happens to be a woman, not as a sex object to be used or feared. Resolving the paradox of sexuality will help you to become the woman you want to be.

PSYCHOSOMATICS

Do you see yourself as:

- sick most of the time?
- susceptible to a variety of illnesses?
- cherished when you are sick and neglected when you are healthy?
- powerless except when ill?
- too weak to get involved in conflicts?
- able to avoid unpleasantness because you are not well?
- having little except your symptoms to talk about?
- cheated out of life by being sick?

Do others see you as:

- always sick?
- deserving of pity?
- needing their cooperation, whether they give it freely or not?
- long suffering, uncomplaining, and deserving of their sacrifices?
- putting limits on their lives?
- enjoying your symptoms?
- controlling them with your illness?
- not helping yourself?

What can you do if, after reading this far, you have the uncomfortable feeling that your illnesses may be psychosomatic? You never intended to get sick, have suffered, have done all you can to get well, and would be ashamed to have others see you as psychosomatically ill. For starters, do not judge yourself harshly. You have not asked that your body react to traumatic situations by developing symptoms. You are the victim of a paradox and deserve understanding rather than blame. Nor do you need to be ashamed of your unconscious way of coping with reality. The world is full of people who have emotional components to their physical illnesses. Few realize it and fewer still will admit it.

Take a positive attitude. Understanding how the paradox of psychosomatics has victimized you can be like a new medicine; it can provide a way to cure the problem. Maybe the particular illness you suffer from will not disappear overnight, but once you assess the price you are paying for being sick, any rewards you are getting will lose their power to reinforce.

Once one is aware of this paradox one feels a strong temptation to diagnose everyone else as being psychosomatically ill. Remember that a little learning is a dangerous thing. Limit your search for psychosomatic symptoms to yourself. Others who may be suffering are having enough pain. They do not need anyone to point out this paradox for them.

If you have held in your emotions in order to appear ladylike you can stop kidding yourself. Those emotions had to go somewhere; they may account for your symptoms. Follow the advice given earlier in this chapter on expressing your emotions. Become spontaneous. If you want to laugh, to cry, to shout with joy, or to express negative feelings, do so. Others will like you for your genuineness, and you will like the healthy way you feel.

Examine whether your sickness has become a way to escape frustration, conflicts, or heavy burdens. Follow the suggestions given to resolve conflicts. Be direct, open, and honest in relating to others. Act upon your rights, and you will feel better about yourself.

If you find that being sick is providing you with the power to control and punish others, look for a more direct way to get their cooperation. They will feel more kindly toward you if they do things for you because they want to, rather than because they feel guilty.

FEAR

Do you see yourself as:

- unable to change because you have too much to lose?
- afraid to take risks because the status quo seems safer?
- full of good intentions that you do not carry out?

- always going to start tomorrow?
- easily giving up?
- overwhelmed by problems too big to handle?
- helpless to change your life?

Do others see you as:

- wishy-washy?
- well intentioned but ineffective?
- always talking, never doing?
- willing to give up when the going gets rough?
- fearful of change?
- stuck in your ruts?
- taking the easy way out?

If you answered yes to many of these questions, it is important for you to explore the rewards you are getting for staying stuck between wanting to want to change and deciding not to take risks. Perhaps these rewards can be gained in other, positive ways. You may be overlooking valuable personal resources because your fears keep you from fully exploring your alternatives. Remember to build on your strengths. Fears are less overwhelming when you have successes and attributes you can admire in yourself and use to accomplish change.

Are you catastrophizing? Is it true that taking constructive steps toward moving out of your rut might mean that you will lose everything? Be sure to examine carefully whether or not your feelings are based on reality. Fear has a way of making dilemmas seem larger than life. This can back you into a corner.

What seems so threatening to you may not, in fact, be so menacing to others. Perhaps if you expressed your fears, they could offer reassurance that would help you get started. If they are unable or unwilling to do this, find a trustworthy, supportive person, perhaps a psychotherapist, who can help you find alternatives that are likely to bring success and give you encouragement to take risks.

Once you have established a support system that you can trust, take a good look at your objective. Perhaps you are like a person standing in the lobby of a sky-scraper and wanting to go to the top floor, only to find that the elevators are out of order. The climb seems insurmountable from where you stand. When you break down your task into little steps and approach the climb one story at a time, however, movement is easy. You can rejoice as you reach each small objective, knowing it is on the way to a final goal.

Give yourself praise and rewards as you move toward your goal, instead of waiting until the end. This will keep your momentum going. Do not be afraid to reevaluate as you go along; you may want to scale down your expectations, branch off in different directions, or even decide to replace one objective with a more attractive or realistic one.

The important thing to remember to escape from the paradox of fear is to do something positive to whittle your fears down to manageable size. You are in charge of what you feel; your fear is not in charge of you. Refuse to back down when fear threatens to chase you into indecision. Instead, talk to your support person, or even to yourself. Do not deny your fear. Say how scared you are, how difficult your task is, and how earnestly you wish you could give up. Then stand up straight and step out and up once again. The only thing you really have to lose is your fear. The reward is in finding a happy, motivated, success-oriented you.

In resolving the paradoxes in your life, you can approach your success in the same way we encourage our clients to view it. Success is not an event. It is unlike the "king of the mountain" concept that you are not successful until you reach the summit, and then you must fight to hold your position. Rather, success is a process involving the little steps along the way to your goal, steps you can cut down to whatever size you feel capable of handling. Accomplishing each step then becomes a success as you expand your efforts toward larger goals. Each step toward the future becomes a continuation of the growth process of risk-taking, confidence-building, and effectiveness.